Readings for Writers

Exploring Yourself, Your Community

and the World

D1304458

Bedford/St. Martin's   BOSTON ◆ NEW YORK

For information, write: Bedford/St. Martin's, 75 Arlington Street, Boston, MA 02116 (617-399-4000)

Contents

THE EDITORS

Introduction   1

Personal and Autobiographical Writing

THE EDITORS

Personal and Autobiographical Writing   3

DAVID SEDARIS

Me Talk Pretty One Day   5

DICK GREGORY

Shame   10

SABAA SALEEM TAHIR

A Proposal I Never Thought I'd Consider   14

SHERMAN ALEXIE

The Lone Ranger and Tonto Fistfight in Heaven   19

BARBARA EHRENREICH

Cultural Baggage   25

JULIA ALVAREZ

I Want to Be Miss America   28

JAMAICA KINCAID

Girl   33

BERNARD COOPER
A Clack of Tiny Sparks: Remembrances of a Gay Boyhood   35

SAVANNAH ODEM
You Act White   44

THOMAS FERRAGUT
Those People   49

THE EDITORS
Personal and Autobiographical Writing: Summative Questions and
Prompts   55

Persuasive and Public Writing

THE EDITORS
Persuasive and Public Writing   56

STEPHEN COLBERT
Higher Education   58

RICHARD DELGADO
Hate Cannot Be Tolerated   67

PAUL ROBERTS
How to Say Nothing in Five Hundred Words   69

JAMES BALDWIN
If Black English Isn't a Language, Then Tell Me, What Is?   82

SUSAN BROWNMILLER
Let's Put Pornography Back in the Closet   86

DAVE EGGERS
Serve or Fail   90

MARTIN LUTHER KING JR.
Letter from Birmingham Jail   94

THE EDITORS
Persuasive and Public Writing: Summative Questions
and Prompts   109

Genre Studies

THE EDITORS

Genre Studies   110

SCOTT MCCLOUD

Understanding Comics   112

PABLO PICASSO

Guernica (*Image*)   119

GRANT WOOD

American Gothic (*Image*)   120

GORDON PARKS

American Gothic (*Image*)   121

JAMES WRIGHT

Lying in a Hammock at William Duffy's Farm in Pine Island,
Minnesota   122

ELIZABETH BISHOP

One Art   123

PHILIP LEVINE

What Work Is   124

FLANNERY O'CONNOR

A Good Man Is Hard to Find   126

CONNOR MAKOWSKI

Making a Documentary: A Short How To Guide   140

THE EDITORS

Genre Studies: Summative Questions and Prompts   153

Research-Based Writing

THE EDITORS

Research-Based Writing   154

AMITAI ETZIONI
Working at McDonald's 155

MICHAEL J. BAMSHAD and STEVE E. OLSON
Does Race Exist? 159

SHERRY TURKLE
How Computers Change the Way We Think 167

CHRISTOPHER CLAUSEN
Against Work 174

JIB FOWLES
Advertising's Fifteen Basic Appeals 181

STEPHANIE COONTZ
A Nation of Welfare Families 199

BRANDON AYERS
The Academic and Social Effects of Homeschooling 204

THE EDITORS
Research-Based Writing: Summative Questions and Prompts 207

Introduction

Welcome to ENGL 1050: Thought & Writing at Western Michigan University! College-level writing is a skill that you will need as you seek to complete your undergraduate writing requirements; consequently, ENGL 1050 is one of the most important and critical courses you will take during your time at WMU.

For many students, ENGL 1050 has long-lasting implications beyond the end of the semester. The course, after all, is called Thought & Writing, and while you'll certainly gain proficiency in a variety of rhetorical approaches—using rhetoric as the art of persuasion, paying attention to tone and audience, identifying appropriate evidence to support claims and arguments, etc.—you'll also be encouraged to consider yourself, your community, and the world in ways that will seem alternately bizarre, thought-provoking, challenging, and revelatory.

It is our task, then, to compile a reader for ENGL 1050 that provides a wealth of texts that are both engaging and intelligently composed, while also ensuring that the content covers issues pertinent to the personal and the political. (Of course, as you'll see, the personal and the political are often very much intertwined.) Additionally, each selection is designed to assist you with rhetorical knowledge for and execution of the writing assignments, large and small, that you will complete in ENGL 1050.

As such, our reader is divided into four sections that parallel the larger writing assignments your instructor may assign in ENGL 1050. These sections consist of the following: Personal and Autobiographical Writing, Persuasive and Public Writing, Genre Studies, and Research-Based Writing. Each of these sections feature a variety of rhetorical approaches, illustrating multiple ways to articulate an argument. The Persuasive and Public Writing section, for example, moves from Colbert's satirical humor to Baldwin's serious tone to King's rational appeals. Each of these texts is successful inasmuch as they make their points cogently and concisely, and yet the authors' approaches are wildly different. It is our hope—and your instructor's, too—that you finish this course feeling comfortable in a wide variety of rhetorical situations, with a great deal of "tools" in your writerly toolbox to ensure you say exactly what it is you mean to say, with an understanding of your purpose and audience.

This reader aims to show you the depth and breadth of experiences and writing styles that occur around the world. We believe the selections within will inspire great discussion in the classroom and introspection outside of it.

Part I: Personal and Autobiographical Writing

You've probably done some type of personal writing on some occasion. Perhaps you've written in a journal or diary that shares your most personal thoughts and feelings about things you've experienced. Or perhaps you've been assigned to write an autobiography that shares your life experiences for a previous class. Likewise, most ENGL 1050 instructors typically assign some sort of autobiographical writing for the first project. These might include literacy autobiographies, where you share your own definitions of literacy in relation to your personal experiences; or memoirs, where you discuss a particular life event or series of life events that have influenced your values, beliefs, or worldview. Other instructors might ask you to discuss your career and/or collegiate goals and how you plan to use your education to achieve them. Of course, these are a few of many examples of personal and autobiographical writing your instructor may assign.

The texts in this section similarly share personal and/or autobiographical accounts of the lived experiences of various authors. David Sedaris' "Me Talk Pretty One Day" humorously describes his fears associated with learning a language in an unfamiliar country. His essay can be used as a lens for examining the ways in which language acquisition affects one's own experiences with acquiring literacy. Dick Gregory's "Shame" can also be used to explore how schooling and higher education shape and impact one's sense of self; however, in contrast to Sedaris, Gregory's tone is much more serious and is complicated by the intersections of race and class.

The sharing of one's personal experiences and autobiographical writing need not only apply to literacy and education. Additional texts, including Sabaa Saleem Tahir's "A Proposal I Thought I'd Never Consider," Sherman Alexie's "The Lone Ranger and Tonto Fistfight in Heaven," Barbara's Ehrenreich's "Cultural Baggage," Julia Alvarez's "I Want to Be Miss America," Jamaica Kincaid's "Girl," and Bernard Cooper's "A Clack of Tiny Sparks: Remembrances of a Gay Boyhood," each provide readers with useful examples of how to make strategic and stylistic choices when sharing personal experiences in memoirs. These texts further examine issues of race, class, gender, and sexuality and how lived experiences shape the author's worldview.

Finally, the sample student texts in this section similarly explore themes that pertain to race, class, gender and sexuality and may serve as topics for discussion as you write your own narratives. These essays, Thomas Ferragut's "Those People," and Savannah Odem's "You Act White," were selected for the 2013 ENGL 1050 Best Essay Award.

As you read these texts, consider the strategies each author uses to appeal to different audiences while sharing very personal--and at times painful--autobiographical experiences.

4

DAVID SEDARIS   [b. 1956]

Me Talk Pretty One Day

Born in 1956 in Johnson City, New York, **David Sedaris** grew up in Raleigh, North Carolina. He is a playwright (in collaboration with his sister Amy) and an essayist whose work has been featured regularly on National Public Radio and in collections such as *Naked* (1997) and *Me Talk Pretty One Day* (2000). Sedaris's work tends toward the satiric, but even the most wickedly pointed of his pieces are marked by an ironic stance that includes the author among those humans whose folly must be satirized. This insistence on turning his satiric eye on himself is evident in "Me Talk Pretty One Day," taken from the collection of the same name, in which he recounts his efforts to learn French, to the chagrin of his teacher and to his own evident amusement.

At the age of forty-one, I am returning to school and have to think of myself as what my French textbook calls "a true debutant." After paying my tuition, I was issued a student ID, which allows me a discounted entry fee at movie theaters, puppet shows, and Festyland, a far-flung amusement park that advertises with billboards picturing a cartoon stegosaurus sitting in a canoe and eating what appears to be a ham sandwich.

I've moved to Paris with hopes of learning the language. My school is an easy ten-minute walk from my apartment, and on the first day of class I arrived early, watching as the returning students greeted one another in the school lobby. Vacations were recounted, and questions were raised concerning mutual friends with names like Kang and Vlatnya. Regardless of their nationalities, everyone spoke in what sounded to me like excellent French. Some accents were better than others, but the students exhibited an ease and confidence I found intimidating. As an added discomfort, they were all young, attractive, and well dressed, causing me to feel not unlike Pa Kettle trapped backstage after a fashion show.

The first day of class was nerve-racking because I knew I'd be expected to perform. That's the way they do it here—it's everybody into the language pool, sink or swim. The teacher marched in, deeply tanned from a recent vacation, and proceeded to rattle off a series of administrative announcements. I've spent quite a few summers in Normandy, and I took a monthlong French class before leaving New York. I'm not completely in the dark, yet I understood only half of what this woman was saying.

"If you have not *meimslsxp* or *lgpdmurct* by this time, then you should not be in this room. Has everyone *apzkiubjxow*? Everyone? Good, we shall begin." She spread out her lesson plan and sighed, saying, "All right, then, who knows the alphabet?"

It was startling because (a) I hadn't been asked that question in a while and (b) I realized, while laughing, that I myself did *not* know the alphabet. They're the same letters, but in France they're pronounced differently. I know the shape of the alphabet but had no idea what it actually sounded like.

"Ahh." The teacher went to the board and sketched the letter *a*. "Do we have anyone in the room whose first name commences with an *ahh*?"

Two Polish Annas raised their hands, and the teacher instructed them to present themselves by stating their names, nationalities, occupations, and a brief list of things they liked and disliked in this world. The first Anna hailed from an industrial town outside of Warsaw and had front teeth the size of tombstones. She worked as a seamstress, enjoyed quiet times with friends, and hated the mosquito.

"Oh, really," the teacher said. "How very interesting. I thought that everyone loved the mosquito, but here, in front of all the world, you claim to detest him. How is it that we've been blessed with someone as unique and original as you? Tell us, please."

The seamstress did not understand what was being said but knew that this was an occasion for shame. Her rabbity mouth huffed for breath, and she stared down at her lap as though the appropriate comeback were stitched somewhere alongside the zipper of her slacks.

The second Anna learned from the first and claimed to love sunshine and detest lies. It sounded like a translation of one of those Playmate of the Month data sheets, the answers always written in the same loopy handwriting: "Turn-ons: Mom's famous five-alarm chili! Turnoffs: insecurity and guys who come on too strong!!!!"

The two Polish Annas surely had clear notions of what they loved and hated, but like the rest of us, they were limited in terms of vocabulary, and this made them appear less than sophisticated. The teacher forged on, and we learned that Carlos, the Argentine bandonion player, loved wine, music, and, in his words, "making sex with the womens of the world." Next came a beautiful young Yugoslav who identified herself as an optimist, saying that she loved everything that life had to offer.

The teacher licked her lips, revealing a hint of the sauce-box we would later come to know. She crouched low for her attack, placed her hands

6

on the young woman's desk, and leaned close, saying, "Oh yeah? And do you love your little war?"

While the optimist struggled to defend herself, I scrambled to think of an answer to what had obviously become a trick question. How often is one asked what he loves in this world? More to the point, how often is one asked and then publicly ridiculed for his answer? I recalled my mother, flushed with wine, pounding the tabletop late one night, saying, "Love? I love a good steak cooked rare. I love my cat, and I love . . ." My sisters and I leaned forward, waiting to hear our names. "Tums," our mother said. "I love Tums."

The teacher killed some time accusing the Yugoslavian girl of masterminding a program of genocide, and I jotted frantic notes in the margins of my pad. While I can honestly say that I love leafing through medical textbooks devoted to severe dermatological conditions, the hobby is beyond the reach of my French vocabulary, and acting it out would only have invited controversy.

When called upon, I delivered an effortless list of things that I detest: 15 blood sausage, intestinal pâtés, brain pudding. I'd learned these words the hard way. Having given it some thought, I then declared my love for IBM typewriters, the French word for *bruise*, and my electric floor waxer. It was a short list, but still I managed to mispronounce *IBM* and assign the wrong gender to both the floor waxer and the typewriter. The teacher's reaction led me to believe that these mistakes were capital crimes in the country of France.

"Were you always this *palicmkrexis*?" she asked. "Even a *fiuscrzsa ticiwelmun* knows that a typewriter is feminine."

I absorbed as much of her abuse as I could understand, thinking—but not saying—that I find it ridiculous to assign a gender to an inanimate object incapable of disrobing and making an occasional fool of itself. Why refer to crack pipe or Good Sir Dishrag when these things could never live up to all that their sex implied?

The teacher proceeded to belittle everyone from German Eva, who hated laziness, to Japanese Yukari, who loved paintbrushes and soap. Italian, Thai, Dutch, Korean, and Chinese—we all left class foolishly believing that the worst was over. She'd shaken us up a little, but surely that was just an act designed to weed out the deadweight. We didn't know it then, but the coming months would teach us what it was like to spend time in the presence of a wild animal, something completely unpredictable. Her temperament was not based on a series of good and bad days but, rather, good and bad moments. We soon learned to dodge chalk and protect our heads and stomachs whenever she approached us with a question. She hadn't yet punched anyone, but it seemed wise to protect ourselves against the inevitable.

Though we were forbidden to speak anything but French, the teacher would occasionally use us to practice any of her five fluent languages.

"I hate you," she said to me one afternoon. Her English was flawless. 20 "I really, really hate you." Call me sensitive, but I couldn't help but take it personally.

After being singled out as a lazy *kfdtinvfm*, I took to spending four hours a night on my homework, putting in even more time whenever we were assigned an essay. I suppose I could have gotten by with less, but I was determined to create some sort of identity for myself: David the hard worker, David the cut-up. We'd have one of those "complete this sentence" exercises, and I'd fool with the thing for hours, invariably settling on something like "A quick run around the lake? I'd love to! Just give me a moment while I strap on my wooden leg." The teacher, through word and action, conveyed the message that if this was my idea of an identity, she wanted nothing to do with it.

My fear and discomfort crept beyond the borders of the classroom and accompanied me out onto the wide boulevards. Stopping for a coffee, asking directions, depositing money in my bank account: these things were out of the question, as they involved having to speak. Before beginning school, there'd been no shutting me up, but now I was convinced that everything I said was wrong. When the phone rang, I ignored it. If someone asked me a question, I pretended to be deaf. I knew my fear was getting the best of me when I started wondering why they don't sell cuts of meat in vending machines.

My only comfort was the knowledge that I was not alone. Huddled in the hallways and making the most of our pathetic French, my fellow students and I engaged in the sort of conversation commonly overheard in refugee camps.

"Sometime me cry alone at night."

"That be common for I, also, but be more strong, you. Much work and 25 someday you talk pretty. People start love you soon. Maybe tomorrow, okay."

Unlike the French class I had taken in New York, here there was no sense of competition. When the teacher poked a shy Korean in the eyelid with a freshly sharpened pencil, we took no comfort in the fact that, unlike Hyeyoon Cho, we all knew the irregular past tense of the verb *to defeat*. In all fairness, the teacher hadn't meant to stab the girl, but neither did she spend much time apologizing, saying only, "Well, you should have been *vkkdyo* more *kdeynfulh*."

Over time it became impossible to believe that any of us would ever improve. Fall arrived and it rained every day, meaning we would now be scolded for the water dripping from our coats and umbrellas. It was mid-October when the teacher singled me out, saying, "Every day spent with you is like having a cesarean section." And it struck me that, for the first time since arriving in France, I could understand every word that someone was saying.

Understanding doesn't mean that you can suddenly speak the language. Far from it. It's a small step, nothing more, yet its rewards are intoxicating and deceptive. The teacher continued her diatribe and I settled back, bathing in the subtle beauty of each new curse and insult.

"You exhaust me with your foolishness and reward my efforts with nothing but pain, do you understand me?"

The world opened up, and it was with great joy that I responded, "I 30 know the thing that you speak exact now. Talk me more, you, plus, please, plus."

[2000]

9

DICK GREGORY [b. 1932]

Shame

Dick Gregory, activist, comedian, and nutrition expert, was born in St. Louis, Missouri, in 1932. While attending Southern Illinois University on an athletic scholarship, Gregory excelled in track, winning the university's Outstanding Athlete Award in 1953. In 1954, he was drafted into the army. After his discharge, he immediately became active in the civil rights movement led by Martin Luther King Jr. In the 1960s, Gregory was an outspoken critic of U.S. involvement in Vietnam, which in turn led to his run for the presidency in 1968 as a write-in candidate for the Freedom and Peace Party. Two of his books from this era are No More Lies: The Myth and Reality of American History (1971) and Dick Gregory's Political Primer (1972). Throughout his life he has crusaded for economic reforms, antidrug issues, and minority rights. In 2000, he published Callus on My Soul, the second volume of his autobiography. In recent years, Gregory has been active in the diet and health food industry.

In the following episode from Nigger (1964), the first volume of his autobiography, Gregory narrates the story of a childhood experience that taught him the meaning of shame. Through his use of dialogue, he dramatically re-creates the experience for readers. Notice how he uses concrete nouns and strong action verbs to describe his experiences and his intense emotional responses to them.

I never learned hate at home, or shame. I had to go to school for that. I was about seven years old when I got my first big lesson. I was in love with a little girl named Helene Tucker, a light-complexioned little girl with pigtails and nice manners. She was always clean and she was smart in school. I think I went to school then mostly to look at her. I brushed my hair and even got me a little old handkerchief. It was a lady's handkerchief, but I didn't want Helene to see me wipe my nose on my hand. The pipes were frozen again, there was no water in the house, but I washed my socks and shirt every night. I'd get a pot, and go over to Mister Ben's grocery store, and stick my pot down into his soda machine. Scoop out some chopped ice. By evening the ice melted to water for washing. I got sick a lot that winter because the fire would go out at night before the clothes were dry. In the morning I'd put them on, wet or dry, because they were the only clothes I had.

Everybody's got a Helene Tucker, a symbol of everything you want. I loved her for her goodness, her cleanness, her popularity. She'd walk down my street and my brothers and sisters would yell, "Here comes Helene," and I'd rub my tennis sneakers on the back of my pants and wish my hair wasn't so nappy and the white folks' shirt fit me better. I'd run out on the street. If I knew my place and didn't come too close, she'd wink at me and say hello. That was a good feeling. Sometimes I'd follow her all the way home, and shovel the snow off her walk and try to make friends with her Momma and her aunts. I'd drop money on her stoop late at night on my way back from shining shoes in the taverns. And she had a Daddy, and he had a good job. He was a paper hanger.

I guess I would have gotten over Helene by summertime, but something happened in that classroom that made her face hang in front of me for the next twenty-two years. When I played the drums in high school it was for Helene and when I broke track records in college it was for Helene and when I started standing behind microphones and heard applause I wished Helene could hear it, too. It wasn't until I was twenty-nine years old and married and making money that I finally got her out of my system. Helene was sitting in that classroom when I learned to be ashamed of myself.

It was on a Thursday. I was sitting in the back of the room, in a seat with a chalk circle drawn around it. The idiot's seat, the troublemaker's seat.

The teacher thought I was stupid. Couldn't spell, couldn't read, couldn't do arithmetic. Just stupid. Teachers were never interested in finding out that you couldn't concentrate because you were so hungry, because you hadn't had any breakfast. All you could think about was noontime, would it ever come? Maybe you could sneak into the cloakroom and steal a bite of some kid's lunch out of a coat pocket. A bite of something. Paste. You can't really make a meal of paste, or put it on bread for a sandwich, but sometimes I'd scoop a few spoonfuls out of the paste jar in the back of the room. Pregnant people get strange tastes. I was pregnant with poverty. Pregnant with dirt and pregnant with smells that made people turn away, pregnant with cold and pregnant with shoes that were never bought for me, pregnant with five other people in my bed and no Daddy in the next room, and pregnant with hunger. Paste doesn't taste too bad when you're hungry.

The teacher thought I was a troublemaker. All she saw from the front of the room was a little black boy who squirmed in his idiot's seat and made noises and poked the kids around him. I guess she couldn't see a kid who made noises because he wanted someone to know he was there.

It was on a Thursday, the day before the Negro payday. The eagle always flew on Friday. The teacher was asking each student how much his father would give to the Community Chest. On Friday night, each kid would get the money from his father, and on Monday he would bring it to the school. I decided I was going to buy me a Daddy right then. I had money in my pocket from shining shoes and selling papers, and whatever Helene Tucker pledged for her Daddy I was going to top it. And I'd hand the money right in. I wasn't going to wait until Monday to buy me a Daddy.

I was shaking, scared to death. The teacher opened her book and 8 started calling out names alphabetically.

"Helene Tucker?"

"My daddy said he'd give two dollars and fifty cents."

"That's very nice, Helene. Very, very nice indeed."

That made me feel pretty good. It wouldn't take too much to top that. I had almost three dollars in dimes and quarters in my pocket. I stuck my hand in my pocket and held onto the money, waiting for her to call my name. But the teacher closed her book after she called everybody else in the class.

I stood up and raised my hand.

"What is it now?"

"You forgot me."

She turned toward the blackboard. "I don't have time to be playing with you, Richard."

"My Daddy said he'd . . ."

"Sit down, Richard, you're disturbing the class."

"My Daddy said he'd give . . . fifteen dollars."

She turned around and looked mad. "We are collecting this money for you and your kind, Richard Gregory. If your Daddy can give fifteen dollars you have no business being on relief."

"I got it right now, I got it right now, my Daddy gave it to me to turn in today, my Daddy said . . ."

"And furthermore," she said, looking right at me, her nostrils getting big and her lips getting thin and her eyes opening wide, "we know you don't have a Daddy."

Helene Tucker turned around, her eyes full of tears. She felt sorry for me. Then I couldn't see her too well because I was crying, too.

"Sit down, Richard."

And I always thought the teacher kind of liked me. She always picked me to wash the blackboard on Friday, after school. That was a big thrill, it made me feel important. If I didn't wash it, come Monday the school might not function right.

"Where are you going, Richard?"

I walked out of school that day, and for a long time I didn't go back very often. There was shame there.

Now there was shame everywhere. It seemed like the whole world had been inside that classroom, everyone had heard what the teacher had said, everyone had turned around and felt sorry for me. There was shame in going to the Worthy Boys Annual Christmas Dinner for you and your kind, because everybody knew what a worthy boy was. Why couldn't they just call it the Boys Annual Dinner; why'd they have to give it a name? There was shame in wearing the brown and orange and white plaid mackinaw the welfare gave to three thousand boys. Why'd it have to be the same for everybody so when you walked down the street the people could see you were on relief? It was a nice warm mackinaw and it had a hood, and my Momma beat me and called me a little rat when she found out I stuffed it in the bottom of a pail full of garbage way over on Cottage Street. There was shame in running over to Mister Ben's at the end of the day and asking for his rotten peaches, there was shame in asking Mrs. Simmons for a spoonful of sugar, there was shame in running out to meet the relief truck. I hated that truck, full of food for you and your kind. I ran into the house and hid when it came. And then I started to sneak through alleys, to take the long way home so the people going into White's Eat Shop wouldn't see me. Yeah, the whole world heard the teacher that day, we all know you don't have a Daddy.

[1964]

A Proposal I Never Thought I'd Consider

Raised in California, **Sabaa Saleem Tahir** is the daughter of Pakistani Muslim immigrants. Tahir, who attended the University of California, Los Angeles, graduated with a degree in communications in 2004. While a student, Tahir, interested in journalism, served as a reporter for UCLA's newspaper, the *Daily Bruin*, and as an intern with the *Washington Post*, where she worked as a copy editor for the newspaper's Foreign desk. After graduating, Tahir continued her work as a copy editor for the *Washington Post*. Tahir met her husband, also a Pakistani Muslim, after publishing "A Proposal I Never Thought I'd Consider," an article about the tradition of arranged marriage in their shared culture. When he contacted her after reading the article, they began correspondence. Their subsequent relationship evolved into a "love-match," and they eventually married with the approval of their parents.

Tahir originally published "A Proposal I Never Thought I'd Consider," which follows, in the *Washington Post* under her maiden name, Saleem, while working as an intern at the newspaper. In the article, Tahir, a self-proclaimed liberal, explains feeling torn between honoring her devout religious beliefs and upholding her feminist ideals, as well as pursuing her career goals.

In spite of myself, I think I may agree to an arranged marriage.

Beginning next month, my parents will contact Muslim family friends around the world with a list of criteria for a husband: a twentysomething, classically handsome, Urdu-speaking Muslim man who is 6 feet tall, with an MD and MBA, as well as a PhD in something respectable like molecular toxicology. He must have a good sense of family and a financial portfolio fat enough to take care of the next 15 generations. My parents will screen the candidates, and after I graduate from college next spring, they will introduce me to the few they deem best. Ultimately, the lucky man will have to pass my own stringent test: Does he own every Radiohead album and listen to them regularly?

Like so many other young South Asians in America, I am the product of two cultures whose conflicting values pull at me with equal urgency. Never have I felt as torn between the two as I do about the question of marriage. I have been a Californian for all but the first year of my life, when my family lived in Britain, where I was born. I grew up in a small town in the Mojave Desert where conservative Republicans were as common as cacti. Inexplicably, I grew up liberal and a feminist.

My mother and father were born and raised in Pakistan, where religion is entrenched in the culture and the culture is explicitly unyielding. Though they left family and comfort decades ago for opportunity in the West, they brought strong religious faith and cultural expectations with them—and tried to instill sobriety and respect in my two older brothers and me. They have more or less succeeded, but they have also endured nearly 30 years of our stubborn refusal to conform. They have grudgingly accepted that, while respectful, their children are also independent, maybe even eccentric—qualities not admired by most traditional Pakistanis.

My parents would casually joke about my marriage while I was grow- 5 ing up. I was uneasy about it, but it seemed so far off that it was easy for me to laugh it off. "When pigs fly!" I'd say, and change the subject.

Now, almost everyone I know—friends, teachers, co-workers—expects me, as a child of the West, to reject the notion of arranged marriage, to proclaim my independence loudly. Sometimes, I still expect that, too. But as a young Muslim woman, I also expect myself to accept the obligations I have as my parents' daughter—regardless of the emotional cost to me.

Pakistani culture and Islam beckon me with security, familiarity and ease. By agreeing to an arranged marriage, I could more easily satisfy my religious obligation to abstain from intimacy with the opposite sex until marriage—not an easy feat, may I say. I would be participating in the ceremony of a culture 11,000 miles removed, a ceremony I've witnessed only twice. By doing so, I could spare my parents the stinging criticism they would face if their daughter chose her own path: barbs from three generations of extended family, all of whom accepted their own arranged marriages without argument—and some of whom complain about them to this day.

At the same time, Pakistani culture repels me with its expectation that I adhere to a tradition that essentially advocates handing me over to a man for safekeeping. From the endless gossip of aunts, uncles, cousins and friends, I know the courtship ritual well. I will briefly meet my parents' choices and pick those who interest me. With each man, after perhaps a month of chaperoned dating, phone calls, no physical contact and little understanding of whether we would mesh, I am supposed to decide whether to marry him.

In the end, the decision will be mine. My parents would never force me to marry a particular man. But they do expect me not to dawdle. Ideally, I should make a decision after no more than five or six meetings. I am supposed to pick a husband, accept my fate and hope the marriage is successful. Our engagement would likely last a year or two, during which we would get to know each other better—and maybe even grow fond of each other. (Breaking it off at that point would be possible, but that would reflect badly on me and on my family and would represent time wasted.) Still, I worry that my filial piety could lead me down an empty road—where independent minds and hearts are given up to the demands of a culture that I often find perplexing.

I am not alone in this struggle. My oldest brother and I have mulled 10 over the marriage question for hours and hours. My other brother, the middle child and black sheep of the family, long ago informed our parents that there would be no arranged marriage for him—in fact, there probably wouldn't be a marriage at all. My parents hope he'll come to his senses. And though their oldest child is 29—marrying age for men in Pakistan—my parents accept his excuse that he's just not ready. Maybe they focus less on him because my father was 31 when he married. Whatever the reason, until I get married, my parents' eyes are on me. Their priorities for me are that I get a bachelor's degree and marry—in that order. Thus, I decided to take an honors thesis class last year to postpone my graduation until next March, when UCLA will have to forcibly boot me out. I am searching for ways to extend my school days so that I can put off the marriage decision again. I have to admit, I'm beginning to feel a creeping sense of desperation because I was imbued with a sense of skepticism toward anything that is overly reliant on tradition rather than reason. But my skepticism is outweighed by an obligation to my mother and father, and to their happiness.

My parents are not evil people who have kept me in a box my whole life, bent on handing me over to a man who will do the same. They've always treated me with love and respect and showed trust in my judgment. And the rules they applied to me when I was younger have remained a part of me, even when I have not wanted them to. For example, my parents never allowed me to date and generally frowned any on male friendships. Dating leads to intimacy, which would be out of the question. In high school, I was far quieter than I am now, and a tight curfew ensured my good behavior.

But the coed dorms, parties and freedom of college have presented a moral dilemma for me. I did not want to disappoint my parents. So I developed a complex method of discouraging in myself behavior that they, and Islam, would consider deviant. When I thought someone was about to ask me out, I used the idea that I wasn't sure about my sexuality as a ruse to get him to keep his distance. Or I ran off, claiming an appointment. But after four years of these tactics—which have not failed me yet—I find it harder to convince others, and myself, that I'm not interested.

Then I think of my parents and their leniency over the years and I stop having the conversation with myself in which I have doubts. Despite their strict upbringing, my parents do not ask me to wear the Islamic head cover. They did not insist that I attend a local college and continue to live at home, as many Muslim girls do. They do not admonish me when I stay out late, and they only occasionally flare up at my decision to forgo medicine for journalism. They remind me to eat and sleep and worry less about grades and career, and, they encourage me to attend concerts and enjoy my youth.

My parents have given me every opportunity for happiness. And I know that their happiness depends on fulfilling their responsibilities as good Muslim parents. They must see their children married to other Muslims of whom they approve.

That took on a new urgency last January when my father, who has a bad heart, also had a stroke. A religious man, he now even more adamantly believes it is his duty to secure my spiritual well-being in whatever time he has left. If he succeeds in marrying me well, ideally to a Muslim from a good Pakistani family, then my soul will be at peace in the afterlife. Moreover, he will be enabling me to follow the rules set out by Islam—to respect my parents' wishes, to start a family and to hand down my religious morals to my children.

That holds nearly as much weight as performing his five daily prayers. For him, my marriage would be the crowning achievement in a life nearly complete. I worry that, if his health deteriorates further and I am not married, I will be the cause of his having an incomplete life.

Similarly, my mother doesn't believe she can perform the pilgrimage to Mecca—of paramount importance to even moderately devout Muslims—with a clear conscience until I am married. If I refused to get married, my parents would be brokenhearted and confused. Like any child close to her parents, I could not watch them suffer.

And so I find myself defending arranged marriage against those who see it as absurd or even barbaric. Yet I'm disturbed by the doubt these critics instill in me. My fifth year of college buys me more time to resolve my career insecurities. But if I can't even decide between writing or editing, philanthropy or graduate school, how can I commit myself to a man I'll know so little about? Beyond my parents' requirements, there are traits I

15

17

need in the man I marry that cannot be discerned from a few meetings. Will he be able to hold his own in a discussion with me? Will he calmly accept that I will be at least a half-hour late to any important event? Will he make fun of Bollywood films with me?

If we marry, it will no doubt be for life. Muslims accept divorce, but usually as a last resort, and many Pakistanis, including my extended family, see divorce as an escape for the weak-willed.

And is it selfish and idealistic to want "true love"? My American 20 instincts tell me that love comes before marriage, not a few years after— if I am lucky. Like a lot of South Asians raised in the United States, I hope for a "love-match"—where parents accept the Muslim their child has met on her own and has decided to marry. My parents have said that this route would please them most, because it would be a compromise between their ideals and mine.

A month ago, I asked my mother about her determination to have me married soon, especially when her own marriage at 21 took her to London, away from the world she knew, preventing her from pursuing a career and establishing her independence. She said, "Do you think I want to you to leave us—to have a man at the center of your life? Maybe even to go away? I want my daughter close to me always, but this is my duty; I don't have a choice—I can't be selfish. I have to let you go."

That day, I decided I would have an arranged marriage.

But now, I marvel at how quickly the summer has passed. I feel like hyperventilating when I think how quickly spring will come, and engagement and marriage will follow. I fantasize about ways to scare off suitors (bringing sock puppets to our first meeting, perhaps?). Briefly, I resolve to put off marriage, for a few years at least.

But then I think of my parents' anguish if I refuse to honor their wishes—I think of my father and the shadowy road ahead of him—and of how empty I will feel. And I wonder, if I have one foot in each world, is it possible to keep from being torn apart?

[2003]

SHERMAN ALEXIE [b. 1966]

The Lone Ranger and Tonto Fistfight in Heaven

Of Spokane/Coeur d'Alene Native American descent, **Sherman Alexie** (b. 1966) was born on the Spokane Indian Reservation in Wellpinit, Washington. He earned his B.A. from Washington State University in Pullman. He has published eight books of poetry and several novels and collections of short fiction, including *The Lone Ranger and Tonto Fistfight in Heaven* (1993), which won a PEN/Hemingway award for a best first book of fiction. He based the script for the film *Smoke Signals* on one of his short stories.

Too hot to sleep so I walked down to the Third Avenue 7-11 for a Creamsicle and the company of a graveyard-shift cashier. I know that game. I worked graveyard for a Seattle 7-11 and got robbed once too often. The last time the bastard locked me in the cooler. He even took my money and basketball shoes.

The graveyard-shift worker in the Third Avenue 7-11 looked like they all do. Acne scars and a bad haircut, work pants that showed off his white socks, and those cheap black shoes that have no support. My arches still ache from my year at the Seattle 7-11.

"Hello," he asked when I walked into his store. "How you doing?"

I gave him a half-wave as I headed back to the freezer. He looked me over so he could describe me to the police later. I knew the look. One of my old girlfriends said I started to look at her that way, too. She left me not long after that. No, I left her and don't blame her for anything. That's how it happened. When one person starts to look at another like a criminal, then the love is over. It's logical.

"I don't trust you," she said to me. "You get too angry."

She was white and I lived with her in Seattle. Some nights we fought so bad that I would just get in my car and drive all night, only stop to fill up on gas. In fact, I worked the graveyard shift to spend as much time away from her as possible. But I learned all about Seattle that way, driving its back ways and dirty alleys.

Sometimes, though, I would forget where I was and get lost. I'd drive for hours, searching for something familiar. Seems like I'd spent my whole life that way, looking for anything I recognized. Once, I ended up in a nice residential neighborhood and somebody must have been worried because the police showed up and pulled me over.

"What are you doing out here?" the police officer asked me as he looked over my license and registration.

"I'm lost."

"Well, where are you supposed to be?" he asked me, and I knew there were plenty of places I wanted to be, but none where I was supposed to be.

"I got in a fight with my girlfriend," I said. "I was just driving around, blowing off steam, you know?"

"Well, you should be more careful where you drive," the officer said. "You're making people nervous. You don't fit the profile of the neighborhood."

I wanted to tell him that I didn't really fit the profile of the country but I knew it would just get me into trouble.

"Can I help you?" the 7-11 clerk asked me loudly, searching for some response that would reassure him that I wasn't an armed robber. He knew this dark skin and long, black hair of mine was dangerous. I had potential.

"Just getting a Creamsicle," I said after a long interval. It was a sick twist to pull on the guy, but it was late and I was bored. I grabbed my Creamsicle and walked back to the counter slowly, scanned the aisles for effect. I wanted to whistle low and menacingly but I never learned to whistle.

"Pretty hot out tonight?" he asked, that old rhetorical weather bullshit question designed to put us both at ease.

"Hot enough to make you go crazy," I said and smiled. He swallowed hard like a white man does in those situations. I looked him over. Same old green, red, and white 7-11 jacket and thick glasses. But he wasn't ugly, just misplaced and marked by loneliness. If he wasn't working there that night, he'd be at home alone, flipping through channels and wishing he could afford HBO or Showtime.

"Will this be all?" he asked me, in that company effort to make me do some impulse shopping. Like adding a clause onto a treaty. *We'll take Washington and Oregon, and you get six pine trees and a brand-new Chrysler Cordoba.* I knew how to make and break promises.

"No," I said and paused. "Give me a Cherry Slushie, too."

"What size?" he asked, relieved.

"Large," I said, and he turned his back to me to make the drink. He realized his mistake but it was too late. He stiffened, ready for the gunshot or the blow behind the ear. When it didn't come, he turned back to me.

"I'm sorry," he said. "What size did you say?"

"Small," I said and changed the story.

"But I thought you said large."

"If you knew I wanted a large, then why did you ask me again?" I asked him and laughed. He looked at me, couldn't decide if I was giving him serious shit or just goofing. There was something about him I liked, even if it was three in the morning and he was white.

"Hey," I said. "Forget the Slushie. What I want to know is if you know all the words to the theme from 'The Brady Bunch'?"

He looked at me, confused at first, then laughed.

"Shit," he said. "I was hoping you weren't crazy. You were scaring me."

"Well, I'm going to get crazy if you don't know the words."

He laughed loudly then, told me to take the Creamsicle for free. He was the graveyard-shift manager and those little demonstrations of power tickled him. All seventy-five cents of it. I knew how much everything cost.

"Thanks," I said to him and walked out the door. I took my time walking home, let the heat of the night melt the Creamsicle all over my hand. At three in the morning I could act just as young as I wanted to act. There was no one around to ask me to grow up.

In Seattle, I broke lamps. She and I would argue and I'd break a lamp, just pick it up and throw it down. At first she'd buy replacement lamps, expensive and beautiful. But after a while she'd buy lamps from Goodwill or garage sales. Then she just gave up the idea entirely and we'd argue in the dark.

"You're just like your brother," she'd yell. "Drunk all the time and stupid."

"My brother don't drink that much."

She and I never tried to hurt each other physically. I did love her, after all, and she loved me. But those arguments were just as damaging as a fist. Words can be like that, you know? Whenever I get into arguments now, I remember her and I also remember Muhammad Ali. He knew the power of his fists but, more importantly, he knew the power of his words, too. Even though he only had an IQ of 80 or so, Ali was a genius. And she was a genius, too. She knew exactly what to say to cause me the most pain.

But don't get me wrong. I walked through that relationship with an executioner's hood. Or more appropriately, with war paint and sharp arrows. She was a kindergarten teacher and I continually insulted her for that.

"Hey, schoolmarm," I asked. "Did your kids teach you anything new today?"

And I always had crazy dreams. I always have had them, but it seemed they became nightmares more often in Seattle.

In one dream, she was a missionary's wife and I was a minor war chief. We fell in love and tried to keep it secret. But the missionary caught us fucking in the barn and shot me. As I lay dying, my tribe learned of the shooting and attacked the whites all across the reservation. I died and my soul drifted above the reservation.

Disembodied, I could see everything that was happening. Whites killing Indians and Indians killing whites. At first it was small, just my tribe and the few whites who lived there. But my dream grew, intensified. Other tribes arrived on horseback to continue the slaughter of whites, and the United States Cavalry rode into battle.

The most vivid image of that dream stays with me. Three mounted soldiers played polo with a dead Indian woman's head. When I first dreamed it, I thought it was just a product of my anger and imagination. But since then, I've read similar accounts of that kind of evil in the old West. Even more terrifying, though, is the fact that those kinds of brutal things are happening today in places like El Salvador.

All I know for sure, though, is that I woke from that dream in terror, packed up all my possessions, and left Seattle in the middle of the night.

"I love you," she said as I left her. "And don't ever come back."

I drove through the night, over the Cascades, down into the plains of central Washington, and back home to the Spokane Indian Reservation.

When I finished the Creamsicle that the 7-11 clerk gave me, I held the wooden stick up into the air and shouted out very loudly. A couple lights flashed on in windows and a police car cruised by me a few minutes later. I waved to the men in blue and they waved back accidentally. When I got home it was still too hot to sleep so I picked up a week-old newspaper from the floor and read.

There was another civil war, another terrorist bomb exploded, and one more plane crashed and all aboard were presumed dead. The crime rate was rising in every city with populations larger than 100,000, and a farmer in Iowa shot his banker after foreclosure on his 1,000 acres.

A kid from Spokane won the local spelling bee by spelling the word *rhinoceros.*

When I got back to the reservation, my family wasn't surprised to see me. They'd been expecting me back since the day I left for Seattle. There's an old Indian poet who said that Indians can reside in the city, but they can never live there. That's as close to truth as any of us can get.

22

Mostly I watched television. For weeks I flipped through channels, searched for answers in the game shows and soap operas. My mother would circle the want ads in red and hand the paper to me.

"What are you going to do with the rest of your life?" she asked.

"Don't know," I said, and normally, for almost any other Indian in the country, that would have been a perfectly fine answer. But I was special, a former college student, a smart kid. I was one of those Indians who was supposed to make it, to rise above the rest of the reservation like a fucking eagle or something. I was the new kind of warrior.

For a few months I didn't even look at the want ads my mother circled, just left the newspaper where she had set it down. After a while, though, I got tired of television and started to play basketball again. I'd been a good player in high school, nearly great, and almost played at the college I attended for a couple years. But I'd been too out of shape from drinking and sadness to ever be good again. Still, I liked the way the ball felt in my hands and the way my feet felt inside my shoes.

At first I just shot baskets by myself. It was selfish, and I also wanted to learn the game again before I played against anybody else. Since I had been good before and embarrassed fellow tribal members, I knew they would want to take revenge on me. Forget about the cowboys versus Indians business. The most intense competition on any reservation is Indians versus Indians.

But on the night I was ready to play for real, there was this white guy at the gym, playing with all the Indians.

"Who is that?" I asked Jimmy Seyler.

"He's the new BIA° chief's kid."

"Can he play?"

"Oh, yeah."

And he could play. He played Indian ball, fast and loose, better than all the Indians there.

"How long's he been playing here?" I asked.

"Long enough."

I stretched my muscles, and everybody watched me. All these Indians watched one of their old and dusty heroes. Even though I had played most of my ball at the white high school I went to, I was still all Indian, you know? I was Indian when it counted, and this BIA kid needed to be beaten by an Indian, any Indian.

I jumped into the game and played well for a little while. It felt good. I hit a few shots, grabbed a rebound or two, played enough defense to keep the other team honest. Then that white kid took over the game. He was too good. Later, he'd play college ball back East and would nearly

BIA: Bureau of Indian Affairs.

make the Knicks team a couple years on. But we didn't know any of that would happen. We just knew he was better that day and every other day.

The next morning I woke up tired and hungry, so I grabbed the want ads, found a job I wanted, and drove to Spokane to get it. I've been working at the high school exchange program ever since, typing and answering phones. Sometimes I wonder if the people on the other end of the line know that I'm Indian and if their voices would change if they did know.

One day I picked up the phone and it was her, calling from Seattle.

"I got your number from your mom," she said. "I'm glad you're working."

"Yeah, nothing like a regular paycheck."

"Are you drinking?"

"No, I've been on the wagon for almost a year."

"Good. "

The connection was good. I could hear her breathing in the spaces between our words. How do you talk to the real person whose ghost has haunted you? How do you tell the difference between the two?

"Listen," I said. "I'm sorry for everything."

"Me, too."

"What's going to happen to us?" I asked her and wished I had the answer for myself.

"I don't know," she said. "I want to change the world."

These days, living alone in Spokane, I wish I lived closer to the river, to the falls where ghosts of salmon jump. I wish I could sleep. I put down my paper or book and turn off all the lights, lie quietly in the dark. It may take hours, even years, for me to sleep again. There's nothing surprising or disappointing in that.

I know how all my dreams end anyway.

[1993]

BARBARA EHRENREICH [b. 1941]

Cultural Baggage

A renowned social critic and prolific essayist, **Barbara Ehrenreich** was born in Butte, Montana, in 1941. In 1963 she graduated with a B.A. in physics from Reed College and went on to earn a Ph.D. in cell biology from Rockefeller University. Initially she had no intention of becoming a writer, but she found herself attracted to a career in social activism rather than research science and began writing investigative articles for small newsletters. Her articles have appeared in the *New York Times, Ms.*, the *Atlantic Monthly, In These Times,* and *The New Republic,* among others. From 1991 to 1997 Ehrenreich was a regular columnist for *Time* magazine and is currently a regular columnist for *The Progressive.* Her national best seller, *Nickel and Dimed* (2001), narrates her efforts to survive on low-income wages and her follow-up book, *Bait and Switch* (2005), recounts her undercover efforts to find a white-collar job in corporate America.

In "Cultural Baggage," Ehrenreich appraises her diverse ethnic and religious heritage and wonders just how much significance she can allot to any one set of traditions. At first despairing of her rootlessness, she concludes that living by her parent's greatest tenets—"Think for yourself" and "Try new things"—are all the cultural roots she needs.

An acquaintance was telling me about the joys of rediscovering her ethnic and religious heritage. "I know exactly what my ancestors were doing 2,000 years ago," she said, eyes gleaming with enthusiasm, "and *I can do the same things now.*" Then she leaned forward and inquired politely, "And what is your ethnic background, if I may ask?"

"None," I said, that being the first word in line to get out of my mouth. Well, not "none," I backtracked. Scottish, English, Irish—that was something, I supposed. Too much Irish to qualify as a WASP; too much of the hated English to warrant a "Kiss Me, I'm Irish" button; plus there are a number of dead ends in the family tree due to adoptions, missing records, failing memories and the like. I was blushing by this time. Did "none" mean I was rejecting my heritage out of Anglo-Celtic self-hate? Or was I revealing a hidden ethnic chauvinism in which the Britannically

Barbara Ehrenreich, "Cultural Baggage" from *The New York Times Magazine,* April 5, 1992. Copyright © 1992 The New York Times. Reprinted by permission.

derived serve as a kind of neutral standard compared with the ethnic "others"?

Throughout the 60's and 70's, I watched one group after another—African-Americans, Latinos, Native Americans—stand up and proudly reclaim their roots while I just sank back ever deeper into my seat. All this excitement over ethnicity stemmed, I uneasily sensed, from a past in which their ancestors had been trampled upon by *my* ancestors, or at least by people who looked very much like them. In addition, it had begun to seem almost un-American not to have some sort of hyphen at hand, linking one to more venerable times and locales.

But the truth is, I was raised with none. We'd eaten ethnic foods in my childhood home, but these were all borrowed, like the pasties, or Cornish meat pies, my father had picked up from his fellow miners in Butte, Mont. If my mother had one rule, it was militant ecumenism in all matters of food and experience. "Try new things," she would say, meaning anything from sweetbreads to clams, with an emphasis on the "new."

As a child, I briefly nourished a craving for tradition and roots. I   5
immersed myself in the works of Sir Walter Scott. I pretended to believe that the bagpipe was a musical instrument. I was fascinated to learn from a grandmother that we were descended from certain Highland clans and longed for a pleated skirt in one of their distinctive tartans.

But in "Ivanhoe," it was the dark-eyed "Jewess" Rebecca I identified with, not the flaxen-haired bimbo Rowena. As for clans: Why not call them "tribes," those bands of half-clad peasants and warriors whose idea of cuisine was stuffed sheep gut washed down with whisky? And then there was the sting of Disraeli's remark— which I came across in my early teens—to the effect that his ancestors had been leading orderly, literate lives when my ancestors were still rampaging through the Highlands daubing themselves with blue paint.

Motherhood put the screws on me, ethnicity-wise. I had hoped that by marrying a man of Eastern European-Jewish ancestry I would acquire for my descendants the ethnic genes that my own forebears so sadly lacked. At one point, I even subjected the children to a seder of my own design, including a little talk about the flight from Egypt and its relevance to modern social issues. But the kids insisted on buttering their matzohs and snickering through my talk. "Give me a break, Mom," the older one said. "You don't even believe in God."

After the tiny pagans had been put to bed, I sat down to brood over Elijah's wine. What had I been thinking? The kids knew that their Jewish grandparents were secular folks who didn't hold seders themselves. And if ethnicity eluded me, how could I expect it to take root in my children, who are not only Scottish-English-Irish, but Hungarian-Polish-Russian to boot?

But, then, on the fumes of Manischewitz, a great insight took form in my mind. It was true, as the kids said, that I didn't "believe in God." But this could be taken as something very different from an accusation—a reminder of a genuine heritage. My parents had not believed in God either, nor had my grandparents or any other progenitors going back to the great-great level. They had become disillusioned with Christianity generations ago—just as, on the in-law side, my children's other ancestors had shaken their Orthodox Judaism. This insight did not exactly furnish me with an "identity," but it was at least something to work with: we are the kind of people, I realized—whatever our distant ancestors' religions—who do *not* believe, who do not carry on traditions, who do not do things just because someone has done them before.

The epiphany went on: I recalled that my mother never introduced a   10 procedure for cooking or cleaning by telling me, "Grandma did it this way." What did Grandma know, living in the days before vacuum cleaners and disposable toilet mops! In my parents' general view, new things were better than old, and the very fact that some ritual had been performed in the past was a good reason for abandoning it now. Because what was the past, as our forebears knew it? Nothing but poverty, superstition and grief. "Think for yourself," Dad used to say. "Always ask why."

In fact, this may have been the ideal cultural heritage for my particular ethnic strain—bounced as it was from the Highlands of Scotland across the sea, out to the Rockies, down into the mines and finally spewed out into high-tech, suburban America. What better philosophy, for a race of migrants, than "Think for yourself"? What better maxim, for a people whose whole world was rudely inverted every 30 years or so, than "Try new things"?

The more tradition-minded, the newly enthusiastic celebrants of Purim and Kwanzaa and Solstice, may see little point to survival if the survivors carry no cultural freight—religion, for example, or ethnic tradition. To which I would say that skepticism, curiosity and wide-eyed ecumenical tolerance are also worthy elements of the human tradition and are at least as old as such notions as "Serbian" or "Croatian," "Scottish" or "Jewish." I make no claims for my personal line of progenitors except that they remained loyal to the values that may have induced all of our ancestors, long, long ago, to climb down from the trees and make their way into the open plains.

A few weeks ago, I cleared my throat and asked the children, now mostly grown and fearsomely smart, whether they felt any stirrings of ethnic or religious identity, etc., which might have been, ahem, insufficiently nourished at home. "None," they said, adding firmly, "and the world would be a better place if nobody else did, either." My chest swelled with pride, as would my mother's, to know that the race of "none" marches on.

27

JULIA ALVAREZ [b. 1950]

I Want to Be Miss America

Julia Alvarez was born in New York City but spent much of her childhood in the Dominican Republic. After learning of the brutal murder of a family involved in the "underground" movement—an episode that Alvarez refers to in her novel *In the Time of the Butterflies* (1994)—she returned with her family to New York. In explaining the forces which have shaped her as a writer and individual, Alvarez refers to the difficult cultural transition she experienced in adapting to the New York City public schools. These early conflicts, in combination with a natural affinity for storytelling, influenced Alvarez to write. After earning degrees at Middlebury College, Syracuse, and the Bread Loaf School of English, Alvarez began teaching creative writing, traveling among cities with the Poetry-in-the Schools program. Her success led to college positions and eventually a tenured job at Middlebury College. Presently, Alvarez divides her time between teaching and writing and lives with her husband on a farm in the Champlain Valley of Vermont. Her major works of fiction include *How the García Girls Lost Their Accent* (1991), *Yo!* (1996), and *In the Name of Salomé: A Novel* (2000). She has also published poetry in a variety of magazines and journals.

As young teenagers in our new country, my three sisters and I searched for clues on how to look as if we belonged here. We collected magazines, studied our classmates and our new TV, which was where we discovered the Miss America contest.

Watching the pageant became an annual event in our family. Once a year, we all plopped down in our parents' bedroom, with Mami and Papi presiding from their bed. In our nightgowns, we watched the fifty young women who had the American look we longed for.

The beginning was always the best part—all fifty contestants came on for one and only one appearance. In alphabetical order, they stepped forward and enthusiastically introduced themselves by name and state. "Hi! I'm! Susie! Martin! Miss! Alaska!" Their voices rang with false cheer. You could hear, not far off, years of high-school cheerleading, pom-poms, bleachers full of moon-eyed boys, and moms on phones, signing them up for all manner of lessons and making dentist appointments.

There they stood, fifty puzzle pieces forming the pretty face of America, so we thought, though most of the color had been left out, except for one, or possibly two, light-skinned black girls. If there was a "Hispanic," she usually looked all-American, and only the last name, López or Rodríguez, often mispronounced, showed a trace of a great-great-grandfather with a dark, curled mustache and a sombrero charging the Alamo. During the initial roll-call, what most amazed us was that some contestants were ever picked in the first place. There were homely girls with cross-eyed smiles or chipmunk cheeks. My mother would inevitably shake her head and say, "The truth is, these Americans believe in democracy—even in looks."

We were beginning to feel at home. Our acute homesickness had 5 passed, and now we were like people recovered from a shipwreck, looking around at our new country, glad to be here. "I want to be in America," my mother hummed after we'd gone to see *West Side Story*, and her four daughters chorused, "OK by me in America." We bought a house in Queens, New York, in a neighborhood that was mostly German and Irish, where we were the only "Hispanics." Actually, no one ever called us that. Our teachers and classmates at the local Catholic schools referred to us as "Porto Ricans" or "Spanish." No one knew where the Dominican Republic was on the map. "South of Florida," I explained, "in the same general vicinity as Bermuda and Jamaica." I could just as well have said west of Puerto Rico or east of Cuba or right next to Haiti, but I wanted us to sound like a vacation spot, not a Third World country, a place they would look down on.

Although we wanted to look like we belonged here, the four sisters, our looks didn't seem to fit in. We complained about how short we were, about how our hair frizzed, how our figures didn't curve like those of the bathing beauties we'd seen on TV.

"The grass always grows on the other side of the fence," my mother scolded. Her daughters looked fine just the way they were.

But how could we trust her opinion about what looked good when she couldn't even get the sayings of our new country right? No, we knew better. We would have to translate our looks into English, iron and tweeze them out, straighten them, mold them into Made-in-the-U.S.A. beauty.

So we painstakingly rolled our long, curly hair round and round, using our heads as giant rollers, ironing it until we had long, shining shanks, like our classmates and the contestants, only darker. Our skin was diagnosed by beauty consultants in department stores as sallow; we definitely needed a strong foundation to tone down that olive. We wore tights even in the summer to hide the legs Mami would not let us shave. We begged for permission, dreaming of the contestants' long, silky limbs. We were ten, fourteen, fifteen, and sixteen—merely children, Mami explained. We had long lives ahead of us in which to shave.

We defied her. Giggly and red-faced, we all pitched in to buy a big tube 10 of Nair at the local drugstore. We acted as if we were purchasing contraceptives. That night we crowded into the bathroom, and I, the most courageous along these lines, offered one of my legs as a guinea pig. When it didn't become gangrenous or fall off as Mami had predicted, we creamed the other seven legs. We beamed at each other; we were one step closer to that runway, those flashing cameras, those oohs and ahhs from the audience.

Mami didn't even notice our Naired legs; she was too busy disapproving of the other changes. Our clothes, for one. "You're going to wear that in public!" She'd gawk, as if to say, What will the Americans think of us?

"This is what the Americans wear," we would argue back.

But the dresses we had picked out made us look cheap, she said, like bad, fast girls—gringas without vergüenza, without shame. She preferred her choices: fuchsia skirts with matching vests, flowered dresses with bows at the neck or gathers where you wanted to look slim, everything bright and busy, like something someone might wear in a foreign country.

Our father didn't really notice our new look at all but, if called upon to comment, would say absently that we looked beautiful. "Like Marilina Monroe." Still, during the pageant, he would offer insights into what he thought made a winner. "Personality, Mami," my father would say from his post at the head of the bed, "Personality is the key," though his favorite contestants, whom he always championed in the name of personality, tended to be the fuller girls with big breasts who gushed shamelessly at Bert Parks. "Ay, Papi," we would groan, rolling our eyes at each other. Sometimes, as the girl sashayed back down the aisle, Papi would break out in a little Dominican song that he sang whenever a girl had a lot of swing in her walk:

> Yo no tumbo caña,
> Que la tumba el viento,
> Que la tumba Dora
> Con su movimiento!

> ("I don't have to cut the cane,
> The wind knocks it down,
> The wind of Dora's movement
> As she walks downtown.")

My father would stop on a New York City street when a young woman   15
swung by and sing this song out loud to the great embarrassment of his
daughters. We were sure that one day when we weren't around to make
him look like the respectable father of four girls, he would be arrested.
My mother never seemed to have a favorite contestant. She was an
ex-beauty herself, and no one seemed to measure up to her high standards. She liked the good girls who had common sense and talked about
their education and about how they owed everything to their mothers.
"Tell that to my daughters," my mother would address the screen, as if
none of us were there to hear her. If we challenged her—how exactly did
we not appreciate her?—she'd maintain a wounded silence for the rest
of the evening. Until the very end of the show, that is, when all our dis-
agreements were forgotten and we waited anxiously to see which of the
two finalists holding hands on that near-empty stage would be the next
reigning queen of beauty. How can they hold hands? I always wondered.
Don't they secretly wish the other person would, well, die?

My sisters and I always had plenty of commentary on all the contestants. We were hardly strangers to this ritual of picking the beauty. In our
own family, we had a running competition as to who was the prettiest of
the four girls. We coveted one another's best feature: the oldest's dark,
almond-shaped eyes, the youngest's great mane of hair, the third oldest's
height and figure. I didn't have a preferred feature, but I was often voted
the cutest, though my oldest sister liked to remind me that I had the kind
of looks that wouldn't age well. Although she was only eleven months
older than I was, she seemed years older, ages wiser. She bragged about
the new kind of math she was learning in high school, called algebra,
which she said I would never be able to figure out. I believed her. Dumb
and ex-cute, that's what I would grow up to be.

As for the prettiest Miss America, we sisters kept our choices secret
until the very end. The range was limited—pretty white women who all
really wanted to be wives and mothers. But even the small and inane set
of options these girls represented seemed boundless compared with
what we were used to. We were being groomed to go from being dutiful
daughters to being dutiful wives with hymens intact. No stops along the
way that might endanger the latter; no careers, no colleges, no shared
apartments with girlfriends, no boyfriends, no social lives. But the
young women on-screen, who were being held up as models in this new
country, were in college, or at least headed there. They wanted to do this,
they were going to do that with their lives. Everything in our native culture had instructed us otherwise: girls were to have no aspirations
beyond being good wives and mothers.

Sometimes there would even be a contestant headed for law school or
medical school. "I wouldn't mind having an office visit with her," my

father would say, smirking. The women who caught my attention were the prodigies who bounded onstage and danced to tapes of themselves playing original compositions on the piano, always dressed in costumes they had sewn, with a backdrop of easels holding paintings they'd painted. "Overkill," my older sister insisted. But if one good thing came out of our watching this yearly parade of American beauties, it was that subtle permission we all felt as a family: a girl could excel outside the home and still be a winner.

Every year, the queen came down the runway in her long gown with a 20 sash like an old-world general's belt of ammunition. Down the walkway she paraded, smiling and waving while Bert sang his sappy song that made our eyes fill with tears. When she stopped at the very end of the stage and the camera zoomed in on her misty-eyed beauty and the credits began to appear on the screen, I always felt let down. I knew I would never be one of those girls, ever. It wasn't just the blond, blue-eyed looks or the beautiful, leggy figure. It was who she was—an American—and we were not. We were foreigners, dark-haired and dark-eyed with olive skin that could never, no matter the sun blocks or foundation makeup, be made into peaches and cream.

Had we been able to see into the future, beyond our noses, which we thought weren't the right shape; beyond our curly hair, which we wanted to be straight; and beyond the screen, which inspired us with a limited vision of what was considered beautiful in America, we would have been able to see the late sixties coming. Soon, ethnic looks would be in. Even Barbie, that quintessential white girl, would suddenly be available in different shades of skin color with bright, colorful outfits that looked like the ones Mami had picked out for us. Our classmates in college wore long braids like Native Americans and embroidered shawls and peasant blouses from South America, and long, diaphanous skirts and dangly earrings from India. They wanted to look exotic—they wanted to look like us.

We felt then a gratifying sense of inclusion, but it had unfortunately come too late. We had already acquired the habit of doubting ourselves as well as the place we came from. To this day, after three decades of living in America, I feel like a stranger in what I now consider my own country. I am still that young teenager sitting in front of the black-and-white TV in my parents' bedroom, knowing in my bones I will never be the beauty queen. There she is, Miss America, but even in my up-to-date, enlightened dreams, she never wears my face.

JAMAICA KINCAID   [b. 1949]

Girl

Born in St. Johns, Antigua, and raised by devoted parents, **Jamaica Kincaid** (b. 1949) entered college in the United States but withdrew to write. After her stories appeared in notable publications, she took a staff position on *The New Yorker.* Her first book, a story collection entitled *At the Bottom of the River* (1984), won a major award from the American Academy and Institute of Arts and Letters. *Annie John* (1985), an interrelated collection, further explored life in the British West Indies as experienced by a young girl. Kincaid now lives in the United States and continues to write about her homeland in works including *A Small Place* (1988), *Lucy* (1990), *Autobiography of My Mother* (1996), and *My Brother* (1997).

Wash the white clothes on Monday and put them on the stone heap; wash the color clothes on Tuesday and put them on the clothesline to dry; don't walk barehead in the hot sun; cook pumpkin fritters in very hot sweet oil; soak your little cloths right after you take them off; when buying cotton to make yourself a nice blouse, be sure that it doesn't have gum on it, because that way it won't hold up well after a wash; soak salt fish overnight before you cook it; is it true that you sing benna° in Sunday school?; always eat your food in such a way that it won't turn someone else's stomach; on Sundays try to walk like a lady and not like the slut you are so bent on becoming; don't sing benna in Sunday school; you mustn't speak to wharf-rat boys, not even to give directions; don't eat fruits on the street—flies will follow you; *but I don't sing benna on Sundays at all and never in Sunday school;* this is how to sew on a button; this is how to make a button-hole for the button you have just sewed on; this is how to hem a dress when you see the hem coming down and so to prevent yourself from looking like the slut I know you are so bent on becoming; this is how you iron your father's khaki shirt so that it doesn't have a crease; this is how you iron your father's khaki pants so that they don't have a crease; this is how you grow okra—far from the house,

Benna: Calypso music.

because okra tree harbors red ants; when you are growing dasheen, make sure it gets plenty of water or else it makes your throat itch when you are eating it; this is how you sweep a corner; this is how you sweep a whole house; this is how you sweep a yard; this is how you smile to someone you don't like too much; this is how you smile to someone you don't like at all; this is how you smile to someone you like completely; this is how you set a table for tea; this is how you set a table for dinner; this is how you set a table for dinner with an important guest; this is how you set a table for lunch; this is how you set a table for breakfast; this is how to behave in the presence of men who don't know you very well, and this way they won't recognize immediately the slut I have warned you against becoming; be sure to wash every day, even if it is with your own spit; don't squat down to play marbles—you are not a boy, you know; don't pick people's flowers—you might catch something; don't throw stones at blackbirds, because it might not be a blackbird at all; this is how to make a bread pudding; this is how to make doukona;° this is how to make pepper pot; this is how to make a good medicine for a cold; this is how to make a good medicine to throw away a child before it even becomes a child; this is how to catch a fish; this is how to throw back a fish you don't like, and that way something bad won't fall on you; this is how to bully a man; this is how a man bullies you; this is how to love a man, and if this doesn't work there are other ways, and if they don't work don't feel too bad about giving up; this is how to spit up in the air if you feel like it, and this is how to move quick so that it doesn't fall on you; this is how to make ends meet; always squeeze bread to make sure it's fresh; *but what if the baker won't let me feel the bread?;* you mean to say that after all you are really going to be the kind of woman who the baker won't let near the bread?

[1978]

Doukona: A spicy plantain pudding.

BERNARD COOPER [b. 1951]

A Clack of Tiny Sparks: Remembrances of a Gay Boyhood

Novelist, essayist, and short-story writer **Bernard Cooper** was born in Los Angeles and earned his B.F.A. and M.F.A. at the California Institute of the Arts. He is the winner of the PEN/Ernest Hemingway Award, an O. Henry Prize, a Guggenheim Fellowship, and a Getty Center for the Arts and Humanities Fellowship. Cooper's publications include two essay collections—*Maps to Anywhere* (1990) and *Truth Serum* (1996), the novel *A Year of Rhymes* (1993), a collection of short stories called *Guess Again* (2000), and *The Bill from My Father: A Memoir* (2006). Cooper's writing has appeared in *Ploughshares*, *Harper's*, the *Paris Review*, and the *New York Times Magazine*. He has taught at the Otis/Parsons Institute of Art and Design, the Southern California Institute of Architecture, and the UCLA Writer's Program, and is currently employed as an art critic for *Los Angeles Magazine*.

Cooper's "A Clack of Tiny Sparks: Remembrances of a Gay Boyhood" (1991), which first appeared in *Harper's*, is an autobiographical coming-of-age story recounting Cooper's dawning awareness of his homosexuality. Anxious and struggling with his sense of self-denial, Cooper applies oft-heard maxims to his own scenario in an effort to appear straight, feel straight, be straight.

Theresa Sanchez sat behind me in ninth-grade algebra. When Mr. Hubbley faced the blackboard, I'd turn around to see what she was reading; each week a new book was wedged inside her copy of *Today's Equations*. The deception worked; from Mr. Hubbley's point of view, Theresa was engrossed in the value of X, but I knew otherwise. One week she perused *The Wisdom of the Orient*, and I could tell from Theresa's contemplative expression that the book contained exotic thoughts, guidelines handed down from high. Another week it was a paperback novel whose title, *Let Me Live My Life*, appeared in bold print atop every page,

Bernard Cooper, "A Clack of Tiny Sparks: Remembrances of a Gay Boyhood" from *Harper's Magazine*, January 1991. Reprinted with special permission.

and whose cover, a gauzy photograph of a woman biting a strand of pearls, head thrown back in an attitude of ecstasy, confirmed my suspicion that Theresa Sanchez was mature beyond her years. She was the tallest girl in school. Her bouffant hairdo, streaked with blond, was higher than the flaccid bouffants of other girls. Her smooth skin, plucked eyebrows, and painted fingernails suggested hours of pampering, a worldly and sensual vanity that placed her within the domain of adults. Smiling dimly, steeped in daydreams, Theresa moved through the crowded halls with a languid, self-satisfied indifference to those around her. "You are merely children," her posture seemed to say. "I can't be bothered." The week Theresa hid *101 Ways to Cook Hamburger* behind her algebra book, I could stand it no longer and, after the bell rang, ventured a question.

"Because I'm having a dinner party," said Theresa. "Just a couple of intimate friends."

No fourteen-year-old I knew had ever given a dinner party, let alone used the word "intimate" in conversation. "Don't you have a mother?" I asked.

Theresa sighed a weary sigh, suffered my strange inquiry. "Don't be so naive," she said. "Everyone has a mother." She waved her hand to indicate the brick school buildings outside the window. "A higher education should have taught you that." Theresa draped an angora sweater over her shoulders, scooped her books from the graffiti-covered desk, and just as she was about to walk away, she turned and asked me, "Are you a fag?"

There wasn't the slightest hint of rancor or condescension in her voice. 5
The tone was direct, casual. Still I was stunned, giving a sidelong glance to make sure no one had heard. "No," I said. Blurted really, with too much defensiveness, too much transparent fear in my response. Octaves lower than usual, I tried a "Why?"

Theresa shrugged. "Oh, I don't know. I have lots of friends who are fags. You remind me of them." Seeing me bristle, Theresa added, "It was just a guess." I watched her erect, angora back as she sauntered out the classroom door.

She had made an incisive and timely guess. Only days before, I'd invited Grady Rogers to my house after school to go swimming. The instant Grady shot from the pool, shaking water from his orange hair, freckled shoulders shining, my attraction to members of my own sex became a matter I could no longer suppress or rationalize. Sturdy and boisterous and gap-toothed, Grady was an inveterate backslapper, a formidable arm wrestler, a wizard at basketball. Grady was a body at home in his body.

My body was a marvel I hadn't gotten used to; my arms and legs would sometimes act of their own accord, knocking over a glass at dinner or

36

flinching at an oncoming pitch. I was never singled out as a sissy, but I could have been just as easily as Bobby Keagan, a gentle, intelligent, and introverted boy reviled by my classmates. And although I had always been aware of a tacit rapport with Bobby, a suspicion that I might find with him a rich friendship, I stayed away. Instead, I emulated Grady in the belief that being seen with him, being like him, would somehow vanquish my self-doubt, would make me normal by association.

Apart from his athletic prowess, Grady had been gifted with all the trappings of what I imagined to be a charmed life: a fastidious, aproned mother who radiated calm, maternal concern; a ruddy, stoic father with a knack for home repairs. Even the Rogerses' small suburban house in Hollywood, with its spindly Colonial furniture and chintz curtains, was a testament to normalcy.

Grady and his family bore little resemblance to my clan of Eastern 10 European Jews, a dark and vociferous people who ate with abandon— matzo and halvah and gefilte fish; foods the goyim couldn't pronounce— who cajoled one another during endless games of canasta, making the simplest remark about the weather into a lengthy philosophical discourse on the sun and the seasons and the passage of time. My mother was a chain-smoker, a dervish in a frowsy housedress. She showed her love in the most peculiar and obsessive ways, like spending hours extracting every seed from a watermelon before she served it in perfectly bite-sized geometric pieces. Preoccupied and perpetually frantic, my mother succumbed to bouts of absentmindedness so profound she'd forget what she was saying midsentence, smile and blush and walk away. A divorce attorney, my father wore roomy, iridescent suits, and the intricacies, the deceits inherent in his profession, had the effect of making him forever tense and vigilant. He was "all wound up," as my mother put it. But when he relaxed, his laughter was explosive, his disposition prankish: "Walk this way," a waitress would say, leading us to our table, and my father would mimic the way she walked, arms akimbo, hips liquid, while my mother and I were wracked with laughter. Buoyant or brooding, my parents' moods were unpredictable, and in a household fraught with extravagant emotion it was odd and awful to keep my longing secret.

One day I made the mistake of asking my mother what a "fag" was. I knew exactly what Theresa had meant but hoped against hope it was not what I thought; maybe "fag" was some French word, a harmless term like "naive." My mother turned from the stove, flew at me, and grabbed me by the shoulders. "Did someone call you that?" she cried.

"Not me," I said. "Bobby Keagan."

"Oh," she said, loosening her grip. She was visibly relieved. And didn't answer. The answer was unthinkable.

* * *

For weeks after, I shook with the reverberations from that afternoon in the kitchen with my mother, pained by the memory of her shocked expression and, most of all, her silence. My longing was wrong in the eyes of my mother, whose hazel eyes were the eyes of the world, and if that longing continued unchecked, the unwieldy shape of my fate would be cast, and I'd be subjected to a lifetime of scorn.

During the remainder of the semester, I became the scientist of my 15 own desire, plotting ways to change my yearning for boys into a yearning for girls. I had enough evidence to believe that any habit, regardless of how compulsive, how deeply ingrained, could be broken once and for all: The plastic cigarette my mother purchased at the Thrifty pharmacy—one end was red to approximate an ember, the other tan like a filtered tip—was designed to wean her from the real thing. To change a behavior required self-analysis, cold resolve, and the substitution of one thing for another: plastic, say, for tobacco. Could I also find a substitute for Grady? What I needed to do, I figured, was kiss a girl and learn to like it.

This conclusion was affirmed one Sunday morning when my father, seeing me wrinkle my nose at the pink slabs of lox he layered on a bagel, tried to convince me of its salty appeal. "You should try some," he said. "You don't know what you're missing."

"It's loaded with protein," added my mother, slapping a platter of sliced onions onto the dinette table. She hovered above us, cinching her housedress, eyes wet from onion fumes, the mock cigarette dangling from her lips.

My father sat there chomping with gusto, emitting a couple of hearty grunts to dramatize his satisfaction. And still I was not convinced. After a loud and labored swallow, he told me I may not be fond of lox today, but sooner or later I'd learn to like it. One's tastes, he assured me, are destined to change.

"Live," shouted my mother over the rumble of the Mixmaster. "Expand your horizons. Try new things." And the room grew fragrant with the batter of a spice cake.

The opportunity to put their advice into practice, and try out my plan 20 to adapt to girls, came the following week when Debbie Coburn, a member of Mr. Hubbley's algebra class, invited me to a party. She cornered me in the hall, furtive as a spy, telling me her parents would be gone for the evening and slipping into my palm a wrinkled sheet of notebook paper. On it were her address and telephone number, the lavender ink in a tidy cursive. "Wear cologne," she advised, wary eyes darting back and forth. "It's a make-out party. Anything can happen."

The Santa Ana wind blew relentlessly the night of Debbie's party, careening down the slopes of the Hollywood hills, shaking the road signs and stoplights in its path. As I walked down Beachwood Avenue, trees thrashed, surrendered their leaves, and carob pods bombarded the pavement. The sky was a deep but luminous blue, the air hot, abrasive, electric. I had to squint in order to check the number of the Coburns' apartment, a three-story building with glitter embedded in its stucco walls. Above the honeycombed balconies was a sign that read BEACH-WOOD TERRACE in lavender script resembling Debbie's.

From down the hall, I could hear the plaintive strains of Little Anthony's "I Think I'm Going Out of My Head." Debbie answered the door bedecked in an Empire dress, the bodice blue and orange polka dots, the rest a sheath of black and white stripes. "Op art," proclaimed Debbie. She turned in a circle, then proudly announced that she'd rolled her hair in orange juice cans. She patted the huge unmoving curls and dragged me inside. Reflections from the swimming pool in the courtyard, its surface ruffled by wind, shuddered over the ceiling and walls. A dozen of my classmates were seated on the sofa or huddled together in corners, their whispers full of excited imminence, their bodies barely discernible in the dim light. Drapes flanking the sliding glass doors bowed out with every gust of wind, and it seemed that the room might lurch from its foundations and sail with its cargo of silhouettes into the hot October night.

Grady was the last to arrive. He tossed a six-pack of beer into Debbie's arms, barreled toward me, and slapped my back. His hair was slicked back with Vitalis, lacquered furrows left by the comb. The wind hadn't shifted a single hair. "Ya ready?" he asked, flashing the gap between his front teeth and leering into the darkened room. "You bet," I lied.

Once the beers had been passed around, Debbie provoked everyone's attention by flicking on the overhead light. "Okay," she called. "Find a partner." This was the blunt command of a hostess determined to have her guests aroused in an orderly fashion. Everyone blinked, shuffled about, and grabbed a member of the opposite sex. Sheila Garabedian landed beside me — entirely at random, though I want to believe she was driven by passion — her timid smile giving way to plain fear as the light went out. Nothing for a moment but the heave of the wind and the distant banter of dogs. I caught a whiff of Sheila's perfume, tangy and sweet as Hawaiian Punch. I probed her face with my own, grazing the small scallop of an ear, a velvety temple, and though Sheila's trembling made me want to stop, I persisted with my mission until I found her lips, tightly sealed as a private letter. I held my mouth over hers and gathered her shoulders closer, resigned to the possibility that, no matter how long we stood there, Sheila would be too scared to kiss me back. Still, she exhaled through her nose, and I listened to the squeak of every breath as though it were a sigh of inordinate pleasure. Diving within myself, I monitored my heartbeat and respiration, trying to will stimulation into being, and all the while an image intruded, an image of Grady erupting from our pool, rivulets of water sliding down his chest. "Change," shouted Debbie, switching on the light. Sheila thanked me, pulled away, and continued her routine of gracious terror with every boy through-out the evening. It didn't matter whom I held—Margaret Sims, Betty Vernon, Elizabeth Lee—my experiment was a failure; I continued to picture Grady's wet chest, and Debbie would bellow "change" with such fervor, it could have been my own voice, my own incessant reprimand.

Our hostess commandeered the light switch for nearly half an hour. 25 Whenever the light came on, I watched Grady pivot his head toward the newest prospect, his eyebrows arched in expectation, his neck blooming with hickeys, his hair, at last, in disarray. All that shuffling across the car-pet charged everyone's arms and lips with static, and eventually, between low moans and soft osculations, I could hear the clack of my tiny sparks and see them flare here and there in the dark like meager, short-lived stars.

I saw Theresa, sultry and aloof as ever, read three more books—*North American Reptiles*, *Bonjour Tristesse*, and *MGM: A Pictorial History*—before she vanished early in December. Rumors of her fate abounded. Debbie Coburn swore that Theresa had been "knocked up" by an older man, a traffic cop, she thought, or a grocer. Nearly quivering with relish, Debbie told me and Grady about the home for unwed mothers in the San Fernando Valley, a compound teeming with pregnant girls who had nothing to do but touch their stomachs and contemplate their mistake. Even Bobby Keagan, who took Theresa's place behind me in algebra, had a theory regarding her disappearance colored by his own wish for escape; he imagined that Theresa, disillusioned with society, booked passage to a tropical island, there to live out the rest of her days without restrictions or ridicule. "No wonder she flunked out of school," I over-heard Mr. Hubbley tell a fellow teacher one afternoon. "Her head was always in a book."

Along with Theresa went my secret, or at least the dread that she might divulge it, and I felt, for a while, exempt from suspicion. I was, however, to run across Theresa one last time. It happened during a period of torrential rain that, according to reports on the six o'clock news, washed houses from the hillsides and flooded the downtown streets. The halls of Joseph Le Conte Junior High were festooned with Christmas decorations: crepe-paper garlands, wreaths studded with plastic berries, and one requisite Star of David twirling above the atten-dance desk. In Arts and Crafts, our teacher, Gerald (he was the only teacher who allowed us—*required* us—to call him by his first name), handed out blocks of balsa wood and instructed us to carve them into bugs. We would paint eyes and antennae with tempera and hang them on a Christmas tree he'd made the previous night. "Voilà," he crooned, unveiling his creation from a burlap sack. Before us sat a tortured scrub, a wardrobe-worth of wire hangers that were bent like branches and soldered together. Gerald credited his inspiration to a Charles Addams cartoon he's seen in which Morticia, grimly preparing for the holidays, hangs vampire bats on a withered pine. "All that red and green," said Gerald. "So predictable. So *boring.*"

As I chiseled a beetle and listened to rain pummel the earth, Gerald handed me an envelope and asked me to take it to Mr. Kendrick, the drama teacher. I would have thought nothing of his request if I hadn't seen Theresa on my way down the hall. She was cleaning out her locker, blithely dropping the sum of its contents — pens and textbooks and mimeographs — into a trash can. "Have a nice life," she sang as I passed. I mustered the courage to ask her what had happened. We stood alone in the silent hall, the reflections of wreaths and garlands submerged in brown linoleum.

"I transferred to another school. They don't have grades or bells, and you get to study whatever you want." Theresa was quick to sense my incredulity. "Honest," she said. "The school is progressive." She gazed into a glass cabinet that held the trophies of track meets and intramural spelling bees. "God," she sighed, "this place is so...barbaric." I was still trying to decide whether or not to believe her story when she asked me where I was headed. "Dear," she said, her exclamation pooling in the silence, "that's no ordinary note, if you catch my drift." The envelope was blank and white; I looked up at Theresa, baffled. "Don't be so naive," she muttered, tossing an empty bottle of nail polish into the trash can. It struck bottom with a resolute thud. "Well," she said, closing her locker and breathing deeply, "bon voyage." Theresa swept through the double doors and in seconds her figure was obscured by rain.

As I walked toward Mr. Kendrick's room, I could feel Theresa's insinu- 30 ation burrow in. I stood for a moment and watched Mr. Kendrick through the pane in the door. He paced intently in front of the class, handsome in his shirt and tie, reading from a thick book. Chalked on the blackboard behind him was THE ODYSSEY BY HOMER. I have no recollection of how Mr. Kendrick reacted to the note, whether he accepted it with pleasure or embarrassment, slipped it into his desk drawer or the pocket of his shirt. I have scavenged that day in retrospect, trying to see Mr. Kendrick's expression, wondering if he acknowledged me in any way as his liaison. All I recall is the sight of his mime through a pane of glass, a lone man mouthing an epic, his gestures ardent in empty air.

Had I delivered a declaration of love? I was haunted by the need to

41

know. In fantasy, a kettle shot steam, the glue released its grip, and I read the letter with impunity. But how would such a letter begin? Did the common endearments apply? This was a message between two men, a message for which I had no precedent, and when I tried to envision the contents, apart from a hasty, impassioned scrawl, my imagination faltered.

Once or twice I witnessed Gerald and Mr. Kendrick walk together into the faculty lounge or say hello at the water fountain, but there was nothing especially clandestine or flirtatious in their manner. Besides, no matter how acute my scrutiny, I wasn't sure, short of a kiss, exactly what to look for—what semaphore of gesture, what encoded word. I suspected there were signs, covert signs that would give them away, just as I'd unwittingly given myself away to Theresa.

In the school library, a *Webster's* unabridged dictionary lay on a wooden podium, and I padded toward it with apprehension; along with clues to the bond between my teachers, I risked discovering information that might incriminate me as well. I had decided to consult the dictionary during lunch period, when most of the students would be on the playground. I clutched my notebook, moving in such a way as to appear both studious and nonchalant, actually believing that, unless I took precautions, someone would see me and guess what I was up to. The closer I came to the podium, the more obvious, I thought, was my endeavor; I felt like the model of The Visible Man in our science class, my heart's undulations, my overwrought nerves legible through transparent skin. A couple of kids riffled through the card catalogue. The librarian, a skinny woman whose perpetual whisper and rubber-soled shoes caused her to drift through the room like a phantom, didn't seem to register my presence. Though I'd looked up dozens of words before, the pages felt strange beneath my fingers. *Homer* was the first word I saw. *Hominid. Homogenize.* I feigned interest and skirted other words before I found the word I was after. Under the heading HO•MO•SEX•U•AL was the terse definition: *adj. Pertaining to, characteristic of, or exhibiting homosexuality. —n. A homosexual person.* I read the definition again and again, hoping the words would yield more than they could. I shut the dictionary, swallowed hard, and, none the wiser, hurried away.

As for Gerald and Mr. Kendrick, I never discovered evidence to prove or dispute Theresa's claim. By the following summer, however, I had overhead from my peers a confounding amount about homosexuals: They wore green on Thursday, couldn't whistle, hypnotized boys with a piercing glance. To this lore, Grady added a surefire test to ferret them out.

"A test?" I said.

"You ask a guy to look at his fingernails, and if he looks at them like this"—Grady closed his fingers into a fist and examined his nails with manly detachment—"then he's okay. But if he does this"—he held out his hands at arm's length, splayed his fingers, and coyly cocked his head—"you'd better watch out." Once he'd completed his demonstration, Grady peeled off his shirt and plunged into our pool. I dove in after. It was early June, the sky immense, glassy, placid. My father was cooking spareribs on the barbecue, an artist with a basting brush. His apron bore the caricature of a frazzled French chef. Mother curled on a chaise lounge, plumes of smoke wafting from her nostrils. In a stupor of contentment she took another drag, closed her eyes, and arched her face toward the sun.

Grady dog-paddled through the deep end, spouting a fountain of chlorinated water. Despite shame and confusion, my longing for him hadn't diminished; it continued to thrive without air and light, like a luminous fish in the dregs of the sea. In the name of play, I swam up behind him, encircled his shoulders, astonished by his taut flesh. The two of us flailed, pretended to drown. Beneath the heavy press of water, Grady's orange hair wavered, a flame that couldn't be doused.

I've lived with a man for seven years. Some nights, when I'm half-asleep and the room is suffused with blue light, I reach out to touch the expanse of his back, and it seems as if my fingers sink into his skin, and I feel the pleasure a diver feels the instant he enters a body of water.

I have few regrets. But one is that I hadn't said to Theresa, "Of course I'm a fag." Maybe I'd have met her friends. Or become friends with her. Imagine the meals we might have concocted: hamburger Stroganoff, Swedish meatballs in a sweet translucent sauce, steaming slabs of Salisbury steak.

SAVANNA ODEM

You Act White

These days, it's not uncommon to see a multi-racial person walking around. I mean it's 2012. So, why does it seem like some people still have a problem with multi-racial people? I'm half black and half white, so being multi-racial was the norm for me. If you were to ask me whether I feel more white or black, I wouldn't be able to pick just one race. Being mixed isn't a lifestyle; it's just who I am.

The first time I felt like I was asked to identify with one race was my first day of 8th grade. As I walked into homeroom in Mrs. Yott's class. I wasn't expecting anything but another normal year. Mrs. Yott was the geography teacher, so her room was full of colorful maps and globes. As I sat in a group with my friends next to a giant globe, I noticed there were a few new people: a girl from Harper Creek Middle School and three other black girls. One of the black girls was tall and chubby, one was regular height and average sized, and one was super tiny. I didn't think anything of it because we got new people all the time. When the bell rang, the group I was sitting with all got up to go to their seats. As I was walking to my seat, I noticed that the new black girls were looking at me and whispering. It struck me as odd and I thought to myself, "Well I guess we're not gonna be friends with each other," and proceeded to my seat.

After homeroom, everyone went to their classes for the day. Gym was my last class of the day. I hadn't seen the new girls all day, but then I walked into the hallway and realized they were walking in the direction of the locker rooms. I didn't want to walk next to them and I didn't want to pass them either, so I started walking more slowly. I thought to myself that this was bad luck, but decided that I was going to give the situation the benefit of the doubt. Everyone got ready for gym class and headed for the gym. Our gym teacher, Mrs. Bussler, told us we were going to be playing dodge ball because she didn't have anything else planned. We all just rolled our eyes because that was a typical Mrs. Bussler move. She split the class right down the middle and put us into two teams. I looked around at who was on my team and, of course, there they were. The three girls who I had a feeling had been talking about me, maybe all day.

The game got started and one by one people got hit with the red, bouncy ball and were sent to sit by the wall. I got hit towards the middle of the game and walked to the side of the wall where one of my best friends, Lynsee, was sitting. We made small talk and then I started getting weird vibes from her. She said with a concerned look on her face, "I don't want you to be upset, but I think Janae, Kamaria and Ty'Asia have been making fun of you all class because I kind of overheard them."

"Oh, so that's their names," I replied. It didn't really come as a surprise since I had a weird feeling about them all day. I shrugged it off and gym class ended, along with the school day.

The next day at lunch, I sat at a big table with a group of my friends and the three girls and some of their friends just happened to be sitting at the table next to us. I ignored them. Then they started getting more obnoxious and I heard one of them say, "She acts weird," and the rest of them snickered.

Lynsee said to me, "I think they're talking about you," so I turned around and asked, "Do you have a problem?"

They all looked at me with smirks on their faces and said, "Not really."

I replied, "Really? I think you do because I'm pretty sure you've been talking about me for the past couple of days," and they snarked back with, "Don't worry about it, mutt." I honestly didn't even know what to say because I've never been called something like that. No one had ever thrown a racial slur at me. So, I rolled my eyes and turned my back to them to continue lunch with my friends.

I went home that day and told my mom what happened. She was immediately furious and wanted to go to the principal. I didn't think that was a good idea because I knew that going to the principal would only make it worse.

However, the situation continued to get worse anyway. For the next few months, they made fun of me to my face and behind my back. They would say, "You act white," and, "You might as well be white." Until then I never thought about what color I acted. How can you act a certain color? I actually started to get a complex about being mixed and for the first time ever, I started to question if I really do "act white." I started looking at how most of my friends acted and what color they were, and I realized that most of my friends were white. I was still confused; I thought we were all past looking at the color of people's skin. I started to think maybe I wasn't black enough and maybe I just would never fit in with any black girls.

Things kept getting worse. Their group of friends got bigger, and at lunch they ganged up on me. Sometimes, if I walked past their table they would yell, "boo!" at me, like I was afraid of them. I didn't want to let them get the best of me, so I always ignored them. I had lots of friends who were there to listen to me, but I never felt any better. I didn't think they could fully understand because they were all 100% white.

One day after school, I was walking to my mom's car to go home and one of the girls picked up a rock and threw it at the back of my head. My mom saw it and right away she got out of the car and dragged me back into the school and into the principal's office. She demanded to see the principal. We went into the office and my mom did all the talking while I just reluctantly sat there. The principal, a black woman, said she'd take care of it and we left.

A couple days later, all their statuses on MySpace were about me being a snitch; they were calling me names and they even had one of their older sisters message me and threaten me. I got so upset over the whole situation that I didn't even want to go to school anymore. I begged my parents to let me stay home, but they told me I had to go to school and hold my head up high. They said, "You can't let people like them dictate what you're gonna do." So I continued to go to school and just took it day by day. The taunting continued, but I held my head high and ignored them like my parents told me to do. Little did I know, they weren't going to stop messing with me that easily.

Sometime later that week when I was at my locker, they threw a container of Vaseline at me and I just lost my cool. I slammed my locker door and whipped around and started yelling at them in the middle of the hallway. Janae walked up to me and got in my face, but I wasn't going to back down. The yelling went on and on and then she pushed me. I lost it. I came back at her and shoved her. A teacher came out of nowhere and stepped in between us. Surprisingly, we didn't get into too much trouble because no one threw any punches. After that our teachers worked extra hard to make sure we weren't near each other because the principal told them what had been going on. A few of our classes got switched around, and I didn't have to deal with Janae, Kamaria and Ty'Asia for the rest of the year.

My situation relates to, "My Ill Literacy Narrative: Growing Up Black, Po and a Girl, in the Hood," by Elaine Richardson. In the story, there is one part about a girl in her neighborhood who was teased because she was light skinned, talked proper, and "acted white." While talking about the how the girl in the book was treated, Richardson said, "Romelda's personal situation, her speech... being 'high yellah' with long flowing hair was read by our female classmates as 'thank[ing] you bedda dan somebody'" (Richardson 53). Looking back, I think maybe my classmates believed I thought I was better than them, and maybe that's why they bullied me. Richardson also talks about how Romelda probably felt being teased by the black girls: "It was their way of critiquing the systems of colourism and discrimination, which lead to feelings of hurt, anger, devaluation and resentment" (Richardson 53). After being bullied by the three girls for months, I started questioning my own race, and I did feel resentment for being mixed. I felt like it would be better if I were just one race or the other. It was like I was having an identity crisis. I wondered if I really did identify with only one race.

Nowadays, I'm more confident about who I am as a mixed person. I still do have a bit of a complex and I still get anxiety when I'm the only mixed person in a group of all white people or all black people, but it's not nearly as bad. I haven't had another experience like that since then. Going through that forced me to re-evaluate and question myself as a mixed person, but it also forced me to figure out who I am as well.

Works Cited

Richardson, Elaine. "My (Ill)Literacy Narrative: Growing Up Black, Po and a Girl, in the Hood." *Gender and Education* 21:6, 753-767. Rpt. In *Mercury Reader: Reading and Writing in the Age of Cultural Diversity*. Ed. Staci Perryman-Clark. Boston: Pearson Learning Solutions, 2012. 41-53. Print.

THOMAS FERRAGUT

Those People

Hi, my name is Thomas. I am six and a half years old.

I like Veggie Tales, peanut butter and jelly sandwiches, and when my sisters let me play with them. I don't like the dark under my bed, going to church, or bread crusts.

Right now, I am watching my very favorite TV show Zoboomafoo. I like this show. I like the monkey, and the animals, and the Kratt Brothers. I especially like when the Kratt Brothers put on their swimsuits and swim with the animals. Actually, they are swimming with some otters right now. The Kratt Brothers should just wear their swimsuits all the time. I'd like that.

"Thomas, do you want some lunch? Your grammie wants to make you a peanut butter and jelly sandwich," my mom calls from the kitchen.

By way of answer I say, "Grammie is here?" Standing up from my seat in front of the TV, I go to give my grammie a hug because you're supposed to hug your grammie. Bracing myself for the inevitable kiss, I steal a peek at the kitchen counter that is about my height. Bread crust. Why do they always make me eat the bread crust? With a sigh, I take my plate off the counter and join my sisters and brother at the nearby table saying, "Thank you, Grammie" because you're supposed to thank people when they give you things even if it's not what you wanted.

About half way through my burden of a meal, I start looking around the room hoping to find a valid reason to not eat my bread crusts. Mom and Grammie are still at the counter talking.

"Erin, I can't believe you would leave your radio on when they were talking about those people. You know you shouldn't be exposing your kids to that" my Grammie said.

"I know, Mom. I guess I just wasn't thinking"

"I just don't get it. Don't they understand what they're doing is wrong?"

"I don't know, Mom. Gay people are just so misguided. All we can really do is pray for them," my Mom replied. My Mom called my Grammie "mom" because she's silly. Grammie isn't mom. Anyway, I don't know what "gay" is, but I'll be sure to avoid it. I wouldn't want to make my mom angry by doing gay.

Hi, my name is Thomas. I am twelve years old.

I like making mayo-ketchup-peanut-butter sandwiches to gross my mom out, playing on the computer, being home schooled, and looking at men with their shirts off. I don't like cleaning the litter box, my grandparents, or my stutter.

"Thomas, can you come into my room for a second? I need to talk to you." my Mom says.

"Uh, yeah." I say calmly. But already my heart has started beating out of my chest. Mom only brings us into her room if we've done something really bad, like sweeping the cat litter under the rug or stealing quarters from the change dish. Something so bad she doesn't want our siblings to know. What could I have done? I don't remember doing anything that bad. Heart thumping, limbs shaking a bit, I follow her into the room. Blue walls, white carpet. It's actually a lot like my room but with a bigger bed and toys aren't everywhere.

"Thomas, you know your dad and I have a program on the computer to let us see what you do on the Internet, right?" I nod, since I know I will stutter if I try to speak. "Well lately it says you've been looking at...

pictures. Pictures of men." That? That must have been bad. I should lie if it's bad.

"P-p-pi-photos? I don't know what you're talking about."

"Well it says you've been looking at pictures of men not fully clothed on various places. Places like gay.com. Listen Thomas, if you have... questions then you can ask your dad and I any time."

"I don't have questions, Mom. I've never been to that site before." That was actually true. I always just used Google image search, but I guess it pulls images from sites like that. There was that word again. Gay. I don't know what it means or why I keep hearing it, but it really seems to bother my Mom a lot. I shouldn't ask or I'll get in trouble. Was gay liking when I look at men? That wouldn't make sense. What could be wrong with that? What if it is though? What if I am this terrible, "gay" person?

Hi, my name is Thomas. I am fourteen years old.

I like video games, reading books, and God. I don't like being home schooled, my mother's parents, or myself.

I kneel down on the red cushion, my face leveling with the screen intended to disguise both my features and the features of my priest. "Bless me father, for I have sinned," I begin going through the verbal ritual, "it has been one week since my last confession. I'm still struggling with a same-sex attraction." I have been for two years actually. Only me and my priest know about it at this point. He says that I shouldn't say I'm struggling with being "gay" because that is the word that people use to try to claim their sin is a part of who they are. In reality, if I were stronger, I could overcome this temptation and be attracted to girls instead. But I'm not strong. I wish I could just die, but the church says I'm not even allowed to do that. People who commit suicide go to hell. It would have to be a genuine accident to be allowed.

We are moving to Michigan soon, but it doesn't really matter to me. I still won't have any close friends. I'll still be broken. If I'm lucky, maybe I'll get to die in a car accident on the way.

Hi, my name is Thomas. I am fifteen years old, but in a week I will be sixteen.

I like video games, living in Michigan, and being a moderator on an internet forum. I don't like my stutter, God, or pretending not to be gay.

I'm lying in my cool basement on a hot day in June, simply lying on the couch alone with my thoughts. I'm not thinking about anything specifically; it's more like I'm thinking about everything. What I want out of life, where I want to go, what I want to do. I want to make enough money to travel a lot, to see the world, to go to college and meet interesting people and do interesting things. I want to be happy with where I am, who I'm with, and who I am. "I'm gay." The words suddenly escape my mouth. I have never actually said that before. Before I've always been "struggling" or something along similar lines. But that's it. I'm not really ok with it, but it's not something I can change. And maybe there isn't anything wrong with it. Maybe I'm not broken after all.

Hi, my name is Thomas. I am sixteen years old.

I like video games, living in Michigan, and going to public school. I don't like my stutter, cold fries, or making my mother upset.

Walking from the kitchen to the living room, I emerge into the brightly lit space. The light from outside shines through the sliding glass door on the far wall, dousing the newly green walls in brilliance. On the couch sits my mother, hurriedly eating so that she can make it to the YMCA where she teaches Zumba. "Hey Mom, when Dad gets back from work, I need to talk to both of you about something important."

"Thomas, if it's so important then just tell me now and I'll call your dad."

"No, I'd rather wait until he's here and talk to you both in person."

"You can't just tell me there's something important to say and then not say it. I'm going to work now, but we'll talk more when I get back."

Well that didn't go quite as intended. Regardless, it's good that I did it. Now I can't chicken out. Today is October 11, 2010, also known as National Coming Out Day. I've already come out to my friends over the past few months, but I've been waiting for the right time to tell my parents. Today is the day. I'm not stupid though. I know my parents are incredibly conservative. I've taken precautions already. My bag is packed in my room upstairs, and I've made arrangements with a friend who says I can stay with him if things go south. Now, however, is the wait.

Trying to divert my thoughts from the confrontation to come, I log onto my laptop to get some homework done. A few hours later, my mother arrives home while I'm making an afternoon snack and immediately she's on my case. "So what do you have to tell me, Thomas?"

Abandoning my half-completed sandwich, I begin to retreat up the open stairway to my room saying, "I already told you that I want to tell both you and Dad in person at the same time!"

"Just tell me Thomas! You're being very rude right now!"

That's it. Spinning on my heel, I'm suddenly facing my mother. The rapid spin displaces the pajamas that I haven't bothered to change out of yet. My two-sizes-too-big shirt hangs lopsided on my frame in contrast to the fire in my eyes, my rigid posture, and my tightly balled fists. "Alright! Fine. Firstly, I'm gay. Secondly, I'm no longer Catholic. There."

Just like that. I'm "out." Her ten second pause seems like an eternity, and her face gives away no reaction. No emotion. "Okay..." she says hesitantly. Then silence. She is still staring at me, her expression betraying nothing of her thoughts. I want her to say something. To react. Say something! I want to scream, but I don't. I stare back, mirroring her stone-faced silence. Finally she continues, carefully trying to control her voice. "Well whatever you're afraid of, don't worry. We still love you, and you won't be kicked out of the house or anything. I need some time to think about this though. We'll talk more later."

I break my stony expression with a grin. Not the most positive reaction possible, but I feel like I could fly right now! "Alright, well while you're thinking I need to go grab my computer and tell all my friends you didn't kick me out."

Hi, my name is Thomas. I am eighteen years old.

In the past two years, my parents slowly got used to the fact that they have a gay son. They started going to PFLAG meetings, also known as Parents and Friends of Lesbians And Gays. "We'll love whoever you love for your sake" turned into "We just want you to be happy and find someone who loves you." My sisters have been ok with it from the start, and in the course of a few months, my little brother went from asserting that I am hell-bound to sticking up for LGBT people whenever he hears someone putting them down.

I like playing video games with my friends, going home to visit my dog, and making videos with the guys on my Youtube collab channel, TheGlobalGays. I don't like studying things I think are useless, walking from Valley 1 to my classes, or waking up early.

That's me. I'm just a freshman in college.

Also, I like men.

Personal and Autobiographical Writing: Summative Questions and Prompts

1. Several of these narratives feature characters attempting to negotiate the norms and values of a different cultural context: for example, the rigorous French language classroom in "Me Talk Pretty One Day" or United States' beauty norms in "I Want to Be Miss America." Write about a time when you needed to negotiate the norms of a different culture. Keep these writing traits, employed by Sedaris and Alvarez, in mind as you write: use of concrete detail, orientation of the reader to the cultural context, and development of yourself as a character.

2. Note that many of the narratives devote much of the text to developing elements other than plot. For example, study the development of characters in paragraphs one and ten in "A Clack of Tiny Sparks," or re-read the description of Dick Gregory's home in paragraph two of "Shame." Note that Cooper and Gregory construct their paragraphs to read like a unified description, not a list of details. After reading, pick a person or place that was/is a significant part of your identity development and write one to two paragraphs of description. Keep your paragraphs focused and vivid, and avoid depending on generalizations that give a reader little information (such as "a nice guy" or "a beautiful place").

3. Re-read Jamaica Kincaid's "Girl" and select one of the following rhetorical devices for analysis: syntax, voice, repetition, or parallelism. In several paragraphs, describe the unique features of your chosen device and explain how this device aids the development of an overall theme or purpose. In your response, use carefully selected direct quotations from the piece.

Part II: Persuasive and Public Writing

Public writing includes writing about others, specific ideas, concepts, or themes. One way people often write about these particular concepts and themes is by using argumentation to persuade readers of their particular stances on, or opinions about, an issue. While the first section consisted of personal narratives, the texts in this section intend to persuade readers of various audiences. Further, while it can be argued that persuasion is at work even when writing about one's self, the approaches necessary to persuade readers may differ significantly when the author considers ideas outside the realm of his/her personal experiences.

In ENGL 1050 you will be expected to write an essay that presents a persuasive argument or stance on an issue. To achieve this task, your instructor may ask you to write to a specific audience, taking a stance on an intellectual or ethical issue. The key here is to develop effective strategies for making your cases to your identified audiences. Consider King's direct address to his fellow clergymen in "Letter From Birmingham Jail," or Eggers' appeal to recent college graduates in "Serve or Fail."

Like King and Eggers, additional readings in this section promote some particular stance on an issue using various rhetorical strategies to persuade readers. Featured topics and issues include the purposes of higher education; accepting citizens of diverse cultural backgrounds; beliefs and values about how the world should operate with regard to equality and public policy, to name a few. These essays include Stephen Colbert's "Higher Education," Richard Delgado's "Hate Cannot Be Tolerated," Paul Roberts' "How to Say Nothing in Five Hundred Words," James Baldwin's "If Black English Isn't a Language, Then Tell Me, What Is?", and Susan Brownmiller's "Let's Put Pornography Back in the Closet."

Despite the different genres and types of publications included in this section, each author has to identify and apply specific strategies to persuade members of particular audiences. When authors apply these strategies, they often do this by appealing to **ethos**, **logos**, and **pathos**, a system of persuasion developed by the Greek philosopher, Aristotle. Ethos, or ethical appeal, pertains to the author's ability to persuade using credibility or character. Logos, or logical appeal, pertains to the author's ability to persuade using reasoning or logic. Pathos, or pathetic (emotional) appeal, pertains to the author's ability to appeal to the audience's emotions.

As you read each of these texts, consider the ways the authors make use of ethos, logos, and pathos. Also, consider how arguments are created for different publications that possess specific audience expectations.

STEPHEN COLBERT [b. 1964]

Higher Education

"Teach your children well."
-David Crosby, bloated folk singer and notorious
lesbian inseminator

If there's a bigger contributor to left-wing elitist brainwashing than colleges and universities, I'd like to see it. There's an old saying, "A little knowledge is a dangerous thing." Which means a lot of knowledge must be a really dangerous thing. And it is. Look no further than the example of Ted Kaczynski, a.k.a. the Unabomber. He skipped sixth grade, got a Bachelor's from Harvard followed by a Master's and a Ph.D., and then embarked on a distinguished academic career of blowing people up. Most Ph.D. biographies have similar endings. *Figure of speech: Don't show it to me.*

Ted Kaczynski's last job before he went into full-time Unabombing? Assistant Professor of Mathematics at the University of California, Berkeley, a.k.a. University of Blame America First, Berkeley. Yes, folks, he capped off all those years of being a student by becoming a professor. Let's face it—he'd have been crazy not to go crazy, which only proves my point: the greatest threat facing America today—outside of flag burning, yoga, and vaccination—is higher education. *Hey Docs! How about a vaccine against yoga?*

Just exactly what makes colleges so dangerous? It's the fact their classrooms and lecture halls are filled with a poison known as New Ideas. *Racism, genocide, and bears were all New Ideas.*

New Ideas hurt Americans in two ways:

The Emotional Cost

Let me ask you this: why were you happier when you were a kid? *Unhappy kids can skip this part.*

Because you didn't know anything.

The more you know, the sadder you get.

Don't Believe Me? By the time you finish reading this chapter, over a hundred dogs and cats in animal shelters around the nation will have been euthanized.

Don't know if this is true.

Bet you wish you could erase that knowledge. But it's too late. You learned a <u>New Idea</u>, and it made you sad. College is just more of the same.

The Physical Cost

Pain is the body's way of telling the brain it's in trouble. Similarly, confusion is the brain's way of telling the body, "All right, buddy, drop that book."

Let's try a little experiment. Look at this equation:

$$x = \frac{-b \pm \sqrt{b^2 - 4ac}}{2a}$$

What you feel right now is your body rejecting an idea that is trying to make you learn it. Don't fight the confusion. That's just your mind scabbing over in a desperate attempt to protect you from that unnatural co-mingling of numbers and letters up there. You can't add it, and you can't read it. Useless.

Numbers and letters?! That's a "Catch-22!"

> **GUT-CHECK:** Son of Sam killer David Berkowitz was a well-adjusted member of society until his neighbor's dog started filling his head with a bunch of <u>New Ideas.</u>

While it's true that you encounter New Ideas in colleges and universities, they aren't the real problem. Some of the buildings are nice, and the lawns are quite lush. It's what infests these hives of higher learning that is the source of the real poison.

Writing fans: Watch for this bee metaphor to reappear later!

I'm talking about Academics.

Not a day goes by without a news of **some** anti-American statement by a lunatic in a mortar board and elbow patches.

> **HERE'S A QUESTION:** Elbow patches? Just what are these lecherous lecturers doing behind their lecterns that wears out their elbows so fast? I've got twenty-year old suits, and the elbows are pristine.

Why can't we fire these "edu-bators"? These men and (all too frequently) women who actually give *credit* for learning a foreign language? Because of a little thing called tenure. Well, I have a modest proposal for changing all that. Doctors don't get tenure. Plumbers don't. Can you imagine if baseball players got tenure, and we had to sit there watching them round the bases in a wheelchair?

"edu-bator" ©Stephen Colbert 2007

I can imagine this.

I propose that we do away with tenure on campus once and for all and replace it with a series of clear-cut requirements for professors. In no particular order:

Actually, in this particular order.

- **Cognitive skills test:** Prospective faculty can demonstrate mental competence by memorizing a small passage of text, say, a secret loyalty oath.

- **U.S. History:** Name the winner of the 1943 World Series. I got this idea from an old World War II movie about a squadron that had been infiltrated by a spy. I can't actually answer this question myself, but I'm not the one whose patriotism is in question.

I may have dreamt it.

- **Penmanship:** Can a professor legibly write a brief paragraph? For instance, a secret loyalty oath?

- **Eat a bug:** Prove you love your country as much as the contestants on *Fear Factor*

- **Public Speaking:** Can the faculty member enunciate the secret loyalty oath when they are called upon to do so by a tribunal?

- **Good-faith attempts at heterosexuality:** Prospective professors would be required to produce evidence of at least five years' worth of heterosexual congress. (I'm open-minded. I don't say you must be straight to teach our youth. I only ask that you try.)

- **Loyalty:** If they fell into enemy hands, could the professor keep the loyalty oath secret? No matter what unspeakable act be visited upon them?

It involves a glass rod and a hammer!

- **Essay:** Why Ayn Rand would thrash Shakespeare in a fair fight. This isn't a metaphor for the disparity in the receptions afforded their differing philosophies in today's left-leaning universities. Professors would be required to describe how she'd kick his ass in a bar.

FROM BAD TO WORDS

The easiest way for college professor "bees" to administer *Told you it* their "idea poison" is through their "though-stingers," *was coming back.* commonly called "books."

> **WAKEUP CALL:** Think books aren't scary? Well, think about this: You can't spell "Book" without "Boo!"

The only good book is the Good Book. Come on, the word "Good" is right there in the title. And if there's one thing you can learn from the Bible, it's that books are responsible for the Fall of Man. Look at the story of Adam and Eve. Their lives were pretty great—until they ate fruit from the Tree of Knowledge.

Now, you don't have to be a biblical scholar to see that the fruit clearly represents a book. First, both come from a tree. Second, if my first point didn't convince you, I'm not going to waste my breath with another.

God's point: Ignorance isn't just bliss, it's Paradise.

Unfortunately, Paradise is Lost, and Ignorance may no longer be an option. The Sad Truth is Knowledge has become a racket, and these days it's nearly impossible for the uneducated to break into the world of highly paid professionals. Doctors and lawyers (even some *dentists*) have to go to college. So to live in the gated communities to which you'd like to become accustomed, you've got to play ball. College Ball.

GETTING IN

First off, if you're going to squander your youth in the Ivory Jungle, at least shoot for the Top Schools. They provide *Note:* something the best firms look for, called *cachet.* *The "t" is silent.*

Rule of Thumb: If they're not in the first two pages of *Classy.* *U.S. News and World Report College Guide*, all they offer is information and the possibility of drunken sex with your *Did your* suitemate—a dangerous potential that will gnaw at you for *suitemate gnaw on* the rest of your life. *you?*

The ultimate goal of going to a Top School is the quiet satisfaction of whipping out your Alma Mater at opportune moments. At first blush, most would peg me as an average Joe, and I'm proud of that. By my sheepskin announces to all assembled that though I may be a man of the people, I also have the keys to the clubhouse. I can't count the number of times I've heard the phrase, "You went to Dartmouth? I find that hard to believe."

Heard it while at Dartmouth, too.

The Bad News

Admissions is an arbitrary and demoralizing process, and no matter how hard you work, the outcome is often determined by personal connections. You know what else is like that?

Life.

Also, love-tester machines. No way I'm a "Cold Fish."

I'm at least a "Pretty Spicy."

The Good News

There's an entire industry in this country devoted to getting kids into college.

And while you may not need Kaplan's or *The Princeton Review* to get into a decent school, you should pay for them anyway. We live in a capitalist society. Love it or leave it.

Applying to college teaches youngsters résumé-building, a.k.a.: lying. Here's how it works, kids. Let's say one day you're bored in class, so to pass the time, you make out with the Danish exchange student across the aisle. No, on your college application, you can say that you carried out and Independent Study in Foreign Tongues.

"Hands" Christian Andersen

BY THE NUMBERS: Even the least-padded résumé can be overcome with a solid application essay. Here's the one that got me into Dartmouth:

I went to Dartmouth.

62

"America is therefore the land of the future, where in the ages that lie before us, the burden of the World's History shall reveal itself," said the philosopher, scholar, and lover-of-thought George Wilhelm Friedrich Hegel.

This tract reminds me of the egregious hardships and unwelcome adversity I faced last summer, when I toiled aboriously on my grandfather's venison farm. It was my duty and task to deal the hinds a deadly coup de grace rifle blow at close range while they grazed luxuriously upon the surrounding foliage. Often, I would summon the impoverished and penurious children who lived adjacent to my grandsire's acreage to assist me with my encumberage, thus imparting to them the sublime significance of firearms. Recieving these pauperized youngsters unto my tutelage was the apex, pinnacle, acme, vertex, and zenith of my life's experience.

In conclusion, my great-great-uncle was Daniel B. Fayerweather of Fayerweather Hall.

There are two secrets that make this essay great.

Secret number one: A Thesaurus. Eggheads love the words, so the more you jam in there, the better. Think of it as a verb sausage.

Secret number two: The last sentence. All it takes is a little research, and you can find the campus library, dormitory, or stadium that most plausibly could have been donated by your family. You'd be surprised how rarely these folks check into your background if you show up to the interview wearing an ascot.

CHASE CUTTING: You got in! Feel good? It should. You were deemed worthy, while your high school rival is going to his safety school.

Baghdad State

NOW WHAT?

When you get to college you'll be on your own, maybe for the first time in your life. You will soon learn that peer pressure is a terrible thing. You're going to be tempted to follow the crowd—into a classroom. Fight it. Because there's no need to attend a single lecture.

Don't believe me? Professor Colbert is going to tell you all you need to know.

You're about to get four years' worth of college in five minutes. I went through the course catalogue for prestigious university—I won't say which, because I might have a shot at an honorary doctorate there—and I found that I could reduce the pertinent content of every class into one sentence. I didn't include graduate classes, because if you're even considering an advanced degree, I've already lost you.

C LIT 211	LITERATURE AND CULTURE NEITHER ONE WILL PROTECT YOU FROM A TERROR ATTACK. PLUS, C LIT IS NOT WHAT YOU THINK.
C LIT 314	THE NORTHERN EUROPEAN BALLAD HEY NONNY, NONNY, WHO GIVES A CRAP?
C LIT 342	LITERATURE OF PACIFIC ISLANDERS BEWARE. THERE'S A LOT MORE LITERATURE BY PACIFIC ISLANDERS THAN YOU'D THINK
CSE 322	INTRODUCTION TO FORMAL MODELS IN COMPUTER SCIENCE SOME PEOPLE JUST DON'T LOSE THEIR VIRGINITY, EVER.
DANCE 306	DANCE FOR MEN GO AHEAD. BREAK YOUR MOTHER'S HEART.
DRAMA 101	INTRODUCTION TO THE THEATRE SOME LUCKY STUDENT IS GOING TO SLEEP WITH THE PROFESSOR. IT COULD BE YOU!
ENG 324	CAREERS IN POETRY JUST MOVE BACK IN WITH YOUR PARENTS NOW.
ETHN 384	INTERRACIAL DYNAMICS BETWEEN WOMEN OF COLOR IT'S NOT WHAT YOU THINK.
H ART 331	NATIVE ART OF THE PACIFIC NORTHWEST COAST OOH, LOOK. SOMEBODY DREW A SALMON!
PHIL 101	INTRODUCTION TO PHILOSOPHY IF A TREE FALLS IN THE FOREST AND NO ONE HEARS IT, I HOPE IT LANDS ON A PHILOSOPHY PROFESSOR.
PHIL 356	INTRODUCTION TO METAPHYSICS NOTHING HERE YOU CAN'T PICK UP BY EATING THE WRONG MUSHROOMS ON A CAMPING TRIP.
PSYCH 101	INTRODUCTION TO PSYCHOLOGY SO THEY MADE YOU USE A TOILET. GET OVER IT.
REL 212	COMPARATIVE RELIGION JESUS WINS.
REL 308	INTRODUCTION TO ISLAM IF YOU TAKE THIS CLASS, THE TERRORISTS HAVE WON.
SCI 252	INSECT BEHAVIOR THERE'S NO WAY I'M GETTING RID OF THOSE CARPENTER ANTS WITHOUT AN EXTERMINATOR
SOC 360	ETHNIC STEREOTYPES AND THE HUMOR OF CRUELTY A PROFESSOR WILL TELL YOU A BUNCH OF HILARIOUS JOKES, AND YOU'RE NOT ALLOWED TO LAUGH
C HIS 416	20TH CENTURY MEXICAN SOCIAL MOVEMENTS THE MOVEMENTS ARE NORTHWARD, TAKE PLACE AT NIGHT
WOMEN 357	WOMEN ON WOMEN: THE LITERATURE OF LIBERATION. IT'S NOT WHAT YOU THINK

Now that you have your education covered, what will you do with all that free time? Well, luckily, college is good for one thing. Can you guess what it is? I'll give you a hint: it starts with "secret" and ends with "societies."

Whether they be Fraternities or Eating Clubs or (in Louisiana) Parishes, universities are the best places a young man can meet and bond with, through an elaborate hazing process, those who can give him a leg up for the rest of his life.

I cemented my lasting relationships with America's future movers and shakers by being forced to strip naked with half my fellow pledges and pass a greased 45 rpm record of Foreigner's "Hot Blooded" from ass crack to ass crack. It could have been worse. The other half of the pledges were passing a greased turntable.

Still played post-crack. Let's see an MP3 do that.

Don't Believe me? While most of his peers at Yale were writing essays about the tension between stasis and dynamism in *Mariana in the Moated Grange,* young George W. Bush was making connections that would eventually lead to him becoming the most Powerful Man in the World.™

I speak, of course, of **Skull and Bones**, a shadowy organization that admits only the most deserving Yalesmen. Its members swear an oath of secrecy, and use their wealth and access to power to promote one another once they graduate into the "real world." For well over a century, Skull and Bones has provided a safe and brotherly environment where future Supreme Court Justices, Presidents, and Captains of Industry can gather to urinate on Geronimo's bones.

THE TAKEAWAY: Contrary to what you'll be taught in college, evolution is a farce, but Darwin did have one good idea: Social Darwinism. You see, in the animal kingdom, God grants long life to whichever lion He thinks is prettiest. But in the world of human society, only the strongest, boldest, and worthiest individuals get the most sex, get the most power, and live the longest. College is the place to meet those people, and once you do, find out their darkest secret.

It may come in handy someday.

[2007]

RICHARD DELGADO

Hate Cannot Be Tolerated

Educated at the University of Washington and the University of California–Berkeley, **Richard Delgado** is a leading commentator on race in the United States. His 1996 book *The Rodrigo Chronicles: Conversations about America and Race* was nominated for the Pulitzer Prize and won the Gustavus Myers Prize for outstanding book on human rights in North America. In addition, he has edited or authored five other books that have won the Gustavus Myers Prize, including the 1995 *The Price We Pay: The Case against Racist Speech, Hate Propaganda, and Pornography*, edited with Laura Lederer, and the 1996 *The Coming Race War? And Other Apocalyptic Tales of America after Affirmative Action and Welfare*, which also won the 1997 American Library Association Choice Outstanding Academic Book Award. Delgado is currently the University Distinguished Professor of Law and Derrick Bell Fellow at the University of Pittsburgh School of Law.

In his essay "Hate Cannot Be Tolerated," Delgado defends hate-speech codes that some colleges have recently enacted. Hate speech, he argues, does not foster conversation and is a veritable "slap in the face" to its victims; thus, rules that govern it should be applauded.

Anonymous vandals scrawl hate-filled graffiti outside a Jewish student center. Black students at a law school find unsigned fliers stuffed inside their lockers screaming that they do not belong there. At a third campus, a group of toughs hurls epithets at a young Latino student walking home late at night.

In response to a rising tide of such incidents, some colleges have enacted hate-speech codes or applied existing rules against individuals whose conduct interferes with the educational opportunities of others. Federal courts have extended "hostile environment" case law to schools that tolerate a climate of hate for women and students of color.

Despite the alarm these measures sometimes elicit, nothing is wrong with them. In each case, the usual and preferred response—"more speech"—is unavailable to the victim. With anonymous hate speech such as the flier or graffiti, the victim cannot talk back, for the hate speaker delivers the message in a cowardly fashion. And talking back to aggressors is rarely an option. Indeed, many hate crimes began just this way: The victim talked back—and paid with his life.

Hate speech is rarely an invitation to a conversation. More like a slap in the face, it reviles and silences. College counselors report that campuses where highly publicized incidents of hate speech have taken place show a decline in minority enrollment as students of color instead choose to attend schools where the environment is healthier.

A few federal courts have declared overly broad hate-speech codes 5 unconstitutional, as well they should. Nothing is gained by a rule so broad it could be construed as forbidding the discussion of controversial subjects such as evolution or affirmative action.

But this is not what most people mean by hate speech, nor are colleges barred from drafting narrow rules that hone in on the conduct they wish to control. And when they do, courts are very likely to find in their favor. Recent Supreme Court rulings striking down laws upholding affirmative action and approving punishment for cross-burning show that the court is not unaware of current trends. Society is becoming more diverse. Reasonable rules aimed at accommodating that diversity and regulating the conduct of bullies and bigots are to be applauded—not feared.

PAUL ROBERTS [1917–1967]

How to Say Nothing in Five Hundred Words

California-born **Paul Roberts** received his B.A. from San Jose State College and his M.A. and Ph.D. from the University of California at Berkeley, where he taught for fourteen years after serving in the merchant marine during World War II. Writing in a down-to-earth, often humorous style, Roberts published several books on English composition, including *Understanding Grammar* (1954), *English Sentences* (1962), and *Modern Grammar* (1954). He died in Rome in 1967.

"How to Say Nothing in Five Hundred Words" is from Roberts's best-known book, *Understanding English* (1958), and is representative of his clarity and wit. Roberts recommends that composition students check their tendency to state the obvious and instead strive for interesting content backed by concrete examples.

NOTHING ABOUT SOMETHING

It's Friday afternoon, and you have almost survived another week of classes. You are just looking forward dreamily to the week end when the English instructor says: "For Monday you will turn in a five-hundred word composition on college football."

Well, that puts a good big hole in the week end. You don't have any strong views on college football one way or the other. You get rather excited during the season and go to all the home games and find it rather more fun than not. On the other hand, the class has been reading Robert Hutchins in the anthology and perhaps Shaw's "Eighty-Yard Run," and from the class discussion you have got the idea that the instructor thinks college football is for the birds. You are no fool, you. You can figure out what side to take.

After dinner you get out the portable typewriter that you got for high school graduation. You might as well get it over with and enjoy Saturday and Sunday. Five hundred words is about two double-spaced pages with normal margins. You put in a sheet of paper, think up a title, and you're off:

WHY COLLEGE FOOTBALL SHOULD BE ABOLISHED

College football should be abolished because it's bad for the school and also bad for the players. The players are so busy practicing that they don't have any time for their studies.

This, you feel, is a mighty good start. The only trouble is that it's only thirty-two words. You still have four hundred and sixty-eight to go, and you've pretty well exhausted the subject. It comes to you that you do your best thinking in the morning, so you put away the typewriter and go to the movies. But the next morning you have to do your washing and some math problems, and in the afternoon you go to the game. The English instructor turns up too, and you wonder if you've taken the right side after all. Saturday night you have a date, and Sunday morning you have to go to church. (You shouldn't let English assignments interfere with your religion.) What with one thing and another, it's ten o'clock Sunday night before you get out the typewriter again. You make a pot of coffee and start to fill out your views on college football. Put a little meat on the bones.

WHY COLLEGE FOOTBALL SHOULD BE ABOLISHED

In my opinion, it seems to me that college football should be abolished. The reason why I think this to be true is because I feel that football is bad for the colleges in nearly every respect. As Robert Hutchins says in his article in our anthology in which he discusses college football, it would be better if the colleges had race horses and had races with one another, because then the horses would not have to attend classes. I firmly agree with Mr. Hutchins on this point, and I am sure that many other students would agree too.

One reason why it seems to me that college football is bad is that it has become too commercial. In the olden times when people played football just for the fun of it, maybe college football was all right, but they do not play football just for the fun of it now as they used to in the old days. Nowadays college football is what you might call a big business. Maybe this is not true at all schools, and I don't think it is especially true here at State, but certainly this is the case at most colleges and universities in America nowadays, as Mr. Hutchins points out in his very interesting article. Actually the coaches and alumni go around to the high schools and offer the high school stars large salaries to come to their colleges and play football for them. There was one case where a high school star was offered a convertible if he would play football for a certain college.

Another reason for abolishing college football is that it is bad for the players. They do not have time to get a college education, because they are so busy playing football. A football player has to practice every afternoon from three to six, and then he is so tired that he can't concentrate on his studies. He just feels like dropping off to sleep after dinner, and then the next day he goes to his classes without having studied and maybe he fails the test.

(Good ripe stuff so far, but you're still a hundred and fifty-one words from home. One more push.)

Also I think college football is bad for the colleges and the universities because not very many students get to participate in it. Out of a college of ten thousand students only seventy-five or a hundred play football, if that many. Football is what you might call a spectator sport. That means that most people go to watch it but do not play it themselves.

(Four hundred and fifteen. Well, you still have the conclusion, and when you retype it, you can make the margins a little wider.)

These are the reasons why I agree with Mr. Hutchins that college football should be abolished in American colleges and universities.

On Monday you turn it in, moderately hopeful, and on Friday it comes 5
back marked "weak in content" and sporting a big "D."

This essay is exaggerated a little, not much. The English instructor will recognize it as reasonably typical of what an assignment on college football will bring in. He knows that nearly half of the class will contrive in five hundred words to say that college football is too commercial and bad for the players. Most of the other half will inform him that college football builds character and prepares one for life and brings prestige to the school. As he reads paper after paper all saying the same thing in almost the same words, all bloodless, five hundred words dripping out of nothing, he wonders how he allowed himself to get trapped into teaching English when he might have had a happy and interesting life as an electrician or a confidence man.

Well, you may ask, what can you do about it? The subject is one on which you have few convictions and little information. Can you be expected to make a dull subject interesting? As a matter of fact, this is precisely what you are expected to do. This is the writer's essential task.

All subjects, except sex, are dull until somebody makes them interesting. The writer's job is to find the argument, the approach, the angle, the wording that will take the reader with him. This is seldom easy, and it is particularly hard in subjects that have been much discussed: College Football, Fraternities, Popular Music, Is Chivalry Dead?, and the like. You will feel that there is nothing you can do with such subjects except repeat the old bromides. But there are some things you can do which will make your papers, if not throbbingly alive, at least less insufferably tedious than they might otherwise be.

AVOID THE OBVIOUS CONTENT

Say the assignment is college football. Say that you've decided to be against it. Begin by putting down the arguments that come to your mind: it is too commercial, it takes the students' minds off their studies, it is hard on the players, it makes the university a kind of circus instead of an intellectual center, for most schools it is financially ruinous. Can you think of any more arguments just off hand? All right. Now when you write your paper, *make sure that you don't use any of the material on this list*. If these are the points that leap to your mind, they will leap to everyone else's too, and whether you get a "C" or a "D" may depend on whether the instructor reads your paper early when he is fresh and tolerant or late, when the sentence "In my opinion, college football has become too commercial," inexorably repeated, has brought him to the brink of lunacy.

Be against college football for some reason or reasons of your own. If they are keen and perceptive ones, that's splendid. But even if they are trivial or foolish or indefensible, you are still ahead so long as they are not everybody else's reasons too. Be against it because the colleges don't spend enough money on it to make it worth while, because it is bad for the characters of the spectators, because the players are forced to attend classes, because the football stars hog all the beautiful women, because it competes with baseball and is therefore un-American and possibly Communist inspired. There are lots of more or less unused reasons for being against college football.

Sometimes it is a good idea to sum up and dispose of the trite and conventional points before going on to your own. This has the advantage of indicating to the reader that you are going to be neither trite nor conventional. Something like this: 10

We are often told that college football should be abolished because it has become too commercial or because it is bad for the players. These

72

arguments are no doubt very cogent, but they don't really go to the heart of the matter.

Then you go to the heart of the matter.

TAKE THE LESS USUAL SIDE

One rather simple way of getting interest into your paper is to take the side of the argument that most of the citizens will want to avoid. If the assignment is an essay on dogs, you can, if you choose, explain that dogs are faithful and lovable companions, intelligent, useful as guardians of the house and protectors of children, indispensable in police work — in short, when all is said and done, man's best friends. Or you can suggest that those big brown eyes conceal more often than not, a vacuity of mind and an inconstancy of purpose; that the dogs you have known most intimately have been mangy, ill-tempered brutes, incapable of instruction; and that only your nobility of mind and fear of arrest prevent you from kicking the flea-ridden animals when you pass them on the street.

Naturally, personal convictions will sometimes dictate your approach. If the assigned subject is "Is Methodism Rewarding to the Individual?" and you are a pious Methodist, you have really no choice. But few assigned subjects, if any, will fall in this category. Most of them will lie in broad areas of discussion with much to be said on both sides. They are intellectual exercises, and it is legitimate to argue now one way and now another, as debaters do in similar circumstances. Always take the side that looks to you hardest, least defensible. It will almost always turn out to be easier to write interestingly on that side.

This general advice applies where you have a choice of subjects. If you are to choose among "The Value of Fraternities" and "My Favorite High School Teacher" and "What I Think About Beetles," by all means plump for the beetles. By the time the instructor gets to your paper, he will be up to his ears in tedious tales about the French teacher at Bloombury High and assertions about how fraternities build character and prepare one for life. Your views on beetles, whatever they are, are bound to be a refreshing change.

Don't worry too much about figuring out what the instructor thinks about the subject so that you can cuddle up with him. Chances are his views are no stronger than yours. If he does have convictions and you oppose them, his problem is to keep from grading you higher than you deserve in order to show he is not biased. This doesn't mean that you should always cantankerously dissent from what the instructor says;

that gets tiresome too. And if the subject assigned is "My Pet Peeve," do not begin, "My pet peeve is the English instructor who assigns papers on 'my pet peeve.'" This was still funny during the War of 1812, but it has sort of lost its edge since then. It is in general good manners to avoid personalities.

SLIP OUT OF ABSTRACTION

If you will study the essay on college football in [the "Nothing about 15 Something" section], you will perceive that one reason for its appalling dullness is that it never gets down to particulars. It is just a series of not very glittering generalities: "football is bad for the colleges," "it has become too commercial," "football is a big business," "it is bad for the players," and so on. Such round phrases thudding against the reader's brain are unlikely to convince him, though they may well render him unconscious.

If you want the reader to believe that college football is bad for the players, you have to do more than say so. You have to display the evil. Take your roommate, Alfred Simkins, the second-string center. Picture poor old Alfy coming home from football practice every evening, bruised and aching, agonizingly tired, scarcely able to shovel the mashed potatoes into his mouth. Let us see him staggering up to the room, getting out his econ textbook, peering desperately at it with his good eye, falling asleep and failing the test in the morning. Let us share his unbearable tension as Saturday draws near. Will he fail, be demoted, lose his monthly allowance, be forced to return to the coal mines? And if he succeeds, what will be his reward? Perhaps a slight ripple of applause when the third-string center replaces him, a moment of elation in the locker room if the team wins, of despair if it loses. What will he look back on when he graduates from college? Toil and torn ligaments. And what will be his future? He is not good enough for pro football, and he is too obscure and weak in econ to succeed in stocks and bonds. College football is tearing the heart from Alfy Simkins and, when it finishes with him, will callously toss aside the shattered hulk.

This is no doubt a weak enough argument for the abolition of college football, but it is a sight better than saying, in three or four variations, that college football (in your opinion) is bad for the players.

Look at the work of any professional writer and notice how constantly he is moving from the generality, the abstract statement, to the concrete example, the facts and figures, the illustration. If he is writing on juvenile delinquency, he does not just tell you that juveniles are (it seems to him) delinquent and that (in his opinion) something should be done

about it. He shows you juveniles being delinquent, tearing up movie the-
atres in Buffalo, stabbing high school principals in Dallas, smoking mar-
ijuana in Palo Alto. And more than likely he is moving toward some
specific remedy, not just a general wringing of the hands.

It is no doubt possible to be *too* concrete, too illustrative or anecdotal,
but few inexperienced writers err this way. For most the soundest advice
is to be seeking always for the picture, to be always turning general
remarks into seeable examples. Don't say, "Sororities teach girls the
social graces." Say, "Sorority life teaches a girl how to carry on a conversation while pouring tea, without sloshing the tea into the saucer." Don't
say, "I like certain kinds of popular music very much." Say, "Whenever I
hear Gerber Spinklittle play 'Mississippi Man' on the trombone, my
socks creep up my ankles."

GET RID OF OBVIOUS PADDING

The student toiling away at his weekly English theme is too often tor-   20
mented by a figure: five hundred words. How, he asks himself, is he to
achieve this staggering total? Obviously by never using one word when
he can somehow work in ten.

He is therefore seldom content with a plain statement like "Fast driving is dangerous." This has only four words in it. He takes thought, and
the sentence becomes:

In my opinion, fast driving is dangerous.

Better, but he can do better still:

In my opinion, fast driving would seem to be rather dangerous.

If he is really adept, it may come out:

In my humble opinion, though I do not claim to be an expert on this complicated subject, fast driving, in most circumstances, would seem to be
rather dangerous in many respects, or at least so it would seem to me.

Thus four words have been turned into forty, and not an iota of content
has been added.

Now this is a way to go about reaching five hundred words, and if you
are content with a "D" grade, it is as good a way as any. But if you aim

higher, you must work differently. Instead of stuffing your sentences with straw, you must try steadily to get rid of the padding, to make your sentences lean and tough. If you are really working at it, your first draft will greatly exceed the required total, and then you will work it down, thus:

> It is thought in some quarters that fraternities do not contribute as much as might be expected to campus life.
> Some people think that fraternities contribute little to campus life.

> The average doctor who practices in small towns or in the country must toil night and day to heal the sick.
> Most country doctors work long hours.

> When I was a little girl, I suffered from shyness and embarrassment in the presence of others.
> I was a shy little girl.

> It is absolutely necessary for the person employed as a marine fireman to give the matter of steam pressure his undivided attention at all times.
> The fireman has to keep his eye on the steam gauge.

You may ask how you can arrive at five hundred words at this rate. Simply. You dig up more real content. Instead of taking a couple of obvious points off the surface of the topic and then circling warily around them for six paragraphs, you work in and explore, figure out the details. You illustrate. You say that fast driving is dangerous, and then you prove it. How long does it take to stop a car at forty and at eighty? How far can you see at night? What happens when a tire blows? What happens in a head-on collision at fifty miles an hour? Pretty soon your paper will be full of broken glass and blood and headless torsos, and reaching five hundred words will not really be a problem.

CALL A FOOL A FOOL

Some of the padding in freshman themes is to be blamed not on anxiety about the word minimum but on excessive timidity. The student writes, "In my opinion, the principal of my high school acted in ways that I believe every unbiased person would have to call foolish." This isn't exactly what he means. What he means is, "My high school principal was a fool." If he was a fool, call him a fool. Hedging the thing about with "in-my-opinion's" and "it-seems-to-me's" and "as-I-see-it's" and "at-least-from-my-point-of-view's" gains you nothing. Delete these phrases whenever they creep into your paper.

The student's tendency to hedge stems from a modesty that in other 25 circumstances would be commendable. He is, he realizes, young and inexperienced, and he half suspects that he is dopey and fuzzy-minded beyond the average. Probably only too true. But it doesn't help to announce your incompetence six times in every paragraph. Decide what you want to say and say it as vigorously as possible, without apology and in plain words.

Linguistic diffidence can take various forms. One is what we call *euphemism*. This is the tendency to call a spade "a certain garden implement" or women's underwear "unmentionables." It is stronger in some eras than others and in some people than others but it always operates more or less in subjects that are touchy or taboo: death, sex, madness, and so on. Thus we shrink from saying "He died last night" but say instead "passed away," "left us," "joined his Maker," "went to his reward." Or we try to take off the tension with a lighter cliché: "kicked the bucket," "cashed in his chips," "handed in his dinner pail." We have found all sorts of ways to avoid saying *mad*: "mentally ill," "touched," "not quite right upstairs," "feeble-minded," "innocent," "simple," "off his trolley," "not in his right mind." Even such a now plain word as *insane* began as a euphemism with the meaning "not healthy."

Modern science, particularly psychology, contributes many polysyllables in which we can wrap our thoughts and blunt their force. To many writers there is no such thing as a bad schoolboy. Schoolboys are maladjusted or unoriented or misunderstood or in need of guidance or lacking in continued success toward satisfactory integration of the personality as a social unit, but they are never bad. Psychology no doubt makes us better men or women, more sympathetic and tolerant, but it doesn't make writing any easier. Had Shakespeare been confronted with psychology, "To be or not to be" might have come out, "To continue as a social unit or not to do so. That is the personality problem. Whether 'tis a better sign of integration at the conscious level to display a psychic tolerance toward the maladjustments and repressions induced by one's lack of orientation in one's environment or—" But Hamlet would never have finished the soliloquy.

Writing in the modern world, you cannot altogether avoid modern jargon. Nor, in an effort to get away from euphemism, should you salt your paper with four-letter words. But you can do much if you will mount guard against those roundabout phrases, those echoing polysyllables that tend to slip into your writing to rob it of its crispness and force.

BEWARE OF THE PAT EXPRESSION

Other things being equal, avoid phrases like "other things being equal." Those sentences that come to you whole, or in two or three doughy lumps, are sure to be bad sentences. They are no creation of yours but pieces of common thought floating in the community soup.

Pat expressions are hard, often impossible, to avoid, because they come too easily to be noticed and seem too necessary to be dispensed with. No writer avoids them altogether, but good writers avoid them more often than poor writers.

By "pat expressions" we mean such tags as "to all practical intents and purposes," "the pure and simple truth," "from where I sit," "the time of his life," "to the ends of the earth," "in the twinkling of an eye," "as sure as you're born," "over my dead body," "under cover of darkness," "took the easy way out," "when all is said and done," "told him time and time again," "parted the best of friends," "stand up and be counted," "gave him the best years of her life," "worked her fingers to the bone." Like other clichés, these expressions were once forceful. Now we should use them only when we can't possibly think of anything else.

Some pat expressions stand like a wall between the writer and thought. Such a one is "the American way of life." Many student writers feel that when they have said that something accords with the American way of life or does not they have exhausted the subject. Actually, they have stopped at the highest level of abstraction. The American way of life is the complicated set of bonds between a hundred and eighty million ways. All of us know this when we think about it, but the tag phrase too often keeps us from thinking about it.

So with many another phrase dear to the politician: "this great land of ours," "the man in the street," "our national heritage." These may prove our patriotism or give a clue to our political beliefs, but otherwise they add nothing to the paper except words.

COLORFUL WORDS

The writer builds with words, and no builder uses a raw material more slippery and elusive and treacherous. A writer's work is a constant struggle to get the right word in the right place, to find that particular word that will convey his meaning exactly, that will persuade the reader or soothe him or startle or amuse him. He never succeeds altogether—sometimes he feels that he scarcely succeeds at all—but such successes as he has are what make die thing worth doing.

There is no book of rules for this game. One progresses through 35 ever-lasting experiment on the basis of ever-widening experience. There are few useful generalizations that one can make about words as words, but there are perhaps a few.

Some words are what we call "colorful." By this we mean that they are calculated to produce a picture or induce an emotion. They are dressy instead of plain, specific instead of general, loud instead of soft. Thus, in place of "Her heart beat," we may write "Her heart *pounded, throbbed, fluttered, danced.*" Instead of "He sat in his chair," we may say, "He *lounged, sprawled, coiled.*" Instead of "It was hot," we may say, "It was *blistering, sultry, muggy, suffocating, steamy, wilting.*"

However, it should not be supposed that the fancy word is always better. Often it is as well to write "Her heart beat" or "It was hot" if that is all it did or all it was. Ages differ in how they like their prose. The nineteenth century liked it rich and smoky. The twentieth has usually preferred it lean and cool. The twentieth century writer, like all writers, is forever seeking the exact word, but he is wary of sounding feverish. He tends to pitch it low, to understate it, to throw it away. He knows that if he gets too colorful, the audience is likely to giggle.

See how this strikes you: "As the rich, golden glow of the sunset died away along the eternal western hills, Angela's limpid blue eyes looked softly and trustingly into Montague's flashing brown ones, and her heart pounded like a drum in time with the joyous song surging in her soul." Some people like that sort of thing, but most modern readers would say, "Good grief," and turn on the television.

COLORED WORDS

Some words we would call not so much colorful as colored—that is, loaded with associations, good or bad. All words—except perhaps structure words—have associations of some sort. We have said that the meaning of a word is the sum of the contexts in which it occurs. When we hear a word, we hear with it an echo of all the situations in which we have heard it before.

In some words, these echoes are obvious and discussable. The word 40 *mother,* for example, has, for most people, agreeable associations. When you hear *mother* you probably think of home, safety, love, food, and various other pleasant things. If one writes, "She was like a mother to me," he gets an effect which he would not get in "She was like an aunt to me." The advertiser makes use of the associations of *mother* by working it in when he talks about his product. The politician works it in when he talks about himself.

So also with such words as *home, liberty, fireside, contentment, patriot, tenderness, sacrifice, childlike, manly, bluff, limpid.* All of these words are loaded with favorable associations that would be rather hard to indicate in a straightforward definition. There is more than a literal difference between "They sat around the fireside" and "They sat around the stove." They might have been equally warm and happy around the stove, but *fireside* suggests leisure, grace, quiet tradition, congenial company, and *stove* does not.

Conversely, some words have bad associations. *Mother* suggests pleasant things, but *mother-in-law* does not. Many mothers-in-law are heroically lovable and some mothers drink gin all day and beat their children insensible, but these facts of life are beside the point. The thing is that *mother* sounds good and *mother-in-law* does not.

Or consider the word *intellectual.* This would seem to be a complimentary term, but in point of fact it is not, for it has picked up associations of impracticality and ineffectuality and general dopiness. So also with such words as *liberal, reactionary, Communist, socialist, capitalist, radical, schoolteacher, truck driver, undertaker, operator, salesman, huckster, speculator.* These convey meanings on the literal level, but beyond that — sometimes, in some places — they convey contempt on the part of the speaker.

The question of whether to use loaded words or not depends on what is being written. The scientist, the scholar, try to avoid them; for the poet, the advertising writer, the public speaker, they are standard equipment. But every writer should take care that they do not substitute for thought. If you write, "Anyone who thinks that is nothing but a Socialist (or Communist or capitalist)" you have said nothing except that you don't like people who think that, and such remarks are effective only with the most naïve readers. It is always a bad mistake to think your readers more naïve than they really are.

COLORLESS WORDS

But probably most student writers come to grief not with words that are 45 colorful or those that are colored but with those that have no color at all. A pet example is *nice,* a word we would find it hard to dispense with in casual conversation but which is no longer capable of adding much to a description. Colorless words are those of such general meaning that in a particular sentence they mean nothing. Slang adjectives, like *cool* ("That's real cool") tend to explode all over the language. They are applied to everything, lose their original force, and quickly die.

Beware also of nouns of very general meaning, like *circumstances, cases, instances, aspects, factors, relationships, attitudes, eventualities,* etc. In most circumstances you will find that those cases of writing which contain too many instances of words like these will in this and other aspects have factors leading to unsatisfactory relationships with the reader resulting in unfavorable attitudes on his part and perhaps other eventualities, like a grade of "D." Notice also what "etc." means. It means "I'd like to make this list longer, but I can't think of any more examples."

JAMES BALDWIN   [1924–1987]

If Black English Isn't a Language, Then Tell Me, What Is?

Born in New York City, the son of a revivalist minister, **James Baldwin** (1924–1987) was raised in poverty in Harlem where, at the age of fourteen, he became a preacher in the Fireside Pentecostal Church. After completing high school he decided to become a writer and, with the help of the black American expatriate writer Richard Wright, won a grant that enabled him to move to Paris, where he lived for most of his remaining years. There he wrote the critically acclaimed *Go Tell It on the Mountain* (1953), a novel about the religious awakening of a fourteen-year-old black youth. Subsequent works, focusing on the intellectual and spiritual trials of black men in a white, racist society, included the novels *Giovanni's Room* (1956), *Another Country* (1962) — both famous at the time for their homosexual themes — *Tell Me How Long the Train's Been Gone* (1968), *If Beale Street Could Talk* (1974), *Just Above My Head* (1979), and *Harlem Quartet* (1987); the play *Blues for Mister Charlie* (1964); and the powerful nonfiction commentaries *Notes of a Native Son* (1955), *Nobody Knows My Name* (1961), and *The Fire Next Time* (1963). Baldwin's short stories are collected in *Going to Meet the Man* (1965).

The argument concerning the use, or the status, or the reality, of black English is rooted in American history and has absolutely nothing to do with the question the argument supposes itself to be posing. The argument has nothing to do with language itself but with the *role* of language. Language, incontestably, reveals the speaker. Language, also, far more dubiously, is meant to define the other — and, in this case, the other is refusing to be defined by a language that has never been able to recognize him.

People evolve a language in order to describe and thus control their circumstances, or in order not to be submerged by a reality that they cannot articulate. (And, if they cannot articulate it, they *are* submerged.) A Frenchman living in Paris speaks a subtly and crucially different language from that of the man living in Marseilles; neither sounds very much like a man living in Quebec; and they would all have great difficulty in apprehending what the man from Guadeloupe, or Martinique, is saying, to say nothing of the man from Senegal—although the "common" language of all these areas is French. But each has paid, and is paying, a different price for this "common" language, in which, as it turns out, they are not saying, and cannot be saying, the same things: they each have very different realities to articulate, or control.

What joins all languages, and all men, is the necessity to confront life, in order, not inconceivably, to outwit death: the price for this is the acceptance, and achievement, of one's temporal identity. So that, for example, though it is not taught in the schools (and this has the potential of becoming a political issue) the south of France still clings to its ancient and musical Provençal, which resists being described as a "dialect." And much of the tension in the Basque countries, and in Wales, is due to the Basque and Welsh determination not to allow their languages to be destroyed. This determination also feeds the flames in Ireland for among the many indignities the Irish have been forced to undergo at English hands is the English contempt for their language.

It goes without saying, then, that language is also a political instrument, means, and proof of power. It is the most vivid and crucial key to identity: it reveals the private identity, and connects one with, or divorces one from, the larger, public, or communal identity. There have been, and are, times, and places, when to speak a certain language could be dangerous, even fatal. Or, one may speak the same language, but in such a way that one's antecedents are revealed, or (one hopes) hidden. This is true in France, and is absolutely true in England: the range (and reign) of accents on that damp little island make England coherent for the English and totally incomprehensible for everyone else. To open your mouth in England is (if I may use black English) to "put your business in the street": You have confessed your parents, your youth, your school, your salary, your self-esteem, and alas, your future.

Now, I do not know what white Americans would sound like if there 5 had never been any black people in the United States, but they would not sound the way they sound. *Jazz,* for example, is a very specific sexual term, as in *jazz me, baby,* but white people purified it into the Jazz Age. *Sock it to me,* which means, roughly, the same thing, has been adopted by Nathaniel Hawthorne's descendants with no qualms or hesitations at all, along with *let it all hang out* and *right on! Beat to his socks,* which was once the black's most total and despairing image of poverty, was transformed into a thing called the Beat Generation, which phenomenon was, largely, composed of *uptight*, middle-class white people, imitating poverty, trying to *get down*, to get *with it*, doing their *thing*, doing their despairing best to be *funky*, which we, the blacks, never dreamed of doing—we *were* funky, baby, like *funk* was going out of style.

Now, no one can eat his cake, and have it, too, and it is late in the day to attempt to penalize black people for having created a language that permits the nation its only glimpse of reality, a language without which the nation would be even more *whipped* than it is.

I say that this present skirmish is rooted in American history, and it is. Black English is the creation of the black diaspora. Blacks came to the United States chained to each other, but from different tribes: neither could speak the other's language. If two black people, at that bitter hour of the world's history, had been able to speak to each other, the institution of chattel slavery could never have lasted as long as it did. Subsequently, the slave was given, under the eye, and the gun, of his master, Congo Square, and the Bible—or, in other words, and under these conditions, the slave began the formation of the black church, and it is within this unprecedented tabernacle that black English began to be formed. This was not, merely, as in the European example, the adoption of a foreign tongue, but an alchemy that transformed ancient elements into a new language: *A language comes into existence by means of brutal necessity, and the rules of the language are dictated by what the language must convey.*

There was a moment, in time, and in this place, when my brother, or my mother, or my father, or my sister, had to convey to me, for example, the danger in which I was standing from the white man standing just behind me, and to convey this with a speed, and in a language, that the white man could not possibly understand, and that, indeed, he cannot understand, until today. He cannot afford to understand it. This understanding would reveal to him too much about himself, and smash that mirror before which he has been frozen for so long.

Now, if this passion, this skill, this (to quote Toni Morrison) "sheer intelligence," this incredible music, the mighty achievement of having brought a people utterly unknown to, or despised by "history"—to have brought this people to their present, troubled, troubling, and unassailable and unanswerable place—if this absolutely unprecedented journey does not indicate that black English is a language, I am curious to know what definition of language is to be trusted.

A people at the center of the Western world, and in the midst of so hostile a population, has not endured and transcended by means of what is patronizingly called a "dialect." We, the blacks, are in trouble, certainly, but we are not doomed, and we are not inarticulate because we are not compelled to defend a morality that we know to be a lie. 10

84

The brutal truth is that the bulk of the white people in America never had any interest in educating black people, except as this could serve white purposes. It is not the black child's language that is in question, it is not his language that is despised: it is his experience. A child cannot be taught by anyone who despises him, and a child cannot afford to be fooled. A child cannot be taught by anyone whose demand, essentially, is that the child repudiate his experience, and all that gives him sustenance, and enter a limbo in which he will no longer be black, and in which he knows that he can never become white. Black people have lost too many black children that way.

And, after all, finally, in a country with standards so untrustworthy, a country that makes heroes of so many criminal mediocrities, a country unable to face why so many of the nonwhite are in prison, or on the needle, or standing, futureless, in the streets — it may very well be that both the child, and his elder, have concluded that they have nothing whatever to learn from the people of a country that has managed to learn so little.

SUSAN BROWNMILLER   [b. 1935]

Let's Put Pornography Back in the Closet

Born in Brooklyn, New York, **Susan Brownmiller** attended Cornell University on a scholarship before dropping out to become an actress. She worked at several jobs, including research and editing, in Manhattan, until, in 1960, the sit-in movement to end lunch-counter segregation in the South awakened her drive toward political activism. She joined the Congress of Racial Equality (CORE) and participated in Freedom Summer in Mississippi. She later protested against the Vietnam War. Brownmiller is most well known as a leader in the feminist movement, which she joined in 1968, and for her book, *Against Our Will: Men, Women, and Rape* (1975). Her other books include *Femininity* (1984) and *In Our Time: Memoir of a Revolution* (1999), a chronicle of the women's liberation movement. She is currently an adjunct professor of women's and gender studies at Pace University in New York City.

In her essay "Let's Put Pornography Back in the Closet," Brownmiller asserts that the First Amendment was not written to protect pornography. While not denying the right for pornography to be produced, she does object to its display in public places.

Free speech is one of the great foundations on which our democracy rests. I am old enough to remember the Hollywood Ten, the screenwriters who went to jail in the late 1940s because they refused to testify before a congressional committee about their political affiliations. They tried to use the First Amendment as a defense, but they went to jail because in those days there were few civil liberties lawyers around who cared to champion the First Amendment right to free speech, when the speech concerned the Communist party.

The Hollywood Ten were correct in claiming the First Amendment. Its high purpose is the protection of unpopular ideas and political dissent. In the dark, cold days of the 1950s, few civil libertarians were willing to declare themselves First Amendment absolutists. But in the brighter, though frantic, days of the 1960s, the principle of protecting unpopular political speech was gradually strengthened.

It is fair to say now that the battle has largely been won. Even the American Nazi party has found itself the beneficiary of the dedicated, tireless work of the American Civil Liberties Union. But—and please notice the quotation marks coming up—"To equate the free and robust exchange of ideas and political debate with commercial exploitation of obscene material demeans the grand conception of the First Amendment and its high purposes in the historic struggle for freedom. It is a misuse of the great guarantees of free speech and free press."

I didn't say that, although I wish I had, for I think the words are thrilling. Chief Justice Warren Burger said it in 1973, in the United States Supreme Court's majority opinion in *Miller v. California*. During the same decades that the right to political free speech was being strengthened in the courts, the nation's obscenity laws also were undergoing extensive revision.

It's amazing to recall that in 1934 the question of whether James   5 Joyce's *Ulysses* should be banned as pornographic actually went before the Court. The battle to protect *Ulysses* as a work of literature with redeeming social value was won. In later decades, Henry Miller's *Tropic* books, *Lady Chatterley's Lover,* and the *Memoirs of Fanny Hill* also were adjudged not obscene. These decisions have been important to me. As the author of *Against Our Will,* a study of the history of rape that does contain explicit sexual material, I shudder to think how my book would have fared if James Joyce, D. H. Lawrence, and Henry Miller hadn't gone before me.

I am not a fan of *Chatterley* or the *Tropic* books, I should quickly mention. They are not to my literary taste, nor do I think they represent female sexuality with any degree of accuracy. But I would hardly suggest that we ban them. Such a suggestion wouldn't get very far anyway. The battle to protect these books is ancient history. Time does march on, quite methodically. What, then is unlawfully obscene, and what does the First Amendment have to do with it?

In the *Miller* case of 1973 (not Henry Miller, by the way, but a porn distributor who sent unsolicited stuff through the mails), the Court came up with new guidelines that it hoped would strengthen obscenity laws by giving more power to the states. What it did in actuality was throw everything into confusion. It set up a three-part test by which materials can be adjudged obscene. The materials are obscene if they depict patently offensive, hard-core sexual conduct; lack serious scientific, literary, artistic, or political value; and appeal to the prurient interest of an average person—as measured by contemporary community standards.

"Patently offensive," "prurient interest," and "hard-core" are indeed words to conjure with. "Contemporary community standards" are what we're trying to redefine. The feminist objection to pornography is not based on prurience, which the dictionary defines as lustful, itching desire. We are not opposed to sex and desire, with or without the itch, and we certainly believe that explicit sexual material has its place in literature, art, science, and education. Here we part company rather swiftly with old-line conservatives who don't want sex education in the high schools, for example.

No, the feminist objection to pornography is based on our belief that pornography represents hatred of women, that pornography's intent is to humiliate, degrade, and dehumanize the female body for the purpose of erotic stimulation and pleasure. We are unalterably opposed to the presentation of the female body being stripped, bound, raped, tortured, mutilated, and murdered in the name of commercial entertainment and free speech.

These images, which are standard pornographic fare, have nothing to 10 do with the hallowed right of political dissent. They have everything to do with the creation of a cultural climate in which a rapist feels he is merely giving in to a normal urge and a woman is encouraged to believe that sexual masochism is healthy, liberated fun. Justice Potter Stewart once said about hard-core pornography, "You know it when you see it," and that certainly used to be true. In the good old days, pornography looked awful. It was cheap and sleazy, and there was no mistaking it for art.

Nowadays, since the porn industry has become a multimillion dollar business, visual technology has been employed in its service. Pornographic movies are skillfully filmed and edited, pornographic still shots using the newest tenets of good design artfully grace the covers of *Hustler, Penthouse,* and *Playboy,* and the public—and the courts—are sadly confused.

The Supreme Court neglected to define "hard-core" in the *Miller* decision. This was a mistake. If "hard-core" refers only to explicit sexual intercourse, then that isn't good enough. When women or children or men—no matter how artfully—are shown tortured or terrorized in the service of sex, that's obscene. And "patently offensive," I would hope, to our "contemporary community standards."

Justice William O. Douglas wrote in his dissent to the *Miller* case that no one is "compelled to look." This is hardly true. To buy a paper at the corner newsstand is to subject oneself to a forcible immersion in pornography, to be demeaned by an array of dehumanized, chopped-up parts of the female anatomy, packaged like cuts of meat at the supermarket. I happen to like my body and I work hard at the gym to keep it in good shape, but I am embarrassed for my body and for the bodies of all women when I see the fragmented parts of us so frivolously, and so flagrantly, displayed.

Some constitutional theorists (Justice Douglas was one) have maintained that any obscenity law is a serious abridgement of free speech.

Others (and Justice Earl Warren was one) have maintained that the First Amendment was never intended to protect obscenity. We live quite compatibly with a host of free-speech abridgements. There are restraints against false and misleading advertising or statements—shouting "fire" without cause in a crowded movie theater, etc.—that do not threaten, but strengthen, our societal values. Restrictions on the public display of pornography belong in this category.

The distinction between permission to publish and permission to display publicly is an essential one and one which I think consonant with First Amendment principles. Justice Burger's words which I quoted above support this without question. We are not saying "Smash the presses" or "Ban the bad ones," but simply "Get the stuff out of our sight." Let the legislatures decide—using realistic and humane contemporary community standards—what can be displayed and what cannot. The courts, after all, will be the final arbiters. 15

DAVE EGGERS [b. 1971]

Serve or Fail

In 1998, **Dave Eggers** founded the literary magazine *Timothy McSweeney's Quarterly Concern*. Three years later, *A Heartbreaking Work of Staggering Genius*, his best-selling memoir about raising his younger brother after the deaths of their parents, was a finalist for the Pulitzer Prize. Since then, he has written several books including *You Shall Know Our Velocity!* (2002) and *What Is the What* (2006). He also edits the *Best American Nonrequired Reading*, a yearly anthology, in addition to being the founding publisher of McSweeney's Press. In 2005, he coauthored *Teachers Have It Easy: The Big Sacrifices and Small Salaries of America's Teachers*.

In "Serve or Fail," a 2004 Op-Ed piece in the *New York Times*, Eggers argues that students required to do community service in college are more likely to become lifelong volunteers. Though he describes his collegiate self as a community service dropout, Eggers later founded 826 National, a network of nonprofit learning centers dedicated to teaching writing to children, and currently teaches at 826 Valencia in San Francisco.

About now, most recent college graduates, a mere week or two beyond their last final, are giving themselves a nice respite. Maybe they're on a beach, maybe they're on a road trip, maybe they're in their rooms, painting their toenails black with a Q-tip and shoe polish. Does it matter? What's important is that they have some time off.

Do they deserve the time off? Well, yes and no. Yes, because finals week is stressful and sleep-deprived and possibly involves trucker-style stimulants. No, because a good deal of the four years of college is spent playing foosball.

I went to a large state school—the University of Illinois—and during my time there, I became one of the best two or three foosball players in the Land of Lincoln. I learned to pass deftly between my rigid players, to play the corners, to strike the ball like a cobra would strike something a cobra would want to strike. I also mastered the dart game called Cricket, and the billiards contest called Nine-ball. I became expert at whiffle ball, at backyard archery, and at a sport we invented that involved one person tossing roasted chickens from a balcony to a group of us waiting below. We got to eat the parts that didn't land on the patio.

The point is that college is too long—it should be three years—and that even with a full course load and part-time jobs (I had my share) there are many hours in the days and weeks that need killing. And because most of us, as students, saw our hours as in need of killing—as opposed to thinking about giving a few of these hours to our communities in one way or another—colleges should consider instituting a service requirement for graduation.

I volunteered a few times in Urbana-Champaign—at a Y.M.C.A. and   5
at a home for senior citizens—and in both cases it was much too easy to quit. I thought the senior home smelled odd, so I left, and though the Y.M.C.A. was a perfect fit, I could have used nudging to continue—nudging the university might have provided. Just as parents and schools need to foster in young people a "reading habit"—a love of reading that becomes a need, almost an addiction—colleges are best-poised to create in their students a lifelong commitment to volunteering even a few hours a month.

Some colleges, and many high schools, have such a thing in place, and last year Michael R. Veon, a Democratic member of Pennsylvania's House of Representatives, introduced a bill that would require the more than 90,000 students at 14 state-run universities to perform 25 hours of community service annually. That comes out to more than two million volunteer hours a year.

College students are, for the most part, uniquely suited to have time for and to benefit from getting involved and addressing the needs of those around them. Unlike high school students, they're less programmed, less boxed-in by family and after-school obligations. They're also more mature, and better able to handle a wide range of tasks. Finally, they're at a stage where exposure to service—and to the people whose lives non-profit service organizations touch—would have a profound effect on them. Meeting a World War II veteran who needs meals brought to him would be educational for the deliverer of that meal, I would think. A college history major might learn something by tutoring a local middle school class that's studying the Underground Railroad. A connection would be forged; a potential career might be discovered.

A service requirement won't work everywhere. It probably wouldn't be feasible, for example, for community college students, who tend to be transient and who generally have considerable family and work demands. But exempt community colleges and you would still have almost 10 million college students enrolled in four-year colleges in the United States. If you exempted a third of them for various reasons, that would leave more than

6 million able-bodied young people at the ready. Even with a modest 10-hour-a-year requirement (the equivalent of two mornings a year) America would gain 60 million volunteer hours to invigorate the nation's non-profit organizations, churches, job corps, conservation groups and college outreach programs.

And with some flexibility, it wouldn't have to be too onerous. Colleges could give credit for service. That is, at the beginning of each year, a student could opt for service, and in return he or she might get credits equal to one class period. Perhaps every 25 hours of service could be traded for one class credit, with a maximum of three credits a year. What a student would learn from working in a shelter for the victims of domestic abuse would surely equal or surpass his or her time spent in racquetball class — at my college worth one full unit.

Alternatively, colleges could limit the service requirement to a student's junior year — a time when the students are settled and have more hours and stability in their schedules. Turning the junior year into a year when volunteering figures prominently could also help colleges bridge the chasm that usually stands between the academic world and the one that lies beyond it. 10

When Gov. Gray Davis of California proposed a service requirement in 1999, an editorial in *The Daily Californian*, the student newspaper at the University of California at Berkeley, opposed the plan: "Forced philanthropy will be as much an oxymoron in action as it is in terms. Who would want to receive community service from someone who is forced to serve? Is forced community service in California not generally reserved for criminals and delinquents?"

First of all, that's putting forth a pretty dim view of the soul of the average student. What, is the unwilling college volunteer going to *throw food* at visitors to the soup kitchen? Volunteering is by nature transformative — reluctant participants become quick converts every day, once they meet those who need their help.

Second, college is largely about fulfilling requirements, isn't it? Students have to complete this much work in the sciences, that much work in the arts. Incoming freshmen accept a tacit contract, submitting to the wisdom of the college's founders and shapers, who decide which experiences are necessary to create a well-rounded scholar, one ready to make a contribution to the world. But while colleges give their students the intellectual tools for life beyond campus, they largely ignore the part about how they might contribute to the world. That is, until the commencement speech, at which time all the "go forth's" and "be helpful's" happen.

But what if such a sentiment happened on the student's first day? What if graduating seniors already knew full well how to balance jobs, studies, family, and volunteer work in the surrounding community? What if campuses were full of underserved high school students meeting with their college tutors? What if the tired and clogged veins of thousands of towns and cities had the energy of millions of college students coursing through them? What if the student who might have become a foosball power — and I say this knowing how much those skills have enhanced my life and those who had the good fortune to have watched me — became instead a lifelong volunteer? That might be pretty good for everybody.

[2004]

MARTIN LUTHER KING JR. [1929–1968]

Letter from Birmingham Jail

The foremost leader of the American civil rights movement of the 1950s and 1960s, **Martin Luther King Jr.** was born in Atlanta, Georgia, in 1929 and assassinated in Memphis, Tennessee, in 1968. He was an ordained minister with a Ph.D., a deliverer of powerful sermons and speeches, and a writer of books. A crusader against segregation, an organizer of the Montgomery, Alabama, bus boycott, and head of the Southern Christian Leadership Conference, King advocated nonviolent resistance in the face of discrimination and violence. The steadfast dignity with which he pursued rights for African Americans earned him worldwide renown and a Nobel Peace Prize.

"Letter from Birmingham Jail" was written while King and hundreds of other protesters were under arrest for demonstrating in Birmingham, Alabama. It is a response to eight of his fellow clergymen who questioned his methods of protest even as they supported his ultimate aims. Note, as you read, the combination in his writing of the cool logic of his argument and his passionate sense of the injustice African Americans have suffered.

MY DEAR FELLOW CLERGYMEN:

While confined here in the Birmingham city jail, I came across your recent statement calling my present activities "unwise and untimely." Seldom do I pause to answer criticism of my work and ideas. If I sought to answer all the criticisms that cross my desk, my secretaries would have little time for anything other than such correspondence in the course of the day, and I would have no time for constructive work. But since I feel that you are men of genuine good will and that your criticisms are sincerely set forth, I want to try to answer your statement in what I hope will be patient and reasonable terms.

I think I should indicate why I am here in Birmingham, since you have been influenced by the view which argues against "outsiders coming in." I have the honor of serving as president of the Southern Christian Leadership Conference, an organization operating in every southern state, with headquarters in Atlanta, Georgia. We have some eighty-five affiliated organizations across the South, and one of them is the Alabama Christian Movement for Human Rights. Frequently we share staff, educational, and financial resources with our affiliates. Several months ago the affiliate here in Birmingham asked us to be on call to engage in a nonviolent direct-action program if such were deemed necessary. We readily consented, and when the hour came we lived up to our promise. So I, along with several members of my staff, am here because I was invited here. I am here because I have organizational ties here.

But more basically, I am in Birmingham because injustice is here. Just as the prophets of the eighth century B.C. left their villages and carried their "thus saith the Lord" far beyond the boundaries of their home towns, and just as the Apostle Paul left his village of Tarsus and carried the gospel of Jesus Christ to the far corners of the Greco-Roman world, so am I compelled to carry the gospel of freedom beyond my own home town. Like Paul, I must constantly respond to the Macedonian call for aid.

Moreover, I am cognizant of the interrelatedness of all communities and states. I cannot sit idly by in Atlanta and not be concerned about what happens in Birmingham. Injustice anywhere is a threat to justice everywhere. We are caught in an inescapable network of mutuality, tied in a single garment of destiny. Whatever affects one directly, affects all indirectly. Never again can we afford to live with the narrow, provincial "outside agitator" idea. Anyone who lives inside the United States can never be considered an outsider anywhere within its bounds.

You deplore the demonstrations taking place in Birmingham. But your statement, I am sorry to say, fails to express a similar concern for the conditions that brought about the demonstrations. I am sure that none of you would want to rest content with the superficial kind of social analysis that deals merely with effects and does not grapple with underlying causes. It is unfortunate that demonstrations are taking place in Birmingham, but it is even more unfortunate that the city's white power structure left the Negro community with no alternative.

In any nonviolent campaign there are four basic steps: collection of the facts to determine whether injustices exist; negotiation; self-purification; and direct action. We have gone through all these steps in Birmingham. There can be no gainsaying the fact that racial injustice engulfs this community. Birmingham is probably the most thoroughly segregated city in the United States. Its ugly record of brutality is widely known. Negroes have experienced grossly unjust treatment in the courts. There have been more unsolved bombings of Negro homes and churches in Birmingham than in any other city in the nation. These are the hard, brutal facts of the case. On the basis of these conditions, Negro leaders sought to negotiate with the city fathers. But the latter consistently refused to engage in good-faith negotiation.

Then, last September, came the opportunity to talk with leaders of Birmingham's economic community. In the course of the negotiations, certain promises were made by the merchants — for example, to remove the stores' humiliating racial signs. On the basis of these promises, the Reverend Fred Shuttlesworth and the leaders of the Alabama Christian Movement for Human Rights agreed to a moratorium on all demonstrations. As the weeks and months went by, we realized that we were the victims of a broken promise. A few signs, briefly removed, returned; the others remained.

As in so many past experiences, our hopes had been blasted, and the shadow of deep disappointment settled upon us. We had no alternative except to prepare for direct action, whereby we would present our very bodies as a means of laying our case before the conscience of the local and the national community. Mindful of the difficulties involved, we decided to undertake a process of self-purification. We began a series of workshops on nonviolence, and we repeatedly asked ourselves: "Are you able to accept blows without retaliating?" "Are you able to endure the ordeal of jail?" We decided to schedule our direct-action program for the Easter season, realizing that except for Christmas, this is the main shopping period of the year. Knowing that a strong economic withdrawal program would be the by-product of direct action, we felt that this would be the best time to bring pressure to bear on the merchants for the needed change.

Then it occurred to us that Birmingham's mayoral election was coming up in March, and we speedily decided to postpone action until after election day. When we discovered that the Commissioner of Public Safety, Eugene "Bull" Connor, had piled up enough votes to be in the run-off, we decided again to postpone action until the day after the runoff so that the demonstrations could not be used to cloud the issues. Like many others, we wanted to see Mr. Connor defeated, and to this end we endured postponement after postponement. Having aided in this community need, we felt that our direct-action program could be delayed no longer.

You may well ask, "Why direct action? Why sit-ins, marches, and so 10 forth? Isn't negotiation a better path?" You are quite right in calling for negotiation. Indeed, this is the very purpose of direct action. Nonviolent direct action seeks to create such a crisis and foster such a tension that a community which has constantly refused to negotiate is forced to confront the issue. It seeks so to dramatize the issue that it can no longer be ignored. My citing the creation of tension as part of the work of the nonviolent-resister may sound rather shocking. But I must confess that I am not afraid of the word "tension." I have earnestly opposed violent tension, but there is a type of constructive, nonviolent tension which is necessary for growth. Just as Socrates felt that it was necessary to create a tension in the mind so that individuals could rise from the bondage of myths and half-truths to the unfettered realm of creative analysis and objective appraisal, so must we see the need for nonviolent gadflies to create the kind of tension in society that will help men rise from the dark depths of prejudice and racism to the majestic heights of understanding and brotherhood.

The purpose of our direct-action program is to create a situation so crisis-packed that it will inevitably open the door to negotiation. I therefore concur with you in your call for negotiation. Too long has our beloved Southland been bogged down in a tragic effort to live in monologue rather than dialogue.

One of the basic points in your statement is that the action that I and my associates have taken in Birmingham is untimely. Some have asked: "Why didn't you give the new city administration time to act?" The only answer that I can give to this query is that the new Birmingham administration must be prodded about as much as the outgoing one, before it will act. We are sadly mistaken if we feel that the election of Albert Boutwell as mayor will bring the millennium to Birmingham. While Mr. Boutwell is a much more gentle person than Mr. Connor, they are both segregationists, dedicated to maintenance of the status quo. I have hoped that Mr. Boutwell will be reasonable enough to see the futility of massive resistance to desegregation. But he will not see this without pressure from devotees of civil rights. My friends, I must say to you that we have not made a single gain in civil rights without determined legal and nonviolent pressure. Lamentably, it is an historical fact that privileged groups seldom give up their privileges voluntarily. Individuals may see the moral light and voluntarily give up their unjust posture, but, as Reinhold Niebuhr has reminded us, groups tend to be more immoral than individuals.

We know through painful experience that freedom is never voluntarily given by the oppressor; it must be demanded by the oppressed. Frankly, I have yet to engage in a direct-action campaign that was "well timed" in the view of those who have not suffered unduly from the disease of segregation. For years now I have heard the word "Wait!" It rings in the ear of every Negro with piercing familiarity. This "Wait" has almost always meant "Never." We must come to see, with one of our distinguished jurists, that "justice too long delayed is justice denied."

We have waited for more than 340 years for our constitutional and God-given rights. The nations of Asia and Africa are moving with jet-like speed toward gaining political independence, but we still creep at horse-

and-buggy pace toward gaining a cup of coffee at a lunch counter. Perhaps it is easy for those who have never felt the stinging darts of segregation to say, "Wait." But when you have seen vicious mobs lynch your mothers and fathers at will and drown your sisters and brothers at whim; when you have seen hate-filled policemen curse, kick, and even kill your black brothers and sisters; when you see the vast majority of your twenty million Negro brothers smothering in an airtight cage of poverty in the midst of an affluent society; when you suddenly find your tongue twisted and your speech stammering as you seek to explain to your six-year-old daughter why she can't go to the public amusement park that has just been advertised on television, and see tears welling up in her eyes when she is told that Funtown is closed to colored children, and see ominous clouds of inferiority beginning to form in her little mental sky, and see her beginning to distort her personality by developing an unconscious bitterness toward white people; when you have to concoct an answer for a five-year-old son who is asking, "Daddy, why do white people treat colored people so mean?"; when you take a cross-country drive and find it necessary to sleep night after night in the uncomfortable corners of your automobile because no motel will accept you; when you are humiliated day in and day out by nagging signs reading "white" and "colored"; when your first name becomes "nigger," your middle name becomes "boy" (however old you are) and your last name becomes "John," and your wife and mother are never given the respected title "Mrs."; when you are harried by day and haunted by night by the fact that you are a Negro, living constantly at tiptoe stance, never quite knowing what to expect next, and are plagued with inner fears and outer resentments; when you are forever fighting a degenerating sense of "nobodiness"—then you will understand why we find it difficult to wait. There comes a time when the cup of endurance runs over, and men are no longer willing to be plunged into the abyss of despair. I hope, sirs, you can understand our legitimate and unavoidable impatience.

You express a great deal of anxiety over our willingness to break laws. 15 This is certainly a legitimate concern. Since we so diligently urge people to obey the Supreme Court's decision of 1954 outlawing segregation in the public schools, at first glance it may seem rather paradoxical for us consciously to break laws. One may well ask: "How can you advocate breaking some laws and obeying others?" The answer lies in the fact that there are two types of laws: just and unjust. I would be the first to advocate obeying just laws. One has not only a legal but a moral responsibility to obey just laws. Conversely, one has a moral responsibility to disobey unjust laws. I would agree with St. Augustine that "an unjust law is no law at all."

Now, what is the difference between the two? How does one determine whether a law is just or unjust? A just law is a man-made code that squares with the moral law or the law of God. An unjust law is a code that is out of harmony with the moral law. To put it in the terms of St. Thomas Aquinas: An unjust law is a human law that is not rooted in eternal law and natural law. Any law that uplifts human personality is just. Any law that degrades human personality is unjust. All segregation statutes are unjust because segregation distorts the soul and damages the personality. It gives the segregator a false sense of superiority and the segregated a false sense of inferiority. Segregation, to use the terminology of the Jewish philosopher Martin Buber, substitutes an "I-it" relationship for an "I-thou" relationship and ends up relegating persons to the status of things. Hence segregation is not only politically, economically, and sociologically unsound, it is morally wrong and sinful. Paul Tillich has said that sin is separation. Is not segregation an existential expression of man's tragic separation, his awful estrangement, his terrible sinfulness? Thus it is that I can urge men to obey the 1954 decision of the Supreme Court, for it is morally right; and I can urge them to disobey segregation ordinances, for they are morally wrong.

Let us consider a more concrete example of just and unjust laws. An unjust law is a code that a numerical or power majority group compels a minority group to obey but does not make binding on itself. This is *difference* made legal. By the same token, a just law is a code that a majority compels a minority to follow and that it is willing to follow itself. This is *sameness* made legal.

Let me give another explanation. A law is unjust if it is inflicted on a minority that, as a result of being denied the right to vote, had no part in enacting or devising the law. Who can say that the legislature of Alabama which set up that state's segregation laws was democratically elected? Throughout Alabama all sorts of devious methods are used to prevent Negroes from becoming registered voters, and there are some counties in which, even though Negroes constitute a majority of the population, not a single Negro is registered. Can any law enacted under such circumstances be considered democratically structured?

Sometimes a law is just on its face and unjust in its application. For instance, I have been arrested on a charge of parading without a permit. Now, there is nothing wrong in having an ordinance which requires a permit for a parade. But such an ordinance becomes unjust when it is used to maintain segregation and to deny citizens the First-Amendment privilege of peaceful assembly and protest.

I hope you are able to see the distinction I am trying to point out. In 20 no sense do I advocate evading or defying the law, as would the rabid segregationist. That would lead to anarchy. One who breaks an unjust law must do so openly, lovingly, and with a willingness to accept the

99

penalty. I submit that an individual who breaks a law that conscience tells him is unjust, and who willingly accepts the penalty of imprisonment in order to arouse the conscience of the community over its injustice, is in reality expressing the highest respect for law.

Of course, there is nothing new about this kind of civil disobedience. It was evidenced sublimely in the refusal of Shadrach, Meshach, and Abednego to obey the laws of Nebuchadnezzar, on the ground that a higher moral law was at stake. It was practiced superbly by the early Christians, who were willing to face hungry lions and the excruciating pain of chopping blocks rather than submit to certain unjust laws of the Roman Empire. To a degree, academic freedom is a reality today because Socrates practiced civil disobedience. In our own nation, the Boston Tea Party represented a massive act of civil disobedience.

We should never forget that everything Adolf Hitler did in Germany was "legal" and everything the Hungarian freedom fighters did in Hungary was "illegal." It was "illegal" to aid and comfort a Jew in Hitler's Germany. Even so, I am sure that, had I lived in Germany at the time, I would have aided and comforted my Jewish brothers. If today I lived in a Communist country where certain principles dear to the Christian faith are suppressed, I would openly advocate disobeying that country's anti-religious laws.

I must make two honest confessions to you, my Christian and Jewish brothers. First, I must confess that over the past few years I have been gravely disappointed with the white moderate. I have almost reached the regrettable conclusion that the Negro's great stumbling block in his stride toward freedom is not the White Citizen's Counciler or the Ku Klux Klanner, but the white moderate, who is more devoted to "order" than to justice; who prefers a negative peace which is the absence of tension to a positive peace which is the presence of justice; who constantly says, "I agree with you in the goal you seek, but I cannot agree with your methods of direct action"; who paternalistically believes he can set the timetable for another man's freedom; who lives by a mythical concept of time and who constantly advises the Negro to wait for a "more convenient season." Shallow understanding from people of good will is more frustrating than absolute misunderstanding from people of ill will. Lukewarm acceptance is much more bewildering than outright rejection.

I had hoped that the white moderate would understand that law and order exist for the purpose of establishing justice and that when they fail in this purpose they become the dangerously structured dams that block the flow of social progress. I had hoped that the white moderate would understand that the present tension in the South is a necessary phase of the transition from an obnoxious negative peace, in which the Negro passively accepted his unjust plight, to a substantive and positive peace, in which all men will respect the dignity and worth of human personality. Actually, we who engage in nonviolent direct action are not the creators of tension. We merely bring to the surface the hidden tension that is already alive. We bring it out in the open, where it can be seen and dealt with. Like a boil that can never be cured so long as it is covered up but must be opened with all its ugliness to the natural medicines of air and light, injustice must be exposed, with all the tension its exposure creates, to the light of human conscience and the air of national opinion, before it can be cured.

In your statement you assert that our actions, even though peaceful, 25 must be condemned because they precipitate violence. But is this a logical assertion? Isn't this like condemning a robbed man because his possession of money precipitated the evil act of robbery? Isn't this like condemning Socrates because his unswerving commitment to truth and his philosophical inquiries precipitated the act by the misguided populace in which they made him drink hemlock? Isn't this like condemning Jesus because his unique God-consciousness and never-ceasing devotion to God's will precipitated the evil act of crucifixion? We must come to see that, as the federal courts have consistently affirmed, it is wrong to urge an individual to cease his efforts to gain his basic constitutional rights because the quest may precipitate violence. Society must protect the robbed and punish the robber.

I had also hoped that the white moderate would reject the myth concerning time in relation to the struggle for freedom. I have just received a letter from a white brother in Texas. He writes: "All Christians know that the colored people will receive equal rights eventually, but it is possible that you are in too great a religious hurry. It has taken Christianity almost two thousand years to accomplish what it has. The teachings of Christ take time to come to earth." Such an attitude stems from a tragic misconception of time, from the strangely irrational notion that there is something in the very flow of time that will inevitably cure all ills. Actually, time itself is neutral; it can be used either destructively or constructively. More and more I feel that the people of ill will have used time much more effectively than have the people of good will. We will have to repent in this generation not merely for the hateful words and actions of the bad people, but for the appalling silence of the good people. Human progress never rolls in on wheels of inevitability; it comes through the tireless efforts of men willing to be co-workers with God, and without this hard work, time itself becomes an ally of the forces of social stagnation. We must use time creatively, in the knowledge that the time is always ripe to do right. Now is the time to make real the promise of democracy and transform our pending national elegy into a creative psalm of brotherhood. Now is the time to lift our national policy from the quicksand of racial injustice to the solid rock of human dignity. You speak of our activity in Birmingham as extreme. At first I was rather disappointed that fellow clergymen would see my nonviolent efforts as those of an extremist. I began thinking about the fact that I stand in the middle of two opposing forces in the Negro community. One is a force of complacency, made up in part of Negroes who, as a result of long years of oppression, are so drained of self-respect and a sense of "somebodiness" that they have adjusted to segregation; and in part of a few middle-class Negroes who, because of a degree of academic and economic security and because in some ways they profit by segregation, have become insensitive to the problems of the masses. The other force is one of bitterness and hatred, and it comes perilously close to advocating violence. It is expressed in the various black nationalist groups that are springing up across the nation, the largest and best-known being Elijah Muhammad's Muslim movement. Nourished by the Negro's frustration over the continued existence of racial discrimination, this movement is made up of people who have lost faith in America, who have absolutely repudiated Christianity, and who have concluded that the white man is an incorrigible "devil."

I have tried to stand between these two forces, saying that we need emulate neither the "do-nothingism" of the complacent nor the hatred and despair of the black nationalist. For there is the more excellent way of love and nonviolent protest. I am grateful to God that, through the influence of the Negro church, the way of nonviolence became an integral part of our struggle.

If this philosophy had not emerged, by now many streets of the South would, I am convinced, be flowing with blood. And I am further convinced that if our white brothers dismiss as "rabblerousers" and "outside agitators" those of us who employ nonviolent direct action, and if they refuse to support our nonviolent efforts, millions of Negroes will, out of frustration and despair, seek solace and security in black-nationalist ideologies—a development that would inevitably lead to a frightening racial nightmare.

Oppressed people cannot remain oppressed forever. The yearning for 30 freedom eventually manifests itself, and that is what has happened to the American Negro. Something within has reminded him of his birthright of freedom, and something without has reminded him that it can be gained. Consciously or unconsciously, he has been caught up by the *Zeitgeist*, and with his black brothers of Africa and his brown and yellow brothers of Asia, South America, and the Caribbean, the United States Negro is moving with a sense of great urgency toward the promised land of racial justice. If one recognizes this vital urge that has engulfed the Negro community, one should readily understand why public demonstrations are taking place. The Negro has many pent-up resentments and latent frustrations, and he must release them. So let him march; let him make prayer pilgrimages to the city hall; let him go on freedom rides—and try to understand why he must do so. If his repressed emotions are not released in nonviolent ways, they will seek expression through violence; this is not a threat but a fact of history. So I have not said to my people, "Get rid of your discontent." Rather, I have tried to say that this normal and healthy discontent can be channeled into the creative outlet of nonviolent direct action. And now this approach is being termed extremist.

But though I was initially disappointed at being categorized as an extremist, as I continued to think about the matter I gradually gained a measure of satisfaction from the label. Was not Jesus an extremist for love: "Love your enemies, bless them that curse you, do good to them that hate you, and pray for them which despitefully use you, and persecute you." Was not Amos an extremist for justice: "Let justice roll down like waters and righteousness like an ever-flowing stream." Was not Paul an extremist for the Christian gospel: "I bear in my body the marks of the Lord Jesus." Was not Martin Luther an extremist: "Here I stand; I cannot do otherwise, so help me God." And John Bunyan: "I will stay in jail to the end of my days before I make a butchery of my conscience." And Abraham Lincoln: "This nation cannot survive half slave and half free." And Thomas Jefferson: "We hold these truths to be self-evident, that all men are created equal. . . ." So the question is not whether we will be extremists, but what kind of extremists we will be. Will we be extremists for hate or for love? Will we be extremists for the preservation of injustice or for the extension of justice? In that dramatic scene on Calvary's hill three men were crucified. We must never forget that all three were crucified for the same crime—the crime of extremism. Two were extremists for immorality, and thus fell below their environment. The other, Jesus Christ, was an extremist for love, truth, and goodness, and thereby rose above his environment. Perhaps the South, the nation, and the world are in dire need of creative extremists.

I had hoped that the white moderate would see this need. Perhaps I was too optimistic; perhaps I expected too much. I suppose I should have realized that few members of the oppressor race can understand the deep groans and passionate yearnings of the oppressed race, and still fewer have the vision to see that injustice must be rooted out by strong, persistent, and determined action. I am thankful, however, that some of our white brothers in the South have grasped the meaning of this social revolution and committed themselves to it. They are still all too few in quantity, but they are big in quality. Some—such as Ralph McGill,

Lillian Smith, Harry Golden, James McBridge Dabbs, Ann Braden, and Sarah Patton Boyle—have written about our struggle in eloquent and prophetic terms. Others have marched with us down nameless streets of the South. They have languished in filthy, roach-infested jails, suffering the abuse and brutality of policemen who view them as "dirty nigger-lovers." Unlike so many of their moderate brothers and sisters, they have recognized the urgency of the moment and sensed the need for powerful "action" antidotes to combat the disease of segregation.

Let me take note of my other major disappointment. I have been so greatly disappointed with the white church and its leadership. Of course, there are some notable exceptions. I am not unmindful of the fact that each of you has taken some significant stands on this issue. I commend you, Reverend Stallings, for your Christian stand on this past Sunday, in welcoming Negroes to your worship service on a nonsegregated basis. I commend the Catholic leaders of this state for integrating Spring Hill College several years ago.

But despite these notable exceptions, I must honestly reiterate that I have been disappointed with the church. I do not say this as one of those negative critics who can always find something wrong with the church. I say this as a minister of the gospel, who loves the church; who was nurtured in its bosom; who has been sustained by its spiritual blessings and who will remain true to it as long as the cord of life shall lengthen.

When I was suddenly catapulted into the leadership of the bus protest 35 in Montgomery, Alabama, a few years ago, I felt we would be supported by the white church. I felt that the white ministers, priests, and rabbis of the South would be among our strongest allies. Instead, some have been outright opponents, refusing to understand the freedom movement and misrepresenting its leaders; all too many others have been more cautious than courageous and have remained silent behind the anesthetizing security of stained-glass windows.

In spite of my shattered dreams, I came to Birmingham with the hope that the white religious leadership of this community would see the justice of our cause and, with deep moral concern, would serve as the channel through which our just grievances could reach the power structure. I had hoped that each of you would understand. But again I have been disappointed.

I have heard numerous southern religious leaders admonish their worshipers to comply with a desegregation decision because it is the law, but I have longed to hear white ministers declare: "Follow this decree because integration is morally right and because the Negro is your brother." In the midst of blatant injustices inflicted upon the Negro, I have watched white churchmen stand on the sideline and mouth pious irrelevancies and sanctimonious trivialities. In the midst of a mighty struggle to rid our nation of racial and economic injustice, I have heard many ministers say: "Those are social issues, with which the gospel has no real concern." And I have watched many churches commit themselves to a completely otherworldly religion which makes a strange, un-Biblical distinction between body and soul, between the sacred and the secular.

I have traveled the length and breadth of Alabama, Mississippi, and all the other southern states. On sweltering summer days and crisp autumn mornings I have looked at the South's beautiful churches with their lofty spires pointing heavenward. I have beheld the impressive outlines of her massive religious-education buildings. Over and over I have found myself asking: "What kind of people worship here? Who is their God? Where were their voices when the lips of Governor Barnett dripped with words of interposition and nullification? Where were they when Governor Wallace gave a clarion call for defiance and hatred? Where were their voices of support when bruised and weary Negro men and women decided to rise from the dark dungeons of complacency to the bright hills of creative protest?"

Yes, these questions are still in my mind. In deep disappointment I have wept over the laxity of the church. But be assured that my tears have been tears of love. There can be no deep disappointment where there is not deep love. Yes, I love the church. How could I do otherwise? I am in the rather unique position of being the son, the grandson, and the great-grandson of preachers. Yes, I see the church as the body of Christ. But, oh! How we have blemished and scarred that body through social neglect and through fear of being nonconformists.

There was a time when the church was very powerful—in the time 40 when the early Christians rejoiced at being deemed worthy to suffer for what they believed. In those days the church was not merely a thermometer that recorded the ideas and principles of popular opinion; it was a thermostat that transformed the mores of society. Whenever the early Christians entered a town, the people in power became disturbed and immediately sought to convict the Christians for being "disturbers of the peace" and "outside agitators." But the Christians pressed on, in the conviction that they were "a colony of heaven," called to obey God rather than man. Small in number, they were big in commitment. They were too God-intoxicated to be "astronomically intimidated." By their effort and example they brought an end to such ancient evils as infanticide and gladiatorial contests.

Things are different now. So often the contemporary church is a weak, ineffectual voice with an uncertain sound. So often it is an archdefender of the status quo. Far from being disturbed by the presence of the church, the power structure of the average community is consoled by the church's silent—and often even vocal—sanction of things as they are.

But the judgment of God is upon the church as never before. If today's church does not recapture the sacrificial spirit of the early church, it will lose its authenticity, forfeit the loyalty of millions, and be dismissed as an irrelevant social club with no meaning for the twentieth century. Every day I meet young people whose disappointment with the church has turned into outright disgust.

Perhaps I have once again been too optimistic. Is organized religion too inextricably bound to the status quo to save our nation and the world? Perhaps I must turn my faith to the inner spiritual church, the church within the church, as the true *ekklesia* and the hope of the world. But again I am thankful to God that some noble souls from the ranks of organized religion have broken loose from the paralyzing chains of conformity and joined us as active partners in the struggle for freedom. They have left their secure congregations and walked the streets of Albany, Georgia, with us. They have gone down the highways of the South on tortuous rides for freedom. Yes, they have gone to jail with us. Some have been dismissed from their churches, have lost the support of their bishops and fellow ministers. But they have acted in the faith that right defeated is stronger than evil triumphant. Their witness has been the spiritual salt that has preserved the true meaning of the gospel in these troubled times. They have carved a tunnel of hope through the dark mountain of disappointment.

I hope the church as a whole will meet the challenge of this decisive hour. But even if the church does not come to the aid of justice, I have no despair about the future. I have no fear about the outcome of our struggle in Birmingham, even if our motives are at present misunderstood. We will reach the goal of freedom in Birmingham and all over the nation, because the goal of America is freedom. Abused and scorned though we may be, our destiny is tied up with America's destiny. Before the pilgrims landed at Plymouth, we were here. Before the pen of Jefferson etched the majestic words of the Declaration of Independence across the pages of history, we were here. For more than two centuries our forebears labored in this country without wages; they made cotton king; they built the homes of their masters while suffering gross injustice and shameful humiliation—and yet out of a bottomless vitality they continued to thrive and develop. If the inexpressible cruelties of slavery could not stop us, the opposition we now face will surely fail. We will win our freedom because the sacred heritage of our nation and the eternal will of God are embodied in our echoing demands.

Before closing I feel impelled to mention one other point in your state- 45
ment that has troubled me profoundly. You warmly commended the

Birmingham police force for keeping "order" and "preventing violence." I doubt that you would have so warmly commended the police force if you had seen its dogs sinking their teeth into unarmed, nonviolent Negroes. I doubt that you would so quickly commend the policemen if you were to observe their ugly and inhumane treatment of Negroes here in the city jail; if you were to watch them push and curse old Negro women and young Negro girls; if you were to see them slap and kick old Negro men and young boys; if you were to observe them, as they did on two occasions, refuse to give us food because we wanted to sing our grace together. I cannot join you in your praise of the Birmingham police department.

It is true that the police have exercised a degree of discipline in handling the demonstrators. In this sense they have conducted themselves rather "nonviolently" in public. But for what purpose? To preserve the evil system of segregation. Over the past few years I have consistently preached that nonviolence demands that the means we use must be as pure as the ends we seek. I have tried to make clear that it is wrong to use immoral means to attain moral ends. But now I must affirm that it is just as wrong, or perhaps even more so, to use moral means to preserve immoral ends. Perhaps Mr. Connor and his policemen have been rather nonviolent in public, as was Chief Pritchett in Albany, Georgia, but they have used the moral means of nonviolence to maintain the immoral end of racial injustice. As T. S. Eliot has said. "The last temptation is the greatest treason: To do the right deed for the wrong reason."

I wish you had commended the Negro sit-inners and demonstrators of Birmingham for their sublime courage, their willingness to suffer, and their amazing discipline in the midst of great provocation. One day the South will recognize its real heroes. They will be the James Merediths, with the noble sense of purpose that enables them to face jeering and hostile mobs, and with the agonizing loneliness that characterizes the life of the pioneer. They will be old, oppressed, battered Negro women, symbolized in a seventy-two-year-old woman in Montgomery, Alabama, who rose up with a sense of dignity and with her people decided not to ride segregated buses, and who responded with ungrammatical profundity to one who inquired about her weariness: "My feets is tired, but my soul is at rest." They will be the young high school and college students, the young ministers of the gospel and a host of their elders, courageously and nonviolently sitting in at lunch counters and willingly going to jail for conscience' sake. One day the South will know that when these disinherited children of God sat down at lunch counters, they were in reality standing up for what is best in the American dream and for the most sacred values in our Judaeo-Christian heritage, thereby bringing our nation back to those great wells of democracy which were dug deep by the founding fathers in their formulation of the Constitution and the Declaration of Independence.

Never before have I written so long a letter. I'm afraid it is much too long to take your precious time. I can assure you that it would have been much shorter if I had been writing from a comfortable desk, but what else can one do when he is alone in a narrow jail cell, other than write long letters, think long thoughts, and pray long prayers?

If I have said anything in this letter that overstates the truth and indicates an unreasonable impatience, I beg you to forgive me. If I have said anything that understates the truth and indicates my having a patience that allows me to settle for anything less than brotherhood, I beg God to forgive me.

I hope this letter finds you strong in the faith. I also hope that circum- 50 stances will soon make it possible for me to meet each of you, not as an integrationist or a civil-rights leader but as a fellow clergyman and a Christian brother. Let us all hope that the dark clouds of racial prejudice will soon pass away and the deep fog of misunderstanding will be lifted from our fear-drenched communities, and in some not too distant to-morrow the radiant stars of love and brotherhood will shine over our great nation with all their scintillating beauty.

Yours for the cause of Peace and Brotherhood,
MARTIN LUTHER KING JR.

[1963]

Persuasive and Public Writing: Summative Questions and Prompts

1. Martin Luther King's renowned "Letter from Birmingham Jail" begins by addressing a particular audience, "My Fellow Clergymen," then attempts to persuade this audience that King's actions toward racial integration are defensible and necessary. Pick a contemporary social or political issue that you care about, then select two different audiences (for example, your first-year classmates, your parents, senators and representatives). Write the first paragraph of two different letters to these two audiences. In both paragraphs, address your audience and introduce your selected issue, but shift your voice, tone, and content based on the person or group to whom you're writing.

2. Select a piece from this section and write a two-paragraph summary/response to a central argument in that piece. In the first paragraph, summarize the writer's central idea faithfully and thoroughly. In the second paragraph, respond by agreeing, disagreeing, or complicating the argument. If you agree with the writer, be sure that your response extends the ideas instead of merely restating them. If you disagree, be sure that you are representing the writer's argument fairly.

3. 3a. Read Dave Eggers' persuasive essay, "Serve or Fail," with Aristotle's three appeals (logos, ethos, and pathos) in mind. For each of the three appeals, find a specific example of Eggers utilizing logos, ethos, and pathos to support his argument. Refer to your selected text by paragraph number, and explain your choices.

   3b. Your selections in 3a likely depend upon how you envision Eggers' audience. Who do you imagine is a primary audience for this piece? College students? Administrators? College-educated adults? Someone else? Explain your response to this question using direct quotations from the text.

Part III: Genre Studies

You may or may not have encountered the term **genre**. For the purposes of this book and the work that you do in ENGL 1050, genre is a way in which readers and writers categorize compositions. Genres can include visual texts composed using images (e.g. photographs, paintings, graphic novels); digital texts designed to be read and interpreted in an electronic platform (e.g. websites, blogs, PowerPoint presentations); and print-based texts that are designed to be read using alphabetic literacy (book, newspaper article; magazine article; poem). As you investigate your genre study, you will begin to see how these categories are not mutually exclusive. For example, Scott McCloud's "Understanding Comics" includes both visual and alphabetic conventions.

When we speak of **conventions**, we are speaking of characteristics that distinguish one genre from another. For example, your autobiography featured a personal voice and storytelling. If you wrote a letter to the editor, it was likely defined in part by the convention of shorter paragraphs and overall length. Depending on your undergraduate major or future profession, you will be required to produce different genres of writing beyond the traditional academic paper or persuasive essay with which you've become most familiar. Successful writing depends on your ability to identify and execute the conventions of each new genre you encounter.

The readings in this section include genres with which you may or may not be familiar. The texts are composed in various genres of writing, with different conventions that adhere to audience expectations. Scott McCloud's "Understanding Comics" helps readers understand how to analyze and employ conventions of visual rhetoric. Additional texts containing visual images include Pablo Picasso's "Guernica," Grant Wood's "American Gothic," and Gordon Parks' "American Gothic." "Guernica," a mural created by Pablo Picasso following the 1937 bombing of a Spanish village, provides an eerie peek into the chaos of war using the close quarters of a single frame. Using realism, Grant Wood's famous "American Gothic" depicts a rural family from the early part of the 20th century, reflecting class and gender roles. This painting has produced a number of references and parodies; one of the first was Gordon Parks' "American Gothic," which removes the man from the picture entirely and illustrates the aloneness of working-class women of color.

This section also includes examples from two alphabetic genres: poetry and fiction. The poetry selections, James Wright's "Lying in a Hammock at William Duffy's Farm in Pine Island, Minnesota," Elizabeth Bishop's "One Art," and Detroit native Philip Levine's "What Work Is," have been selected for their wit, originality, and tone. Likewise, the mystical, straightforward, and hauntingly beautiful "A Good Man is Hard to Find" by Flannery O'Connor represents some of the finest American short writing from the past century. The final text, "How to Make a Documentary," by Connor Makowski, is one of four recipients of the 2013 ENGL 1050 Best Essay Award. Makowski's "how-to" manual serves as an example for how students might understand and produce a documentary as a genre.

As you read, consider how conventions and form shape the content and purpose of different genres.

SCOTT McCLOUD [b. 1960]

Understanding Comics

Born in Boston, Massachusetts, and raised in Lexington, **Scott McCloud** is a cartoonist and comics theorist. After graduating from Syracuse University with a fine arts degree in illustration, McCloud worked in the production department of DC Comics before creating *Zot!*—a lighthearted, thirty-six-issue alternative series published by Eclipse Comics between 1984 and 1991—in response to the darker, violent comics that dominated the scene during the 1980s. McCloud followed *Zot!* with *Destroy!!* (1986), a single, oversized volume parodying the archetypal, violent superhero; *The New Adventures of Abraham Lincoln* (1998), his first attempt with computer-generated artwork; and *Superman: Adventures of the Man of Steel* (1998), a compilation of the first six of twelve superman stories scripted for DC Comics. Cited as the "Aristotle of comics," McCloud is best known as the author of *Understanding Comics: The Invisible Art* (1993), in which his self-caricature guides the reader through a study of sequential art, by tracing the relationship between words and images. Following the belated success of *Understanding Comics*, he published *Reinventing Comics* (2000) and *Making Comics* (2006), in which his self-caricature reemerged.

In the following excerpts from *Understanding Comics*, McCloud suggests that the influence of new media on the written word is often misunderstood, and that comics are more than simple juxtapositions of words and images. Drawing first on the idea of "show and tell," McCloud proposes "unlimited" benefits to the interdependent use of words and images in comics, comparing the two to dance partners: "[E]ach one takes turns leading."

THE ART FORM OF COMICS IS MANY CENTURIES OLD, BUT IT'S *PERCEIVED* AS A RECENT INVENTION AND SUFFERS THE CURSE OF *ALL* NEW MEDIA.

THE CURSE OF BEING JUDGED BY THE STANDARDS OF THE OLD.

EVER SINCE THE INVENTION OF THE WRITTEN WORD, NEW MEDIA HAVE BEEN *MISUNDERSTOOD.*

CAREFUL, JACOB! IF YOU KEEP DOING THIS, YOU'LL STOP USING YOUR *MEMORY!*

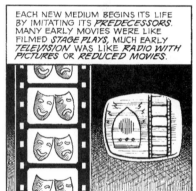

EACH NEW MEDIUM BEGINS ITS LIFE BY IMITATING ITS *PREDECESSORS.* MANY EARLY MOVIES WERE LIKE FILMED *STAGE PLAYS,* MUCH EARLY *TELEVISION* WAS LIKE *RADIO WITH PICTURES* OR *REDUCED MOVIES.*

FAR TOO MANY COMICS CREATORS HAVE NO HIGHER GOAL THAN TO MATCH THE ACHIEVEMENTS OF OTHER MEDIA, AND VIEW ANY CHANCE TO *WORK* IN OTHER MEDIA AS A *STEP UP.*

AND *AGAIN,* AS LONG AS WE VIEW COMICS AS A *GENRE* OF WRITING OR A *STYLE* OF GRAPHIC ART THIS ATTITUDE MAY *NEVER* DISAPPEAR.

WORDS AND PICTURES IN COMBINATION MAY NOT BE MY *DEFINITION* OF COMICS, BUT THE COMBINATION HAS HAD *TREMENDOUS INFLUENCE* ON ITS *GROWTH.*

com·ics (kom'iks)**n.** p... form, used with a singula... Juxtaposed pictoria... ...er images in deliberate... ...ence, intended to conve... ...n and/or to produ... response in t... **2.** Superheroe... costumes, fight... villians who want ... ...e world, in violent s... ...use...

A HUGE RANGE OF HUMAN EXPERIENCES CAN BE *PORTRAYED* IN COMICS THROUGH EITHER WORDS OR PICTURES.

AS A RESULT--AND DESPITE ITS MANY *OTHER* POTENTIAL USES -- COMICS HAVE BECOME *FIRMLY IDENTIFIED* WITH THE ART OF *STORYTELLING.*

AND *INDEED,* WORDS AND PICTURES HAVE *GREAT* POWERS TO TELL STORIES WHEN CREATORS FULLY EXPLOIT THEM *BOTH.*

DADA
BIOGRAPHY   HORROR
ROMANCE   SURREALISM
BLANK
VERSE   HISTORICAL
                FICTION
EPIC
POETRY   FOLK TALES
              EROTICA
SOCIAL
ALLEGORY   MYSTERY
              RELIGIOUS
ADAPTATIONS   TOPICS
STREAM
OF CONSCIOUSNESS
SATIRE

SEQUENTIAL ART

AND SO FAR, WE'VE ONLY SEEN THE *TIP OF THE ICEBERG!*

AS CHILDREN, WE "SHOW AND TELL" *INTERCHANGEABLY,* WORDS AND IMAGES COMBINING TO TRANSMIT A *CONNECTED SERIES OF IDEAS.*

IT'S GOT ONE OF *THESE* THINGS.

THE DIFFERENT WAYS IN WHICH WORDS AND PICTURES CAN *COMBINE* IN COMICS IS VIRTUALLY *UNLIMITED.*

BUT LET'S TRY TO BREAK IT DOWN INTO SOME DISTINCT *CATEGORIES.*

IN COMICS AT ITS *BEST,* WORDS AND PICTURES ARE LIKE *PARTNERS* IN A *DANCE* AND EACH ONE TAKES TURNS *LEADING.*

WHEN *BOTH* PARTNERS TRY TO LEAD, THE COMPETITION CAN *SUBVERT* THE OVERALL GOALS...

YOW!

...THOUGH A LITTLE *PLAYFUL* *COMPETITION* CAN SOMETIMES PRODUCE *ENJOYABLE RESULTS.*

BUT WHEN THESE PARTNERS EACH *KNOW* THEIR ROLES--

--AND *SUPPORT* EACH OTHER'S *STRENGTHS--*

--COMICS CAN MATCH *ANY* OF THE ART FORMS IT DRAWS SO MUCH OF ITS STRENGTH FROM.

[1993]

Pablo Picasso, *Guernica*, 1937. Picasso's cubist painting depicts the bombing of Guernica, a town in Spain's Basque Country, by Nazi Germany on April 26, 1937. (Copyright © 2008 Estate of Pablo Picasso/Artists Rights Society (ARS), New York. Photo by John Bigelow Taylor/Art Resource, New York.)

Grant Wood, *American Gothic*, 1930. Grant Wood's painting, *American Gothic*, is one of the most famous, and most parodied, works of art in American popular culture. (Copyright © Art Institute of Chicago.)

Gordon Parks, *American Gothic*, **1942.** A photograph of government charwoman Ella Watson by Gordon Parks parodies Grant Wood's 1930 painting of the same name. (Courtesy Gordon Parks/Corbis.)

JAMES WRIGHT   [1927–1980]

Lying in a Hammock
at William Duffy's Farm
in Pine Island, Minnesota

Raised in Martin's Ferry, Ohio, **James Wright** attended Kenyon College, where the influence of John Crowe Ransom sent his early poetry in a formalist direction. After spending a year in Austria on a Fulbright fellowship, he returned to the United States and earned an M.A. and a Ph.D. at the University of Washington, studying under Theodore Roethke and Stanley Kunitz. He went on to teach at the University of Minnesota, Macalester College, and Hunter College. His working-class background and the poverty that he witnessed during the Depression stirred in him a sympathy for the poor and for "outsiders" of various sorts that shaped the tone and content of his poetry. He published numerous books of poetry; his *Collected Poems* received the Pulitzer Prize in 1972. "Lying in a Hammock" explores the themes of nature and environment as well as the personal decisions and values of the speaker.

Over my head, I see the bronze butterfly,
Asleep on the black trunk,
Blowing like a leaf in green shadow.
Down the ravine behind the empty house,   5
The cowbells follow one another
Into the distances of the afternoon.
To my right,
In a field of sunlight between two pines,
The droppings of last year's horses
Blaze up into golden stones.   10
I lean back, as the evening darkens and comes on.
A chicken hawk floats over, looking for home.
I have wasted my life.

[1963]

ELIZABETH BISHOP [1911–1979]

One Art

Born in Worcester, Massachusetts, **Elizabeth Bishop** (1911–1979) was raised in Nova Scotia by her grandparents after her father died and her mother was committed to an asylum. She attended Vassar College intending to study medicine but was encouraged by Marianne Moore to be a poet. From 1935 to 1937 she traveled in France, Spain, northern Africa, Ireland, and Italy. She settled in Key West, Florida, for four years and then in Rio de Janeiro for almost twenty. She wrote slowly and carefully, producing a small body of technically sophisticated, formally varied, witty, and thoughtful poetry, revealing in precise, true-to-life images her impressions of the physical world. She served as Consultant in Poetry at the Library of Congress from 1949 to 1950.

The art of losing isn't hard to master;
so many things seem filled with the intent
to be lost that their loss is no disaster.

Lose something every day. Accept the fluster
of lost door keys, the hour badly spent.   5
The art of losing isn't hard to master.

Then practice losing farther, losing faster:
places, and names, and where it was you meant
to travel. None of these will bring disaster.

I lost my mother's watch. And look! my last, or   10
next-to-last, of three loved houses went.
The art of losing isn't hard to master.

I lost two cities, lovely ones. And, vaster,
some realms I owned, two rivers, a continent.
I miss them, but it wasn't a disaster.   15

—Even losing you (the joking voice, a gesture
I love) I shan't have lied. It's evident
the art of losing's not too hard to master
though it may look like (*Write* it!) like disaster.

[1976]

PHILIP LEVINE   [b. 1928]

What Work Is

Born in Detroit, **Philip Levine** (b. 1928) received his degrees from
Wayne State University and the University of Iowa. He is the author of
many books of poetry, including *The Simple Truth* (1994), which won
the Pulitzer Prize. He has also published a collection of essays, edited
The Essential Keats (1987), and co-edited and translated two books
of poetry by the Spanish poet Gloria Fuertes and the Mexican poet
Jamie Sabines. He lives in New York City and Fresno, California, and
teaches at New York University.

We stand in the rain in a long line
waiting at Ford Highland Park. For work.
You know what work is—if you're
old enough to read this you know what
work is, although you may not do it.   5
Forget you. This is about waiting,
shifting from one foot to another.
Feeling the light rain falling like mist
into your hair, blurring your vision
until you think you see your own brother   10
ahead of you, maybe ten places.
You rub your glasses with your fingers,
and of course it's someone else's brother,
narrower across the shoulders than
yours but with the same sad slouch, the grin   15
that does not hide the stubbornness,
the sad refusal to give in to
rain, to the hours wasted waiting,
to the knowledge that somewhere ahead
a man is waiting who will say, "No,   20
we're not hiring today," for any
reason he wants. You love your brother,
now suddenly you can hardly stand
the love flooding you for your brother,

who's not beside you or behind or   25
ahead because he's home trying to
sleep off a miserable night shift
at Cadillac so he can get up
before noon to study his German.
Works eight hours a night so he can sing   30
Wagner, the opera you hate most,
the worst music ever invented.
How long has it been since you told him
you loved him, held his wide shoulders,
opened your eyes wide and said those words,   35
and maybe kissed his cheek? You've never
done something so simple, so obvious,
not because you're too young or too dumb,
not because you're jealous or even mean
or incapable of crying in   40
the presence of another man, no,
just because you don't know what work is.

[1991]

FLANNERY O'CONNOR [1925–1964]

A Good Man Is Hard to Find

The dragon is by the side of the road, watching those who pass.
Beware lest he devour you. We go to the Father of Souls, but it is
necessary to pass by the dragon. —ST. CYRIL OF JERUSALEM

Born in Savannah, Georgia, and raised on a farm in Milledgeville, Georgia, **Flannery O'Connor** (1925–1964) graduated from Georgia State College for Women in 1945 and attended the Writers' Workshop at the University of Iowa, from which she received a master's degree in 1947. From Iowa she moved to New York City to begin her writing career but, after little more than two years, was forced by illness to return to her mother's Georgia farm. Confined as an invalid by the degenerative disease lupus, O'Connor spent her remaining fourteen years raising peacocks and writing fiction set in rural Georgia. Her works are distinguished by irreverent humor, often grotesque characters, and intense, almost mystical affirmation of the challenges of religious belief. Her work includes two novels, *Wise Blood* (1952) and *The Violent Bear It Away* (1960), and two short story collections, *A Good Man Is Hard to Find* (1955) and *Everything That Rises Must Converge* (1965). After her death at the age of thirty-nine, a selection of occasional prose, *Mystery and Manners* (1969) was edited by her friends Sally and Robert Fitzgerald, and a collection of letters, *The Habit of Being* (1979), was edited by Sally Fitzgerald. *The Complete Stories* (1971) received the National Book Award.

The grandmother didn't want to go to Florida. She wanted to visit some of her connections in east Tennessee and she was seizing at every chance to change Bailey's mind. Bailey was the son she lived with, her only boy. He was sitting on the edge of his chair at the table, bent over the orange sports section of the *Journal*. "Now look here, Bailey," she said, "see here, read this," and she stood with one hand on her thin hip and the other rattling the newspaper at his bald head. "Here this fellow that calls himself The Misfit is aloose from the Federal Pen and headed toward

Florida and you read here what it says he did to these people. Just you read it. I wouldn't take my children in any direction with a criminal like that aloose in it. I couldn't answer to my conscience if I did."

Bailey didn't look up from his reading so she wheeled around then and faced the children's mother, a young woman in slacks, whose face was as broad and innocent as a cabbage and was tied around with a green head-kerchief that had two points on the top like rabbit's ears. She was sitting on the sofa, feeding the baby his apricots out of a jar. "The children have been to Florida before," the old lady said. "You all ought to take them somewhere else for a change so they would see different parts of the world and be broad. They never have been to east Tennessee."

The children's mother didn't seem to hear her but the eight-year-old boy, John Wesley, a stocky child with glasses, said, "If you don't want to go to Florida, why dontcha stay at home?" He and the little girl, June Star, were reading the funny papers on the floor.

"She wouldn't stay at home to be queen for a day," June Star said without raising her yellow head.

"Yes and what would you do if this fellow, The Misfit, caught you?" the grandmother asked.

"I'd smack his face," John Wesley said.

"She wouldn't stay at home for a million bucks," June Star said. "Afraid she'd miss something. She has to go everywhere we go."

"All right, Miss," the grandmother said. "Just remember that the next time you want me to curl your hair."

June Star said her hair was naturally curly.

The next morning the grandmother was the first one in the car, ready to go. She had her big black valise that looked like the head of a hippopotamus in one corner, and underneath it she was hiding a basket with Pitty Sing, the cat, in it. She didn't intend for the cat to be left alone in the house for three days because he would miss her too much and she was afraid he might brush against one of the gas burners and accidentally asphyxiate himself. Her son, Bailey, didn't like to arrive at a motel with a cat.

She sat in the middle of the back seat with John Wesley and June Star on either side of her. Bailey and the children's mother and the baby sat in front and they left Atlanta at eight forty-five with the mileage on the car at 55890. The grandmother wrote this down because she thought it would be interesting to say how many miles they had been when they got back. It took them twenty minutes to reach the outskirts of the city.

The old lady settled herself comfortably, removing her white cotton gloves and putting them up with her purse on the shelf in front of the back window. The children's mother still had on slacks and still had her head tied up in a green kerchief, but the grandmother had on a navy blue

127

straw sailor hat with a bunch of white violets on the brim and a navy blue dress with a small white dot in the print. Her collars and cuffs were white organdy trimmed with lace and at her neckline she had pinned a purple spray of cloth violets containing a sachet. In case of an accident, anyone seeing her dead on the highway would know at once that she was a lady.

She said she thought it was going to be a good day for driving, neither too hot nor too cold, and she cautioned Bailey that the speed limit was fifty-five miles an hour and that the patrolmen hid themselves behind billboards and small clumps of trees and sped out after you before you had a chance to slow down. She pointed out interesting details of the scenery: Stone Mountain; the blue granite that in some places came up to both sides of the highway; the brilliant red clay banks slightly streaked with purple; and the various crops that made rows of green lace-work on the ground. The trees were full of silver-white sunlight and the meanest of them sparkled. The children were reading comic magazines and their mother had gone back to sleep.

"Let's go through Georgia fast so we won't have to look at it much," John Wesley said.

"If I were a little boy," said the grandmother, "I wouldn't talk about my native state that way. Tennessee has the mountains and Georgia has the hills."

"Tennessee is just a hillbilly dumping ground," John Wesley said, "and Georgia is a lousy state too."

"You said it," June Star said.

"In my time," said the grandmother, folding her thin veined fingers, "children were more respectful of their native states and their parents and everything else. People did right then. Oh look at the cute little pickaninny!" she said and pointed to a Negro child standing in the door of a shack. "Wouldn't that make a picture, now?" she asked and they all turned and looked at the little Negro out of the back window. He waved.

"He didn't have any britches on," June Star said.

"He probably didn't have any," the grandmother explained. "Little niggers in the country don't have things like we do. If I could paint, I'd paint that picture," she said.

The children exchanged comic books.

The grandmother offered to hold the baby and the children's mother passed him over the front seat to her. She set him on her knee and bounced him and told him about the things they were passing. She rolled her eyes and screwed up her mouth and stuck her leathery thin face into his smooth bland one. Occasionally he gave her a faraway smile. They passed a large cotton field with five or six graves fenced in the middle of it, like a small island. "Look at the graveyard!" the grandmother said, pointing it out. "That was the old family burying ground. That belonged to the plantation."

"Where's the plantation?" John Wesley asked.

"Gone with the Wind," said the grandmother. "Ha. Ha."

When the children finished all the comic books they had brought, they opened the lunch and ate it. The grandmother ate a peanut butter sandwich and an olive and would not let the children throw the box and the paper napkins out the window. When there was nothing else to do they played a game by choosing a cloud and making the other two guess what shape it suggested. John Wesley took one the shape of a cow and June Star guessed a cow and John Wesley said, no, an automobile, and June Star said he didn't play fair, and they began to slap each other over the grandmother.

The grandmother said she would tell them a story if they would keep quiet. When she told a story, she rolled her eyes and waved her head and was very dramatic. She said once when she was a maiden lady she had been courted by a Mr. Edgar Atkins Teagarden from Jasper, Georgia. She said he was a very good-looking man and a gentleman and that he brought her a watermelon every Saturday afternoon with his initials cut in it, E. A. T. Well, one Saturday, she said, Mr. Teagarden brought the watermelon and there was nobody at home and he left it on the front porch and returned in his buggy to Jasper, but she never got the watermelon, she said, because a nigger boy ate it when he saw the initials, E. A. T.! This story tickled John Wesley's funny bone and he giggled and giggled but June Star didn't think it was any good. She said she wouldn't marry a man that just brought her a watermelon on Saturday. The grandmother said she would have done well to marry Mr. Teagarden because he was a gentleman and had bought Coca-Cola stock when it first came out and that he had died only a few years ago, a very wealthy man.

They stopped at The Tower for barbecued sandwiches. The Tower was a part stucco and part wood filling station and dance hall set in a clearing outside of Timothy. A fat man named Red Sammy Butts ran it and there were signs stuck here and there on the building and for miles up and down the highway saying, TRY RED SAMMY'S FAMOUS BARBE-CUE. NONE LIKE FAMOUS RED SAMMY'S! RED SAM! THE FAT BOY WITH THE HAPPY LAUGH. A VETERAN! RED SAMMY'S YOUR MAN!

Red Sammy was lying on the bare ground outside The Tower with his head under a truck while a gray monkey about a foot high, chained to a small chinaberry tree, chattered nearby. The monkey sprang back into the tree and got on the highest limb as soon as he saw the children jump out of the car and run toward him.

Inside, The Tower was a long dark room with a counter at one end and tables at the other and dancing space in the middle. They all sat down at a board table next to the nickelodeon and Red Sam's wife, a tall burnt-brown woman with hair and eyes lighter than her skin, came and took their order. The children's mother put a dime in the machine and played "The Tennessee Waltz," and the grandmother said that tune always made her want to dance. She asked Bailey if he would like to dance but he only glared at her. He didn't have a naturally sunny disposition like she did and trips made him nervous. The grandmother's brown eyes were very bright. She swayed her head from side to side and pretended she was dancing in her chair. June Star said play something she could tap to so the children's mother put in another dime and played a fast number and June Star stepped out onto the dance floor and did her tap routine.

"Ain't she cute?" Red Sam's wife said, leaning over the counter. "Would you like to come be my little girl?"

"No I certainly wouldn't," June Star said. "I wouldn't live in a broken-down place like this for a million bucks!" and she ran back to the table.

"Ain't she cute?" the woman repeated, stretching her mouth politely.

"Aren't you ashamed?" hissed the grandmother.

Red Sam came in and told his wife to quit lounging on the counter and hurry up with these people's order. His khaki trousers reached just to his hip bones and his stomach hung over them like a sack of meal swaying under his shirt. He came over and sat down at a table nearby and let out a combination sigh and yodel. "You can't win," he said. "You can't win," and he wiped his sweating red face off with a gray handkerchief. "These days you don't know who to trust," he said. "Ain't that the truth?"

"People are certainly not nice like they used to be," said the grandmother.

"Two fellers come in here last week," Red Sammy said, "driving a Chrysler. It was a old beat-up car but it was a good one and these boys looked all right to me. Said they worked at the mill and you know I let them fellers charge the gas they bought? Now why did I do that?"

"Because you're a good man!" the grandmother said at once.

"Yes'm, I suppose so," Red Sam said as if he were struck with this answer.

His wife brought the orders, carrying the five plates all at once without a tray, two in each hand and one balanced on her arm. "It isn't a soul in this green world of God's that you can trust," she said. "And I don't count nobody out of that, not nobody," she repeated, looking at Red Sammy.

"Did you read about that criminal, The Misfit, that's escaped?" asked the grandmother.

"I wouldn't be a bit surprised if he didn't attack this place right here," said the woman. "If he hears about it being here, I wouldn't be none surprised to see him. If he hears it's two cent in the cash register, I wouldn't be a tall surprised if he . . ."

"That'll do," Red Sam said. "Go bring these people their Co'-Colas," and the woman went off to get the rest of the order.

"A good man is hard to find," Red Sammy said. "Everything is getting terrible. I remember the day you could go off and leave your screen door unlatched. Not no more."

He and the grandmother discussed better times. The old lady said that in her opinion Europe was entirely to blame for the way things were now. She said the way Europe acted you would think we were made of money and Red Sam said it was no use talking about it, she was exactly right. The children ran outside into the white sunlight and looked at the monkey in the lacy chinaberry tree. He was busy catching fleas on himself and biting each one carefully between his teeth as if it were a delicacy.

They drove off again into the hot afternoon. The grandmother took cat naps and woke up every few minutes with her own snoring. Outside of Toombsboro she woke up and recalled an old plantation that she had visited in this neighborhood once when she was a young lady. She said the house had six white columns across the front and that there was an avenue of oaks leading up to it and two little wooden trellis arbors on either side in front where you sat down with your suitor after a stroll in the garden. She recalled exactly which road to turn off to get to it. She knew that Bailey would not be willing to lose any time looking at an old house, but the more she talked about it, the more she wanted to see it once again and find out if the little twin arbors were still standing. "There was a secret panel in this house," she said craftily, not telling the truth but wishing that she were, "and the story went that all the family silver was hidden in it when Sherman came through but it was never found . . ."

"Hey!" John Wesley said. "Let's go see it! We'll find it! We'll poke all the woodwork and find it! Who lives there? Where do you turn off at? Hey Pop, can't we turn off there?"

"We never have seen a house with a secret panel!" June Star shrieked. "Let's go to the house with the secret panel! Hey Pop, can't we go see the house with the secret panel!"

"It's not far from here, I know," the grandmother said. "It wouldn't take over twenty minutes."

Bailey was looking straight ahead. His jaw was as rigid as a horseshoe. "No," he said.

The children began to yell and scream that they wanted to see the house with the secret panel. John Wesley kicked the back of the front seat and June Star hung over her mother's shoulder and whined desperately into her ear that they never had any fun even on their vacation, that they could never do what THEY wanted to do. The baby began to scream and John Wesley kicked the back of the seat so hard that his father could feel the blows in his kidney.

"All right!" he shouted and drew the car to a stop at the side of the road. "Will you all shut up? Will you all just shut up for one second? If you don't shut up, we won't go anywhere."

"It would be very educational for them," the grandmother murmured.

"All right," Bailey said, "but get this: this is the only time we're going to stop for anything like this. This is the one and only time."

"The dirt road that you have to turn down is about a mile back," the grandmother directed. "I marked it when we passed."

"A dirt road," Bailey groaned.

After they had turned around and were headed toward the dirt road, the grandmother recalled other points about the house, the beautiful glass over the front doorway and the candle-lamp in the hall. John Wesley said that the secret panel was probably in the fireplace.

"You can't go inside this house," Bailey said. "You don't know who lives there."

"While you all talk to the people in front, I'll run around behind and get in a window," John Wesley suggested.

"We'll all stay in the car," his mother said.

They turned onto the dirt road and the car raced roughly along in a swirl of pink dust. The grandmother recalled the times when there were no paved roads and thirty miles was a day's journey. The dirt road was hilly and there were sudden washes in it and sharp curves on dangerous embankments. All at once they would be on a hill, looking down over the blue tops of trees for miles around, then the next minute, they would be in a red depression with the dust-coated trees looking down on them.

"This place had better turn up in a minute," Bailey said, "or I'm going to turn around."

The road looked as if no one had traveled on it in months.

"It's not much farther," the grandmother said and just as she said it, a horrible thought came to her. The thought was so embarrassing that she turned red in the face and her eyes dilated and her feet jumped up, upsetting her valise in the corner. The instant the valise moved, the newspaper top she had over the basket under it rose with a snarl and Pitty Sing, the cat, sprang onto Bailey's shoulder.

The children were thrown to the floor and their mother, clutching the baby, was thrown out the door onto the ground; the old lady was thrown into the front seat. The car turned over once and landed right-side-up in a gulch off the side of the road. Bailey remained in the driver's seat with the cat—gray-striped with a broad white face and an orange nose—clinging to his neck like a caterpillar.

As soon as the children saw they could move their arms and legs, they scrambled out of the car, shouting, "We've had an ACCIDENT!" The grandmother was curled up under the dashboard, hoping she was injured so that Bailey's wrath would not come down on her all at once. The horrible thought she had had before the accident was that the house she had remembered so vividly was not in Georgia but in Tennessee.

Bailey removed the cat from his neck with both hands and flung it out the window against the side of a pine tree. Then he got out of the car and started looking for the children's mother. She was sitting against the side of the red gutted ditch, holding the screaming baby, but she only had a cut down her face and a broken shoulder. "We've had an ACCIDENT!" the children screamed in a frenzy of delight.

"But nobody's killed," June Star said with disappointment as the grandmother limped out of the car, her hat still pinned to her head but the broken front brim standing up at a jaunty angle and the violet spray hanging off the side. They all sat down in the ditch, except the children, to recover from the shock. They were all shaking.

"Maybe a car will come along," said the children's mother hoarsely.

"I believe I have injured an organ," said the grandmother, pressing her side, but no one answered her. Bailey's teeth were clattering. He had on a yellow sport shirt with bright blue parrots designed in it and his face was as yellow as the shirt. The grandmother decided that she would not mention that the house was in Tennessee.

The road was about ten feet above and they could only see the tops of the trees on the other side of it. Behind the ditch they were sitting in there were more woods, tall and dark and deep. In a few minutes they saw a car some distance away on top of a hill, coming slowly as if the occupants were watching them. The grandmother stood up and waved both arms dramatically to attract their attention. The car continued to come on slowly, disappeared around a bend and appeared again, moving even slower, on top of the hill they had gone over. It was a big black battered hearse-like automobile. There were three men in it.

It came to a stop just over them and for some minutes, the driver looked down with a steady expressionless gaze to where they were sitting, and didn't speak. Then he turned his head and muttered something to the other two and they got out. One was a fat boy in black trousers and a red sweat shirt with a silver stallion embossed on the front of it. He moved around on the right side of them and stood staring, his mouth partly open in a kind of loose grin. The other had on khaki pants and a blue striped coat and a gray hat pulled very low, hiding most of his face. He came around slowly on the left side. Neither spoke.

The driver got out of the car and stood by the side of it, looking down at them. He was an older man than the other two. His hair was just beginning to gray and he wore silver-rimmed spectacles that gave him a scholarly look. He had a long creased face and didn't have on any shirt or undershirt. He had on blue jeans that were too tight for him and was holding a black hat and a gun. The two boys also had guns.

"We've had an ACCIDENT!" the children screamed.

The grandmother had the peculiar feeling that the bespectacled man was someone she knew. His face was as familiar to her as if she had known him all her life but she could not recall who he was. He moved away from the car and began to come down the embankment, placing his feet carefully so that he wouldn't slip. He had on tan and white shoes and no socks, and his ankles were red and thin. "Good afternoon," he said. "I see you all had you a little spill."

"We turned over twice!" said the grandmother.

"Oncet," he corrected. "We seen it happen. Try their car and see will it run, Hiram," he said quietly to the boy with the gray hat.

"What you got that gun for?" John Wesley asked. "Whatcha gonna do with that gun?"

"Lady," the man said to the children's mother, "would you mind calling them children to sit down by you? Children make me nervous. I want all you all to sit down right together there where you're at."

"What are you telling US what to do for?" June Star asked.

Behind them the line of woods gaped like a dark open mouth. "Come here," said the mother.

"Look here now," Bailey began suddenly, "we're in a predicament! We're in . . ."

The grandmother shrieked. She scrambled to her feet and stood staring. "You're The Misfit!" she said. "I recognized you at once!"

"Yes'm," the man said, smiling slightly as if he were pleased in spite of himself to be known, "but it would have been better for all of you, lady, if you hadn't of reckernized me."

Bailey turned his head sharply and said something to his mother that shocked even the children. The old lady began to cry and The Misfit reddened.

"Lady," he said, "don't you get upset. Sometimes a man says things he don't mean. I don't reckon he meant to talk to you thataway."

"You wouldn't shoot a lady, would you?" the grandmother said and removed a clean handkerchief from her cuff and began to slap at her eyes with it.

The Misfit pointed the toe of his shoe into the ground and made a little hole and then covered it up again. "I would hate to have to," he said.

"Listen," the grandmother almost screamed, "I know you're a good man. You don't look a bit like you have common blood. I know you must come from nice people!"

"Yes mam," he said, "finest people in the world." When he smiled he showed a row of strong white teeth. "God never made a finer woman than my mother and my daddy's heart was pure gold," he said. The boy with the red sweat shirt had come around behind them and was standing with his gun at his hip. The Misfit squatted down on the ground. "Watch them children, Bobby Lee," he said. "You know they make me nervous." He looked at the six of them huddled together in front of him and he seemed to be embarrassed as if he couldn't think of anything to say. "Ain't a cloud in the sky," he remarked, looking up at it. "Don't see no sun but don't see no cloud neither."

"Yes, it's a beautiful day," said the grandmother. "Listen," she said, "you shouldn't call yourself The Misfit because I know you're a good man at heart. I can just look at you and tell."

"Hush!" Bailey yelled. "Hush! Everybody shut up and let me handle this!" He was squatting in the position of a runner about to sprint forward but he didn't move.

"I pre-chate that, lady," The Misfit said and drew a little circle in the ground with the butt of his gun.

"It'll take a half a hour to fix this here car," Hiram called, looking over the raised hood of it.

"Well, first you and Bobby Lee get him and that little boy to step over yonder with you," The Misfit said, pointing to Bailey and John Wesley. "The boys want to ast you something," he said to Bailey. "Would you mind stepping back in them woods there with them?"

"Listen," Bailey began, "we're in a terrible predicament! Nobody realizes what this is," and his voice cracked. His eyes were as blue and intense as the parrots in his shirt and he remained perfectly still.

The grandmother reached up to adjust her hat brim as if she were going to the woods with him but it came off in her hand. She stood staring at it and after a second she let it fall on the ground. Hiram pulled Bailey up by the arm as if he were assisting an old man. John Wesley caught hold of his father's hand and Bobby Lee followed. They went off toward the woods and just as they reached the dark edge, Bailey turned and supporting himself against a gray naked pine trunk, he shouted, "I'll be back in a minute, Mamma, wait on me!"

"Come back this instant!" his mother shrilled but they all disappeared into the woods.

"Bailey Boy!" the grandmother called in a tragic voice but she found she was looking at The Misfit squatting on the ground in front of her. "I just know you're a good man," she said desperately. "You're not a bit common!"

"Nome, I ain't a good man," The Misfit said after a second as if he had considered her statement carefully, "but I ain't the worst in the world neither. My daddy said I was a different breed of dog from my brothers and sisters. 'You know,' Daddy said, 'it's some that can live their whole life out without asking about it and it's others has to know why it is, and this boy is one of the latters. He's going to be into everything!'" He put on his black hat and looked up suddenly and then away deep into the woods as if he were embarrassed again. "I'm sorry I don't have on a shirt before you ladies," he said, hunching his shoulders slightly. "We buried our clothes that we had on when we escaped and we're just making do until we can get better. We borrowed these from some folks we met," he explained.

"That's perfectly all right," the grandmother said. "Maybe Bailey has an extra shirt in his suitcase."

"I'll look and see terrectly," The Misfit said.

"Where are they taking him?" the children's mother screamed.

"Daddy was a card himself," The Misfit said. "You couldn't put anything over on him. He never got in trouble with the Authorities though. Just had the knack of handling them."

"You could be honest too if you'd only try," said the grandmother. "Think how wonderful it would be to settle down and live a comfortable life and not have to think about somebody chasing you all the time."

The Misfit kept scratching in the ground with the butt of his gun as if he were thinking about it. "Yes'm, somebody is always after you," he murmured.

The grandmother noticed how thin his shoulder blades were just behind his hat because she was standing up looking down at him. "Do you ever pray?" she asked.

He shook his head. All she saw was the black hat wiggle between his shoulder blades. "Nome," he said.

There was a pistol shot from the woods, followed closely by another. Then silence. The old lady's head jerked around. She could hear the wind move through the tree tops like a long satisfied insuck of breath. "Bailey Boy!" she called.

"I was a gospel singer for a while," The Misfit said. "I been most everything. Been in the arm service, both land and sea, at home and abroad, been twict married, been an undertaker, been with the railroads, plowed Mother Earth, been in a tornado, seen a man burnt alive oncet," and he looked up at the children's mother and the little girl who were sitting close together, their faces white and their eyes glassy; "I even seen a woman flogged," he said.

"Pray, pray," the grandmother began, "pray, pray . . ."

"I never was a bad boy that I remember of," The Misfit said in an almost dreamy voice, "but somewheres along the line I done something wrong and got sent to the penitentiary. I was buried alive," and he looked up and held her attention to him by a steady stare.

"That's when you should have started to pray," she said. "What did you do to get sent to the penitentiary, that first time?"

"Turn to the right, it was a wall," The Misfit said, looking up again at the cloudless sky. "Turn to the left, it was a wall. Look up it was a ceiling, look down it was a floor. I forgot what I done, lady. I set there and set there, trying to remember what it was I done and I ain't recalled it to this day. Oncet in a while, I would think it was coming to me, but it never come."

"Maybe they put you in by mistake," the old lady said vaguely.

"Nome," he said. "It wasn't no mistake. They had the papers on me."

"You must have stolen something," she said.

The Misfit sneered slightly. "Nobody had nothing I wanted," he said. "It was a head-doctor at the penitentiary said what I had done was kill my daddy but I known that for a lie. My daddy died in nineteen ought nineteen of the epidemic flu and I never had a thing to do with it. He was buried in the Mount Hopewell Baptist churchyard and you can go there and see for yourself."

"If you would pray," the old lady said, "Jesus would help you."

"That's right," The Misfit said.

"Well then, why don't you pray?" she asked trembling with delight suddenly.

"I don't want no hep," he said. "I'm doing all right by myself."

Bobby Lee and Hiram came ambling back from the woods. Bobby Lee was dragging a yellow shirt with bright blue parrots in it.

"Thow me that shirt, Bobby Lee," The Misfit said. The shirt came flying at him and landed on his shoulder and he put it on. The grandmother couldn't name what the shirt reminded her of. "No, lady," The Misfit said while he was buttoning it up, "I found out the crime don't matter. You can do one thing or you can do another, kill a man or take a tire off his car, because sooner or later you're going to forget what it was you done and just be punished for it."

The children's mother had begun to make heaving noises as if she couldn't get her breath. "Lady," he asked, "would you and that little girl like to step off yonder with Bobby Lee and Hiram and join your husband?"

"Yes, thank you," the mother said faintly. Her left arm dangled helplessly and she was holding the baby, who had gone to sleep, in the other. "Hep that lady up, Hiram," The Misfit said as she struggled to climb out of the ditch, "and Bobby Lee, you hold onto that little girl's hand."

137

"I don't want to hold hands with him," June Star said. "He reminds me of a pig."

The fat boy blushed and laughed and caught her by the arm and pulled her off into the woods after Hiram and her mother.

Alone with The Misfit, the grandmother found that she had lost her voice. There was not a cloud in the sky nor any sun. There was nothing around her but woods. She wanted to tell him that he must pray. She opened and closed her mouth several times before anything came out. Finally she found herself saying, "Jesus. Jesus," meaning, Jesus will help you, but the way she was saying it, it sounded as if she might be cursing.

"Yes'm," The Misfit said as if he agreed. "Jesus thown everything off balance. It was the same case with Him as with me except He hadn't committed any crime and they could prove I had committed one because they had the papers on me. Of course," he said, "they never shown me my papers. That's why I sign myself now. I said long ago, you get you a signature and sign everything you do and keep a copy of it. Then you'll know what you done and you can hold up the crime to the punishment and see do they match and in the end you'll have something to prove you ain't been treated right. I call myself The Misfit," he said, "because I can't make what all I done wrong fit what all I gone through in punishment."

There was a piercing scream from the woods, followed closely by a pistol report. "Does it seem right to you, lady, that one is punished a heap and another ain't punished at all?"

"Jesus!" the old lady cried. "You've got good blood! I know you wouldn't shoot a lady! I know you come from nice people! Pray! Jesus, you ought not to shoot a lady. I'll give you all the money I've got!"

"Lady," The Misfit said, looking beyond her far into the woods, "there never was a body that give the undertaker a tip."

There were two more pistol reports and the grandmother raised her head like a parched old turkey hen crying for water and called, "Bailey Boy, Bailey Boy!" as if her heart would break.

"Jesus was the only One that ever raised the dead," The Misfit continued, "and He shouldn't have done it. He thown everything off balance. If He did what He said, then it's nothing for you to do but thow away everything and follow Him, and if He didn't, then it's nothing for you to do but enjoy the few minutes you got left the best you can — by killing somebody or burning down his house or doing some other meanness to him. No pleasure but meanness," he said and his voice had become almost a snarl.

"Maybe He didn't raise the dead," the old lady mumbled, not knowing what she was saying and feeling so dizzy that she sank down in the ditch with her legs twisted under her.

"I wasn't there so I can't say He didn't," The Misfit said. "I wisht I had of been there," he said, hitting the ground with his fist. "It ain't right I wasn't there because if I had of been there I would of known. Listen lady," he said in a high voice, "if I had of been there I would of known and I wouldn't be like I am now." His voice seemed about to crack and the grandmother's head cleared for an instant. She saw the man's face twisted close to her own as if he were going to cry and she murmured, "Why you're one of my babies. You're one of my own children!" She reached out and touched him on the shoulder. The Misfit sprang back as if a snake had bitten him and shot her three times through the chest. Then he put his gun down on the ground and took off his glasses and began to clean them.

Hiram and Bobby Lee returned from the woods and stood over the ditch, looking down at the grandmother who half sat and half lay in a puddle of blood with her legs crossed under her like a child's and her face smiling up at the cloudless sky.

Without his glasses, The Misfit's eyes were red-rimmed and pale and defenseless-looking. "Take her off and thow her where you thown the others," he said, picking up the cat that was rubbing itself against his leg.

"She was a talker, wasn't she?" Bobby Lee said, sliding down the ditch with a yodel.

"She would of been a good woman," The Misfit said, "if it had been somebody there to shoot her every minute of her life."

"Some fun!" Bobby Lee said.

"Shut up, Bobby Lee," The Misfit said. "It's no real pleasure in life."

[1955]

CONNOR MAKOWSKI

Making a Documentary:
A Short How-to Guide

A BRIEF HISTORY

The history of documentary films begins with the birth of the cinema. In 1895, the Lumiere brothers introduced a moving picture to a paying audience in Paris, France for the first time. The first show was composed only of documentaries (Aitken). Some early documentaries include *Nanook of the North* and *Man of Aran*. Documentaries have changed little since then in comparison to many other motion media forms. These include changes in filming style, changes in audio capturing, and changes in post-production editing to create a specific mood. The biggest change did not occur until the advent of the digital video camera. Paired with the Internet, this gave people the ability to share their ideas and experiences with others.

Documentaries contain many different topics including visual poems, trips to exotic lands, and artful propaganda (Nichols). Even though these different topics are addressed, most documentaries allow the viewer to see a given topic from a specific standpoint (Aitken).

Some recent films have yielded huge profits even with limited theatrical releases. These include *Food Inc.*, *U.N. Me*, *Earth*, and *March of the Penguins*.

SO YOU THINK YOU WANT TO MAKE A DOCUMENTARY?

There are certain things that filmmakers must consider before starting any project, especially a documentary. If you answer no to any of these questions I suggest that you do not make a documentary, at least for now (Lanier and Nichols).

1. Do you love movies? Documentaries?
2. Have you wanted to do this for a while?
3. Are you observant, insightful, funny, odd or a little bit of each?
4. Are you willing to put in the time to do any of the following?

    a.   Video editing?

    b.   Finding people?

    c.   Setting up interviews?

    d.   Researching for hours?

5. Do you feel comfortable meeting new people?

If you answered all questions with a yes, then you are ready to start the long process of making a documentary.

GENERAL INFORMATION

In this Manual I address all the tasks necessary to make a documentary. I assume that the reader (a.k.a.: you) is going to be doing all of the hard work, possibly including some acting.

Most amateur filmmaking will consist of one motivated person: YOU (Lanier and Nichols)! Although I would not recommend doing the project by yourself, you may have to do most of the work independently Get used to it. many of your early films will probably be done independently.

While I would never recommend the lone wolf style as it puts a lot of strain on the filmmaker, almost inevitably, you will do most of the video by yourself. With this, the person who will be the biggest factor in determining if this film will ever be finished is you. Finishing a first project is an important part of beginning any film career. It is important that you do not get easily discouraged. There will be no easy way out for the long hours that you spend on research, writing scripts, and the all-powerful boredom devil of editing. Completing this shows the filmmaker that (s)he has the endurance and power to finish a film. The result will probably not be exactly as the filmmaker imagined, but at least it will be complete. There will be a result. Something about finishing just allows the filmmaker to move on. With many years of experience I can say that if you can't make it through the first process, you are unlikely to make it through subsequent ones. In other words: This is a lot of work. It requires you to really want to do it. You really should finish your first project, so don't give up.

The following are materials you should have before you start any filming process:

1. A high resolution camera (at least 1920x1080) with a good built in microphone. These usually cost around $700.

2. A separate high quality microphone. These usually cost around $100

3. Some video editing program.

   a. If on a PC, I recommend Windows Movie Maker (free), or Sony Movie Studio (around $50)

   b. If on a Mac, I recommend iMovie(free) or Final Cut Pro (around $300)

WHAT TOPIC WILL YOUR DOCUMENTARY COVER?

A documentary is essentially an argument (Rabiger). Before any point is argued, one has to know about which (s)he is arguing. It is important that you, as the creator of this film, know what you will cover within your documentary. I recommend using these tips to pick a topic. Your thought process may be circular here. If you have recurring issues during this process, continue further into the chapter to find some help. Once completing this cycle three times you should continue on to the next chapter.

1. Brainstorm

2. Isolate one idea or topic that you would like to cover

   a.   If stuck move back to step 1.

3. Determine if it is possible to cover that idea or topic

   a.   Can you afford to cover this?

   b.   Would you be able to cover the topic in less than 15 minutes? (This is the limit you should put on your first few documentaries. You will find that this is an extremely large amount of work as it is. Remember that it is important to finish your first few projects.)

   c.   If you are unable to do **a.** or **b.** move back to step 2.

4. Make sure you are able to properly support your argument

   a.   Will you be able to exhibit (explained later in this chapter):

      i.   Ethos

      ii.   Pathos

      iii.   Logos

b. Will you be able to find evidence to support your topic?

c. If you are unable to do **a.** or **b.** move back to step 2.

5. If you have made it this far you have a good topic. You should restart the process and complete it two more times so that you have three Ideas or topics to choose from.

BRAINSTORMING STAGE

Here are some generic subjects that may help to get the creative juices flowing. Think about making a film on:

1. Historical records

2. Social issues

3. Propaganda

4. Current events

5. An encounter

Here are a few exercises that I have found helpful in the past:

1. Elaborate on one of the topics listed above. Give your interpretation of the word or phrase. From this interpretation, think about possible topics you might be able to film. It is imperative that you write these topics down as they come to you. Don't do too much thinking. (Lanier and Nichols)

2. Free write. Jot down what comes to your mind without any censoring of ideas.

3. Think about what it is that gets you hot headed. What makes you want to just punch the person who is disagreeing with you in the

left eyeball? We all have these subjects. To give you some examples you might think about political issues like taxes, abortion, and foreign involvement. You could also think about all of the things that you might say you hate in a hate video such as dogs with clothing, people who eat only meat, or just about anything else that you can get creative about and support with a documentary.

EXPLANATION OF ETHOS, PATHOS, LOGOS

Ethos is defined as the character of the rhetor (the one making the argument or claim); however, this is more specifically targeted towards the establishment of the credibility of the filmmaker. Ask yourself this: Can you exhibit knowledge and accurate information on the topic that you chose? Thendetermine how you are going to do this.

Pathos is translated from Greek into English as suffering, but this form of rhetorical argument is more commonly established by exhibiting emotions and compassion. It is imperative that you are able to influence the emotions of the viewer. Can your idea or topic accomplish this? Then determine how you are going to do this.

Logos literally translates as "I say."This refers to the facts as evidence that you are presenting on the topic. Are your presentations of the facts ones that can be accepted by others? Then determine how you are going to do this.

RESEARCH

This stage is by far one of the least exciting stages of the movie making process. It requires you to spend hours online in archives and talking to people for small amounts of information on your topic. This is process is going to have to be specific to the particular idea that you are presenting. Some general advice is to get more information than necessary.

General things that you will want to find on each topic include:

1. Eyewitnesses of your topic

2. Experts on your topic

3. Statistical data

4. Empirical data

5. If possible a good financial statement is always helpful

EYEWITNESSES OF YOUR TOPIC

When making a documentary, eyewitness accounts are a primary source that will make the difference between a decent film and a good one(Rabiger). Finding these sources for your film requires you to research who may have been involved in a particular event. Google is your friend! Use Google. In almost all situations a name will appear that you can use to start getting connected to people. An author of a book on the subject or an expert (you could take out two birds with one stone here) in that subject might be able to connect you to people. It will require you to email, call, and flatout pester a person from whom you want information. Don't be scared; be polite, and remember that you will probably get rejected.

Finding eyewitnesses can be difficult if you are covering an event that has long passed, such as the Titanic. A good alternative is to find the grandkids of a survivor to receive a secondhand account. This is not optimal; however, you need to take what you can get. If it happened hundreds of years ago, it is always feasible to take a firsthand written account and either display that with music or read it while images are shown.

CASTING A CREW

This is where the fun begins. Casting a good crew is important for any documentary. As a starting filmmaker, you should not expect people to just hop in your lap and say "I want to volunteer my time to help you support your opinion." This does not happen. You need to search around.

You are looking for particular traits to fill roles within any film (Weston). In the documentary film industry you will need at least one other person that will conduct interviews, guide the viewers, be the face of the performance, or will be the person filming you. For the sake of this guide I will assume that you want to make your film on the cheap with limited help and will only require one person other than yourself. This is only for the filming and voiceover stage. You will still be doing all of the editing by yourself.

You need to determine the role at which you will be best. Then start searching for the other role to fill. The two generic roles of any documentary including their specific attributes include:

1. Cameraman
    a. Steady hands
        i. To keep the shot steady and centered on the subject being filmed
    b. Patience

        i.   To wait for shots when actors continually mess up

  c. Quietness

        i.   Does not move around much

       ii. Breathes quietly

  d. Seriousness

        i.   Does not laugh much

       ii. Keeps most emotions inside

      iii. Does not allow things being filmed to affect him

2. Actor/Interviewer

  a. Face/Body

        i.   A face that stands out

       ii. Avoid a face that you feel will distract viewers

      iii. A face/body that fits the context of your documentary (a man with lots of piercings and tattoos should probably not present on the topic of making good first impressions at work)

  b. Voice

        i.   A good tone

       ii. A moderate amount of inflection

      iii. A voice that fits the context of your topic

  c. Compassionate toward subject being filmed

        i.   Allows for genuine emotions

      ii. Cares about what he/she is talking about

  d. Able to connect with viewers and interviewees

      i. Has natural charm

      ii. Genuinely likes people

      iii. Can work with just about anyone

It is always nice to be able to have another person who can do voiceover with the actor only appearing on screen and giving interviews. This allows you to find a more specific person for conducting interviews and guiding viewers. It also helps you find a specific person who can lay down a perfect documentary voice.

Start with friends, but BE CAREFUL!!! I cannot stress this enough. It only takes one person who cannot keep his/her mouth shut or sit still during a shot. This will invariably wreck a scene, interview, or any other shot that may require audio. If you are filming in a house, this may cause the camera to shake as well. It is better to tell him or her, "no way; you can't handle this!" than to have a horrible documentary. You don't have to be that blunt about it, but if it is necessary do it! You will thank me later. Still, BE CAREFUL!

If you are unable to find a friend, move on to asking friends if they know someone who can fill that part. After this point you're on your own. Be creative.

FILMING

Finally! You are ready to start filming. You have an idea/topic, research, interviews set up, and a crew.

This is when you determine your own style. Keep in mind that you will throw away more than half of your footage, so make sure to film everything. Think about how your video is going to flow and make sure that you get all of the shots here that you need. I cannot stress this enough. FILM EVERYTHING. You can always take out later, but you cannot add in unless you go back to film more.

Here are some tips that I recommend for filming an interview:

· Get your subject comfortable.

· Have him/her/them keep a one eye perspective (looking at you or at the camera. No Switching).

· Explain what your intentions with this footage are if you have not already.

· Ask the questions clearly and correctly (rehearse prior to filming).

· Thank the subject(s) afterward.

When filming, remember that you must keep shots quick and simple to keep the audience attentive. Consider filming the same scene from multiple angles. Long shots with no cuts will only bore people. As one of your first videos you must focus on finding your own style. Experiment and see what you like.

THE EDITING PROCESS

This is where all the magic happens (Lanier and Nichols). All of your work raps up with this step. It is important that you set a deadline. This gives you a goal to aim for. This also ensures that you will finish your project and not let it sit around forever.

I offer tips and tricks about the editing process here:

1. Find your style

    a. How do you arrange your clips?

   b. What do you do to keep attention?

   c. Mesh you filmed shots with your editing cuts.

2. Keep your cuts quick

   a. Cut your already short filmed shots to contain only necessary material.

   b. Focus on making the video flow with shots that are cohesive.

   c. Condensing your video keeps it interesting.

3. Editing in scenes

   a. Group your videos so you can work on one scene at a time

       i.   (personal preference) organize your work chronologically

       ii. It is easier to stay organized

       iii. It saves time.

   b. Focus on keeping each scene interesting

   c. Make each scene perfect.

4. Get your audio right

   a. Make sure all scenes allow the subject to be heard

   b. Try to isolate and remove unnecessary sounds

       i. A good sound editing program like Sony Sound forge is an excellent helper here.

   c. Record a voice over that corresponds with your video

5. Add in music that reflects the mood of your piece

a. Make sure you do not block out other necessary audio parts

b. Keep audio light and vary it as necessary.

FINISH UP

You're all done!!! Enjoy your work and show it off to the world or all of your friends. If it's not so good, you can always just show it to your mom.

Works Cited

Aitken, Ian. Encyclopedia of the documentary film, Volume 1. New York: Routledge, 2006.

Lanier, Troy and Clay Nichols. Filmmaking For Teens Pulling Off Your Shorts. Studio City: Michael Wiese Productions, 2005.

Nichols, Bill. Introduction to Documentary, Second Edition. Bloomington: Indiana University Press, 2010.

Rabiger, Michael. Directing the Documentary. Waltham: Focal, 2009.

Weston, Judith. Directing Actors: Creating Memorable Performances for Film & Television. Studio City: Michael Wiese Productions, 1996.

Genre Studies: Summative Questions and Prompts

1. Use the content from one of your previously written essays and transform it into one of the following short genres: a Tweet, a Facebook status update, a haiku, or a newspaper headline. After you have done this, write a paragraph describing some of the decisions that you made as you recast your essay in this new genre. Also consider how the conventions of the genre impact the content.

2. Select one of the three images in this section and respond to this prompt in two or three paragraphs: "If this image were an alphabetic text, what would it say?" Note that the prompt is not asking you to describe the painting or photo, but to convert your sense of the image--its tone, content, composition--into words.

3. Choose a single frame from Scott McCloud's "Understanding Comics" and carefully analyze the interaction of alphabetic text and image. Explain how the visual elements of the frame work together with the text to create meaning. In your analysis, you might consider some of the following details: use of negative space, foregrounding of particular elements, degree of realism, placement of text, stylization of figures, etc. Also consider how your selected frame works within the context of the entire excerpt.

Part IV: Research Writing

At some point or another, you've probably heard someone use the term **research**, whether it be in the classroom, on television, in a newspaper, or in a magazine. Although the term research may be quite common, its meaning may change depending on whom you ask. For the purposes of this book and the work you do in ENGL 1050, research means more than reporting what you found through Google or Wikipedia. Instead, research involves the ability to collect, synthesize, and evaluate information and data in order to draw carefully formulated conclusions about a topic. Oftentimes, researchers begin by asking a specific question about the topic they plan to investigate, and then consulting **secondary sources** that help them answer their research questions. Additionally researchers can design studies themselves and collect data from individuals, animals, or other **primary sources** and artifacts to answer their questions.

The readings in this section will encourage you to think critically about the purposes, decisions, and methods that guide different types of research. Ultimately, research texts formulate an informed opinion after conducting research on a topic. Amitai Etzioni's 1986 study "Working at McDonalds," for example, takes the overlooked topic of teenage employment and examines it using the few studies available alongside his own personal knowledge of the subject. Similarly, Jib Fowles' "Advertising's Fifteen Basic Appeals" and Stephanie Coontz's "A Nation of Welfare Families" analyze several primary sources in order to reach a specific conclusion about the cultural impact of advertising and government funding, respectively.

Additionally, research texts can study particular social phenomena using primary and secondary sources in order to inform the reader and/or draw specific conclusions. In "Against Work," Christopher Clausen examines the nascent word "workaholic" and its impact on American culture. Other texts that take this approach include Michael J. Bamshad and Steve E. Olson's "Does Race Exist?" and Sherry Turkle's "How Computers Change the Way We Think." The final text in this section is our fourth winner of the 2013 ENGL 1050 Best Essay Award by Brendon Ayers, entitled "The Academic and Social Effects of Homeschooling."

As you read the texts in this section, consider the ways that research is described, analyzed, critiqued, and performed.

AMITAI ETZIONI [b. 1929]

Working at McDonald's

Born Werner Falk in 1929 in Cologne, Germany, Amitai Etzioni fled from Nazi Germany to Palestine in the 1930s, ultimately studying at the Hebrew University in Jerusalem. A prominent sociologist, he received his Ph.D. in 1958 from the University of California, Berkeley, and then taught for two decades at Columbia University. From 1979 to 1980 he served at the White House as a senior adviser on domestic affairs. The author of twenty-four books, including *The Monochrome Society* (2001), *The Limits of Privacy* (1999), and *The New Golden Rule* (1996), Etzioni has taught at George Washington University since 1980. As director of the university's Institute for Communitarian Policy Studies, Etzioni founded the Communitarian Network, a nonprofit, nonpartisan organization that provides a forum for discussing the impact of moral, social, and political issues on society's well being. He is also the founder of the journal *Responsive Community* and has been awarded numerous honors, including the 2001 John P. McGovern Award in Behavioral Sciences and the Seventh James Wilbur Award for Extraordinary Contributions to the Appreciation and Advancement of Human Values by the Conference on Value Inquiry.

Etzioni's "Working at McDonald's," originally published in the *Miami Herald* in 1986, evaluates the educational merits of adolescents' holding down part-time, paying jobs in fast-food restaurants. Critical of the long hours, the managerial role models, the failure of these jobs to foster independent thought and decision making skills, and the enticements of a questionable consumerism, Etzioni insists that teens "go back to school."

McDonald's is bad for your kids. I do not mean the flat patties and the white-flour buns; I refer to the jobs teen-agers undertake, mass-producing these choice items.

As many as two-thirds of America's high school juniors and seniors now hold down part-time paying jobs, according to studies. Many of these are in fast-food chains, of which McDonald's is the pioneer, trendsetter, and symbol.

Amitai Etzioni, "Working at McDonald's" from *The Miami Herald*, August 24, 1986. Reprinted by permission of the author.

At first, such jobs may seem right out of the Founding Fathers' educational manual for how to bring up self-reliant, work-ethic-driven, productive youngsters. But in fact, these jobs undermine school attendance and involvement, impart few skills that will be useful in later life, and simultaneously skew the values of teen-agers—especially their ideas about the worth of a dollar.

It has been a longstanding American tradition that youngsters ought to get paying jobs. In folklore, few pursuits are more deeply revered than the newspaper route and the sidewalk lemonade stand. Here the youngsters are to learn how sweet are the fruits of labor and self-discipline (papers are delivered early in the morning, rain or shine), and the ways of trade (if you price your lemonade too high or too low . . .).

Roy Rogers, Baskin Robbins, Kentucky Fried Chicken, *et al.*, may at 5 first seem nothing but a vast extension of the lemonade stand. They provide very large numbers of teen jobs, provide regular employment, pay quite well compared to many other teen jobs, and, in the modern equivalent of toiling over a hot stove, test one's stamina.

Closer examination, however, finds the McDonald's kind of job highly uneducational in several ways. Far from providing opportunities for entrepreneurship (the lemonade stand) or self- discipline, self-supervision, and self-scheduling (the paper route), most teen jobs these days are highly structured—what social scientists call "highly routinized."

True, you still have to have the gumption to get yourself over to the hamburger stand, but once you don the prescribed uniform, your task is spelled out in minute detail. The franchise prescribes the shape of the coffee cups; the weight, size, shape, and color of the patties; and the texture of the napkins (if any). Fresh coffee is to be made every eight minutes. And so on. There is no room for initiative, creativity, or even elementary rearrangements. These are breeding grounds for robots working for yesterday's assembly lines, not tomorrow's high-tech posts.

There are very few studies of the matter. One of the few is a 1984 study by Ivan Charper and Bryan Shore Fraser. The study relies mainly on what teen-agers write in response to questionnaires rather than actual observations of fast-food jobs. The authors argue that the employees develop many skills such as how to operate a food-preparation machine and a cash register. However, little attention is paid to how long it takes to acquire such a skill, or what its significance is.

What does it matter if you spend 20 minutes to learn to use a cash register, and then—"operate" it? What skill have you acquired? It is a long way from learning to work with a lathe or carpenter tools in the olden days or to program computers in the modern age.

A 1980 study by A. V. Harrell and P. W. Wirtz found that, among those 10 students who worked at least 25 hours per week while in school, their unemployment rate four years later was half of that of seniors who did not work. This is an impressive statistic. It must be seen, though, together with the finding that many who begin as part-time employees in fast-food chains drop out of high school and are gobbled up in the world of low-skill jobs.

Some say that while these jobs are rather unsuited for college-bound, white, middle-class youngsters, they are "ideal" for lower-class, "non-academic," minority youngsters. Indeed, minorities are "over-represented" in these jobs (21 percent of fast-food employees). While it is true that these places provide income, work, and even some training to such youngsters, they also tend to perpetuate their disadvantaged status. They provide no career ladders, few marketable skills, and undermine school attendance and involvement.

The hours are often long. Among those 14 to 17, a third of fast-food employees (including some school dropouts) labor more than 30 hours per week, according to the Charper-Fraser study. Only 20 percent work 15 hours or less. The rest: between 15 to 30 hours.

Often the stores close late, and after closing one must clean up and tally up. In affluent Montgomery County, Md., where child labor would not seem to be a widespread economic necessity, 24 percent of the seniors at one high school in 1985 worked as much as five to seven days a week; 27 percent, three to five. There is just no way such amounts of work will not interfere with school work, especially homework. In an informal survey published in the most recent yearbook of the high school, 58 percent of the seniors acknowledged that their jobs interfere with their school work.

The Charper-Fraser study sees merit in learning teamwork and working under supervision. The authors have a point here. However, it must be noted that such learning is not automatically educational or wholesome. For example, much of the supervision in fast-food places leans toward teaching one the wrong kinds of compliance: blind obedience, or shared alienation with the "boss."

Supervision is often both tight and woefully inappropriate. Today, 15 fast-food chains and other such places of work (record shops, bowling alleys) keep costs down by having teens supervise teens with often no adult on the premises.

There is no father or mother figure with which to identify, to emulate, to provide a role model and guidance. The work-culture varies from one place to another: Sometimes it is a tightly run shop (must keep the cash registers ringing); sometimes a rather loose pot party interrupted by customers. However, only rarely is there a master to learn from, or much worth learning. Indeed, far from being places where solid adult work values are being transmitted, these are places where all too often delinquent teen values dominate. Typically, when my son Oren was dishing out ice cream for Baskin Robbins in upper Manhattan, his fellow teen-workers considered him a sucker for not helping himself to the till. Most youngsters felt they were entitled to $50 severance "pay" on their last day on the job.

The pay, oddly, is the part of the teen work-world that is most difficult to evaluate. The lemonade stand or paper route money was for your allowance. In the old days, apprentices learning a trade from a master contributed most, if not all of their income to their parents' household. Today, the teen pay may be low by adult standards, but it is often, especially in the middle class, spent largely or wholly by the teens. That is, the youngsters live free at home ("after all, they are high school kids") and are left with very substantial sums of money.

Where this money goes is not quite clear. Some use it to support themselves, especially among the poor. More middle-class kids set some money aside to help pay for college, or save it for a major purchase—often a car. But large amounts seem to flow to pay for an early introduction into the most trite aspects of American consumerism: Flimsy punk clothes, trinkets, and whatever else is the last fast-moving teen craze.

One may say that this is only fair and square; they are being good American consumers and spend their money on what turns them on. At least, a cynic might add, these funds do not go into illicit drugs and booze. On the other hand, an educator might bemoan that these young, yet unformed individuals, so early in life are driven to buy objects of no intrinsic educational, cultural, or social merit, learn so quickly the dubious merit of keeping up with the Joneses in ever-changing fads, promoted by mass merchandising.

Many teens find the instant reward of money, and the youth status 20 symbols it buys, much more alluring than credits in calculus courses, European history, or foreign languages. No wonder quite a few would rather skip school—and certainly homework—and instead work longer at a Burger King. Thus, most teen work these days is not providing early lessons in work ethic; it fosters escape from school and responsibilities, quick gratification, and a short cut to the consumeristic aspects of adult life.

Thus, parents should look at teen employment not as automatically educational. It is an activity—like sports—that can be turned into an educational opportunity. But it can also easily be abused. Youngsters must learn to balance the quest for income with the needs to keep growing and pursue other endeavors that do not pay off instantly—above all education.

Go back to school.

MICHAEL J. BAMSHAD
STEVE E. OLSON

Does Race Exist?

Michael J. Bamshad is a professor of pediatrics and genome sciences in the University of Washington's School of Medicine and a member of Seattle Children's Hospital's Genetics Care Team. A recipient of the Society for Pediatric Research's Young Investigator Award, Bamshad is interested in the relationship between evolution and genetics. With colleagues Lynn B. Jorde and John C. Carey, Bamshad also coauthored the textbook *Medical Genetics*. **Steve E. Olson**, a graduate of Yale University with a degree in physics, is a freelance science and public policy writer based in Washington, D.C., and Seattle, Washington. Olson has written for various publications including the *Smithsonian*, the *Atlantic Monthly*, the *Washington Post*, and *Wired*. He also has served as a consultant writer for organizations such as the National Academy of Sciences and National Research Council, the White House Office of Science and Technology Policy, the National Institutes of Health, and the Institute for Genomic Research. Olson's books include the 2002 National Book Award finalist *Mapping Human History: Genes, Race, and Our Common Origins* (2003); *Count Down: Six Kids Vie for Glory at the World's Toughest Math Competition* (2004); and *Anarchy Evolution: Faith, Science, and Bad Religion in a World without God* (2010), which was coauthored with musician Greg Graffin.

First published in *Scientific American* in December 2003, "Does Race Exist?" explores both the social definitions and biological components of race. Examining implications for the diagnosis and treatment of diseases such as sickle cell anemia and AIDS, Bamshad and Olson consider four classifications of race based on genetics, as well as the risks and benefits of genetic testing and the controversy surrounding the use of race as a variable in scientific research.

Look around on the streets of any major city, and you will see a sampling of the outward variety of humanity: skin tones ranging from milk-white to dark brown; hair textures running the gamut from fine and stick-straight to thick and wiry. People often use physical characteristics such as these—along with area of geographic origin and shared culture—to group themselves and others into "races." But how valid is the concept of race from a biological standpoint? Do physical features reliably say anything informative about a person's genetic makeup beyond indicating that the individual has genes for blue eyes or curly hair?

The problem is hard in part because the implicit definition of what makes a person a member of a particular race differs from region to region across the globe. Someone classified as "black" in the U.S., for instance, might be considered "white" in Brazil and "colored" (a category distinguished from both "black" and "white") in South Africa.

Yet common definitions of race do sometimes work well to divide groups according to genetically determined propensities for certain diseases. Sickle cell disease is usually found among people of largely African or Mediterranean descent, for instance, whereas cystic fibrosis is far more common among those of European ancestry. In addition, although the results have been controversial, a handful of studies have suggested that African-Americans are more likely to respond poorly to some drugs for cardiac disease than are members of other groups.

Over the past few years, scientists have collected data about the genetic constitution of populations around the world in an effort to probe the link between ancestry and patterns of disease. These data are now providing answers to several highly emotional and contentious questions: Can genetic information be used to distinguish human groups having a common heritage and to assign individuals to particular ones? Do such groups correspond well to predefined descriptions now widely used to specify race? And, more practically, does dividing people by familiar racial definitions or by genetic similarities say anything useful about how members of those groups experience disease or respond to drug treatment?

In general, we would answer the first question yes, the second no, and 5 offer a qualified yes to the third. Our answers rest on several generalizations about race and genetics. Some groups do differ genetically from others, but how groups are divided depends on which genes are examined; simplistically put, you might fit into one group based on your skin-color genes but another based on a different characteristic. Many studies have demonstrated that roughly 90 percent of human genetic variation occurs within a population living on a given continent, whereas about 10 percent of the variation distinguishes continental populations. In other words, individuals from different populations are, on average, just slightly more different from one another than are individuals from the same population. Human populations are very similar, but they often can be distinguished.

160

CLASSIFYING HUMANS

As a first step to identifying links between social definitions of race and genetic heritage, scientists need a way to divide groups reliably according to their ancestry. Over the past 100,000 years or so, anatomically modern humans have migrated from Africa to other parts of the world, and members of our species have increased dramatically in number. This spread has left a distinct signature in our DNA.

To determine the degree of relatedness among groups, geneticists rely on tiny variations, or polymorphisms, in the DNA—specifically in the sequence of base pairs, the building blocks of DNA. Most of these polymorphisms do not occur within genes, the stretches of DNA that encode the information for making proteins (the molecules that constitute much of our bodies and carry out the chemical reactions of life). Accordingly, these common variations are neutral, in that they do not directly affect a particular trait. Some polymorphisms do occur in genes, however; these can contribute to individual variation in traits and to genetic diseases.

As scientists have sequenced the human genome (the full set of nuclear DNA), they have also identified millions of polymorphisms. The distribution of these polymorphisms across populations reflects the history of those populations and the effects of natural selection. To distinguish among groups, the ideal genetic polymorphism would be one that is present in all the members of one group and absent in the members of all other groups. But the major human groups have separated from one another too recently and have mixed too much for such differences to exist.

Polymorphisms that occur at different frequencies around the world can, however, be used to sort people roughly into groups. One useful class of polymorphisms consists of the Alus, short pieces of DNA that are similar in sequence to one another. Alus replicate occasionally, and the resulting copy splices itself at random into a new position on the original chromosome or on another chromosome, usually in a location that has no effect on the functioning of nearby genes. Each insertion is a unique event. Once an Alu sequence inserts itself, it can remain in place for eons, getting passed from one person to his or her descendants. Therefore, if two people have the same Alu sequence at the same spot in their genome, they must be descended from a common ancestor who gave them that specific segment of DNA.

One of us (Bamshad), working with University of Utah scientists Lynn B. Jorde, Stephen Wooding, and W. Scott Watkins and with Mark A. Batzer of Louisiana State University, examined 100 different Alu polymorphisms in 565 people born in sub-Saharan Africa, Asia, and Europe. 10

161

First we determined the presence or absence of the 100 Alus in each of the 565 people. Next we removed all the identifying labels (such as place of origin and ethnic group) from the data and sorted the people into groups using only their genetic information.

Our analysis yielded four different groups. When we added the labels back to see whether each individual's group assignment correlated to common, predefined labels for race or ethnicity, we saw that two of the groups consisted only of individuals from sub-Saharan Africa, with one of those two made up almost entirely of Mbuti Pygmies. The other two groups consisted only of individuals from Europe and East Asia, respectively. We found that we needed 60 Alu polymorphisms to assign individuals to their continent of origin with 90 percent accuracy. To achieve nearly 100 percent accuracy, however, we needed to use about 100 Alus.

Other studies have produced comparable results. Noah A. Rosenberg and Jonathan K. Pritchard, geneticists formerly in the laboratory of Marcus W. Feldman of Stanford University, assayed approximately 375 polymorphisms called short tandem repeats in more than 1,000 people from 52 ethnic groups in Africa, Asia, Europe, and the Americas. By looking at the varying frequencies of these polymorphisms, they were able to distinguish five different groups of people whose ancestors were typically isolated by oceans, deserts or mountains: sub-Saharan Africans; Europeans and Asians west of the Himalayas; East Asians; inhabitants of New Guinea and Melanesia; and Native Americans. They were also able to identify subgroups within each region that usually corresponded with each member's self-reported ethnicity.

The results of these studies indicate that genetic analyses can distinguish groups of people according to their geographic origin. But caution is warranted. The groups easiest to resolve were those that were widely separated from one another geographically. Such samples maximize the genetic variation among groups. When Bamshad and his co-workers used their 100 Alu polymorphisms to try to classify a sample of individuals from southern India into a separate group, the Indians instead had more in common with either Europeans or Asians. In other words, because India has been subject to many genetic influences from Europe and Asia, people on the subcontinent did not group into a unique cluster. We concluded that many hundreds—or perhaps thousands—of polymorphisms might have to be examined to distinguish between groups whose ancestors have historically interbred with multiple populations.

THE HUMAN RACE

Given that people can be sorted broadly into groups using genetic data, do common notions of race correspond to underlying genetic differences among populations? In some cases they do, but often they do not. For instance, skin color or facial features—traits influenced by natural selection—are routinely used to divide people into races. But groups with similar physical characteristics as a result of selection can be quite different genetically. Individuals from sub-Saharan Africa and Australian Aborigines might have similar skin pigmentation (because of adapting to strong sun), but genetically they are quite dissimilar.

In contrast, two groups that are genetically similar to each other 15 might be exposed to different selective forces. In this case, natural selection can exaggerate some of the differences between groups, making them appear more dissimilar on the surface than they are underneath. Because traits such as skin color have been strongly affected by natural selection, they do not necessarily reflect the population processes that have shaped the distribution of neutral polymorphisms such as Alus or short tandem repeats. Therefore, traits or polymorphisms affected by natural selection may be poor predictors of group membership and may imply genetic relatedness where, in fact, little exists.

Another example of how difficult it is to categorize people involves populations in the U.S. Most people who describe themselves as African-American have relatively recent ancestors from West Africa, and West Africans generally have polymorphism frequencies that can be distinguished from those of Europeans, Asians, and Native Americans. The fraction of gene variations that African-Americans share with West Africans, however, is far from uniform, because over the centuries African-Americans have mixed extensively with groups originating from elsewhere in Africa and beyond.

Over the past several years, Mark D. Shriver of Pennsylvania State University and Rick A. Kittles of Howard University have defined a set of polymorphisms that they have used to estimate the fraction of a person's genes originating from each continental region. They found that the West African contribution to the genes of individual African-Americans averages about 80 percent, although it ranges from 20 to 100 percent. Mixing of groups is also apparent in many individuals who believe they have only European ancestors. According to Shriver's analyses, approximately 30 percent of Americans who consider themselves "white" have less than 90 percent European ancestry. Thus, self-reported ancestry is not necessarily a good predictor of the genetic composition of a large number of Americans. Accordingly, common notions of race do not always reflect a person's genetic background.

MEMBERSHIP HAS ITS PRIVILEGES

Understanding the relation between race and genetic variation has important practical implications. Several of the polymorphisms that differ in frequency from group to group have specific effects on health. The mutations responsible for sickle cell disease and some cases of cystic fibrosis, for instance, result from genetic changes that appear to have risen in frequency because they were protective against diseases prevalent in Africa and Europe, respectively. People who inherit one copy of the sickle cell polymorphism show some resistance to malaria; those with one copy of the cystic fibrosis trait may be less prone to the dehydration resulting from cholera. The symptoms of these diseases arise only in the unfortunate individuals who inherit two copies of the mutations.

Genetic variation also plays a role in individual susceptibility to one of the worst scourges of our age: AIDS. Some people have a small deletion in both their copies of a gene that encodes a particular cell-surface receptor called chemokine receptor 5 (CCR5). As a result, these individuals fail to produce CCR5 receptors on the surface of their cells. Most strains of HIV-1, the virus that causes AIDS, bind to the CCR5 receptor to gain entry to cells, so people who lack CCR5 receptors are resistant to HIV-1 infection. This polymorphism in the CCR5 receptor gene is found almost exclusively in groups from northeastern Europe.

Several polymorphisms in CCR5 do not prevent infection but instead 20 influence the rate at which HIV-1 infection leads to AIDS and death. Some of these polymorphisms have similar effects in different populations; others only alter the speed of disease progression in selected groups. One polymorphism, for example, is associated with delayed disease progression in European-Americans but accelerated disease in African-Americans. Researchers can only study such population-specific effects—and use that knowledge to direct therapy—if they can sort people into groups.

In these examples—and others like them—a polymorphism has a relatively large effect in a given disease. If genetic screening were inexpensive and efficient, all individuals could be screened for all such disease-related gene variants. But genetic testing remains costly. Perhaps more significantly, genetic screening raises concerns about privacy and consent: some people might not want to know about genetic factors that could increase their risk of developing a particular disease. Until these issues are resolved further, self-reported ancestry will continue to be a potentially useful diagnostic tool for physicians.

Ancestry may also be relevant for some diseases that are widespread in particular populations. Most common diseases, such as hypertension and diabetes, are the cumulative results of polymorphisms in several genes, each of which has a small influence on its own. Recent research suggests that polymorphisms that have a particular effect in one group may have a different effect in another group. This kind of complexity would make it much more difficult to use detected polymorphisms as a guide to therapy. Until further studies are done on the genetic and environmental contributions to complex diseases, physicians may have to rely on information about an individual's ancestry to know how best to treat some diseases.

RACE AND MEDICINE

But the importance of group membership as it relates to health care has been especially controversial in recent years. Last January the U.S. Food and Drug Administration issued guidelines advocating the collection of race and ethnicity data in all clinical trials. Some investigators contend that the differences between groups are so small and the historical abuses associated with categorizing people by race so extreme that group membership should play little if any role in genetic and medical studies. They assert that the FDA should abandon its recommendation and instead ask researchers conducting clinical trials to collect genomic data on each individual. Others suggest that only by using group membership, including common definitions of race based on skin color, can we understand how genetic and environmental differences among groups contribute to disease. This debate will be settled only by further research on the validity of race as a scientific variable.

A set of articles in the March 20 issue of the *New England Journal of Medicine* debated both sides of the medical implications of race. The authors of one article—Richard S. Cooper of the Loyola Stritch School of Medicine, Jay S. Kaufman of the University of North Carolina at Chapel Hill and Ryk Ward of the University of Oxford—argued that race is not an adequate criterion for physicians to use in choosing a particular drug for a given patient. They pointed out two findings of racial differences that are both now considered questionable: that a combination of certain blood vessel-dilating drugs was more effective in treating heart failure in people of African ancestry and that specific enzyme inhibitors (angiotensin converting enzyme, or ACE, inhibitors) have little efficacy in such individuals. In the second article, a group led by Neil Risch of Stanford University countered that racial or ethnic groups can differ from one another genetically and that the differences can have medical importance. They cited a study showing that the rate of complications from type 2 diabetes varies according to race, even after adjusting for such factors as disparities in education and income. The intensity of these arguments reflects both scientific and social factors. Many biomedical studies have not rigorously defined group membership, relying instead on inferred relationships based on racial categories. The dispute over the importance of group membership also illustrates how strongly the perception of race is shaped by different social and political perspectives.

In cases where membership in a geographically or culturally defined group has been correlated with health-related genetic traits, knowing something about an individual's group membership could be important for a physician. And to the extent that human groups live in different environments or have different experiences that affect health, group membership could also reflect nongenetic factors that are medically relevant.

Regardless of the medical implications of the genetics of race, the research findings are inherently exciting. For hundreds of years, people have wondered where various human groups came from and how those groups are related to one another. They have speculated about why human populations have different physical appearances and about whether the biological differences between groups are more than skin deep. New genetic data and new methods of analysis are finally allowing us to approach these questions. The result will be a much deeper understanding of both our biological nature and our human interconnectedness.

[2003]

SHERRY TURKLE   [b. 1948]

How Computers Change
the Way We Think

Sherry Turkle is the Abby Rockefeller Mauzé Professor of the Social
Studies of Science and Technology at the Massachusetts Institute of
Technology (MIT) as well as the director and founder of MIT's Initia-
tive on Technology and Self. A licensed clinical psychologist, Turkle
holds a joint doctorate in sociology and personality psychology from
Harvard University. She is the author of several books, including *Life
on the Screen: Identity in the Age of the Internet* (1997) and *Falling for
Science: Objects in Mind* (2008).

  In "How Computers Change the Way We Think," Turkle suggests
that technology is changing how we understand and interact with the
world—not necessarily for the better. As an example, Turkle notes how
the ease of online friendships makes face-to-face interaction all the
more difficult. She also argues that computers have become a mode
for thinking and knowledge. Because of this, she believes there are few
left who are not "computer people."

The tools we use to think change the ways in which we think. The invention of written language brought about a radical shift in how we process,
organize, store, and transmit representations of the world. Although
writing remains our primary information technology, today when we
think about the impact of technology on our habits of mind, we think
primarily of the computer.

  My first encounters with how computers change the way we think
came soon after I joined the faculty at the Massachusetts Institute of
Technology in the late 1970s, at the end of the era of the slide rule and
the beginning of the era of the personal computer. At a lunch for new
faculty members, several senior professors in engineering complained
that the transition from slide rules to calculators had affected their students' ability to deal with issues of scale. When students used slide rules,
they had to insert decimal points themselves. The professors insisted
that that required students to maintain a mental sense of scale, whereas

Sherry Turkle, "How Computers Change the Way We Think" from the *Chronicle of
Higher Education*, January 30, 2004. Reprinted by permission of the author.

those who relied on calculators made frequent errors in orders of magnitude. Additionally, the students with calculators had lost their ability to do "back of the envelope" calculations, and with that, an intuitive feel for the material.

That same semester, I taught a course in the history of psychology. There, I experienced the impact of computational objects on students' ideas about their emotional lives. My class had read Freud's essay on slips of the tongue, with its famous first example: the chairman of a parliamentary session opens a meeting by declaring it closed. The students discussed how Freud interpreted such errors as revealing a person's mixed emotions. A computer-science major disagreed with Freud's approach. The mind, she argued, is a computer. And in a computational dictionary—like we have in the human mind—"closed" and "open" are designated by the same symbol, separated by a sign for opposition. "Closed" equals "minus open." To substitute "closed" for "open" does not require the notion of ambivalence or conflict.

"When the chairman made that substitution," she declared, "a bit was dropped; a minus sign was lost. There was a power surge. No problem."

The young woman turned a Freudian slip into an information- 5 processing error. An explanation in terms of meaning had become an explanation in terms of mechanism.

Such encounters turned me to the study of both the instrumental and the subjective sides of the nascent computer culture. As an ethnographer and psychologist, I began to study not only what the computer was doing *for* us, but what it was doing *to* us, including how it was changing the way we see ourselves, our sense of human identity.

In the 1980s, I surveyed the psychological effects of computational objects in everyday life—largely the unintended side effects of people's tendency to project thoughts and feelings onto their machines. In the twenty years since, computational objects have become more explicitly designed to have emotional and cognitive effects. And those "effects by design" will become even stronger in the decade to come. Machines are being designed to serve explicitly as companions, pets, and tutors. And they are introduced in school settings for the youngest children.

Today, starting in elementary school, students use e-mail, word processing, computer simulations, virtual communities, and PowerPoint software. In the process, they are absorbing more than the content of what appears on their screens. They are learning new ways to think about what it means to know and understand.

What follows is a short and certainly not comprehensive list of areas where I see information technology encouraging changes in thinking. There can be no simple way of cataloging whether any particular change is good or bad. That is contested terrain. At every step we have to ask, as educators and citizens, whether current technology is leading us in directions that serve our human purposes. Such questions are not technical; they are social, moral, and political. For me, addressing that subjective side of computation is one of the more significant challenges for the next decade of information technology in higher education. Technology does not determine change, but it encourages us to take certain directions. If we make those directions clear, we can more easily exert human choice.

THINKING ABOUT PRIVACY

Today's college students are habituated to a world of online blogging, 10 instant messaging, and Web browsing that leaves electronic traces. Yet they have had little experience with the right to privacy. Unlike past generations of Americans, who grew up with the notion that the privacy of their mail was sacrosanct, our children are accustomed to electronic surveillance as part of their daily lives.

I have colleagues who feel that the increased incursions on privacy have put the topic more in the news, and that this is a positive change. But middle-school and high-school students tend to be willing to provide personal information online with no safeguards, and college students seem uninterested in violations of privacy and in increased governmental and commercial surveillance. Professors find that students do not understand that in a democracy, privacy is a right, not merely a privilege. In ten years, ideas about the relationship of privacy and government will require even more active pedagogy. (One might also hope that increased education about the kinds of silent surveillance that technology makes possible may inspire more active political engagement with the issue.)

AVATARS OR A SELF?

Chat rooms, role-playing games, and other technological venues offer us many different contexts for presenting ourselves online. Those possibilities are particularly important for adolescents because they offer what Erik Erikson described as a moratorium, a time out or safe space for the personal experimentation that is so crucial for adolescent development. Our dangerous world—with crime, terrorism, drugs, and AIDS—offers little in the way of safe spaces. Online worlds can provide valuable spaces for identity play.

169

But some people who gain fluency in expressing multiple aspects of self may find it harder to develop authentic selves. Some children who write narratives for their screen avatars may grow up with too little experience of how to share their real feelings with other people. For those who are lonely yet afraid of intimacy, information technology has made it possible to have the illusion of companionship without the demands of friendship.

FROM POWERFUL IDEAS TO POWERPOINT

In the 1970s and early 1980s, some educators wanted to make programming part of the regular curriculum for K–12 education. They argued that because information technology carries ideas, it might as well carry the most powerful ideas that computer science has to offer. It is ironic that in most elementary schools today, the ideas being carried by information technology are not ideas from computer science like procedural thinking, but more likely to be those embedded in productivity tools like PowerPoint presentation software.

PowerPoint does more than provide a way of transmitting content. It 15 carries its own way of thinking, its own aesthetic—which not surprisingly shows up in the aesthetic of college freshmen. In that aesthetic, presentation becomes its own powerful idea.

To be sure, the software cannot be blamed for lower intellectual standards. Misuse of the former is as much a symptom as a cause of the latter. Indeed, the culture in which our children are raised is increasingly a culture of presentation, a corporate culture in which appearance is often more important than reality. In contemporary political discourse, the bar has also been lowered. Use of rhetorical devices at the expense of cogent argument regularly goes without notice. But it is precisely because standards of intellectual rigor outside the educational sphere have fallen that educators must attend to how we use, and when we introduce, software that has been designed to simplify the organization and processing of information.

In *The Cognitive Style of PowerPoint* (Graphics Press, 2003), Edward R. Tufte suggests that PowerPoint equates bulleting with clear thinking. It does not teach students to begin a discussion or construct a narrative. It encourages presentation, not conversation. Of course, in the hands of a master teacher, a PowerPoint presentation with few words and powerful images can serve as the jumping-off point for a brilliant lecture. But in the hands of elementary-school students, often introduced to Power-Point in the third grade, and often infatuated with its swooshing sounds, animated icons, and flashing text, a slide show is more likely to close down debate than open it up.

Developed to serve the needs of the corporate boardroom, the software is designed to convey absolute authority. Teachers used to tell students that clear exposition depended on clear outlining, but presentation software has fetishized the outline at the expense of the content.

Narrative, the exposition of content, takes time. PowerPoint, like so much in the computer culture, speeds up the pace.

WORD PROCESSING VERSUS THINKING

The catalog for the Vermont Country Store advertises a manual type- 20 writer, which the advertising copy says "moves at a pace that allows time to compose your thoughts." As many of us know, it is possible to manipulate text on a computer screen and see how it looks faster than we can think about what the words mean.

Word processing has its own complex psychology. From a pedagogical point of view, it can make dedicated students into better writers because it allows them to revise text, rearrange paragraphs, and experiment with the tone and shape of an essay. Few professional writers would part with their computers; some claim that they simply cannot think without their hands on the keyboard. Yet the ability to quickly fill the page, to see it before you can think it, can make bad writers even worse.

A seventh grader once told me that the typewriter she found in her mother's attic is "cool because you have to type each letter by itself. You have to know what you are doing in advance or it comes out a mess." The idea of thinking ahead has become exotic.

TAKING THINGS AT INTERFACE VALUE

We expect software to be easy to use, and we assume that we don't have to know how a computer works. In the early 1980s, most computer users who spoke of transparency meant that, as with any other machine, you could "open the hood" and poke around. But only a few years later, Macintosh users began to use the term when they talked about seeing their documents and programs represented by attractive and easy-to-interpret icons. They were referring to an ability to make things work without needing to go below the screen surface. Paradoxically, it was the screen's opacity that permitted that kind of transparency. Today, when people say that something is transparent, they mean that they can see how to make it work, not that they know how it works. In other words, transparency means epistemic opacity.

The people who built or bought the first generation of personal computers understood them down to the bits and bytes. The next generation of operating systems were more complex, but they still invited that old-time reductive understanding. Contemporary information technology encourages different habits of mind. Today's college students are already used to taking things at (inter)face value; their successors in 2014 will be even less accustomed to probing below the surface.

SIMULATION AND ITS DISCONTENTS

Some thinkers argue that the new opacity is empowering, enabling any- 25
one to use the most sophisticated technological tools and to experiment with simulation in complex and creative ways. But it is also true that our tools carry the message that they are beyond our understanding. It is possible that in daily life, epistemic opacity can lead to passivity.

I first became aware of that possibility in the early 1990s, when the first generation of complex simulation games were introduced and immediately became popular for home as well as school use. SimLife teaches the principles of evolution by getting children involved in the development of complex ecosystems; in that sense it is an extraordinary learning tool. During one session in which I played SimLife with Tim, a thirteen-year-old, the screen before us flashed a message: "Your orgot is being eaten up." "What's an orgot?" I asked. Tim didn't know. "I just ignore that," he said confidently. "You don't need to know that kind of stuff to play."

For me, that story serves as a cautionary tale. Computer simulations enable their users to think about complex phenomena as dynamic, evolving systems. But they also accustom us to manipulating systems whose core assumptions we may not understand and that may not be true.

We live in a culture of simulation. Our games, our economic and political systems, and the ways architects design buildings, chemists envisage molecules, and surgeons perform operations all use simulation technology. In ten years the degree to which simulations are embedded in every area of life will have increased exponentially. We need to develop a new form of media literacy: readership skills for the culture of simulation.

We come to written text with habits of readership based on centuries of civilization. At the very least, we have learned to begin with the journalist's traditional questions: who, what, when, where, why, and how. Who wrote these words, what is their message, why were they written,

172

and how are they situated in time and place; politically and socially? A central project for higher education during the next ten years should be creating programs in information-technology literacy, with the goal of teaching students to interrogate simulations in much the same spirit, challenging their built-in assumptions.

Despite the ever-increasing complexity of software, most computer 30 environments put users in worlds based on constrained choices. In other words, immersion in programmed worlds puts us in reassuring environments where the rules are clear. For example, when you play a video game, you often go through a series of frightening situations that you escape by mastering the rules—you experience life as a reassuring dichotomy of scary and safe. Children grow up in a culture of video games, action films, fantasy epics, and computer programs that all rely on that familiar scenario of almost losing but then regaining total mastery: there is danger. It is mastered. A still-more-powerful monster appears. It is subdued. Scary. Safe.

Yet in the real world, we have never had a greater need to work our way out of binary assumptions. In the decade ahead, we need to rebuild the culture around information technology. In that new sociotechnical culture, assumptions about the nature of mastery would be less absolute. The new culture would make it easier, not more difficult, to consider life in shades of gray, to see moral dilemmas in terms other than a battle between Good and Evil. For never has our world been more complex, hybridized, and global. Never have we so needed to have many contradictory thoughts and feelings at the same time. Our tools must help us accomplish that, not fight against us.

Information technology is identity technology. Embedding it in a culture that supports democracy, freedom of expression, tolerance, diversity, and complexity of opinion is one of the next decade's greatest challenges. We cannot afford to fail.

When I first began studying the computer culture, a small breed of highly trained technologists thought of themselves as "computer people." That is no longer the case. If we take the computer as a carrier of a way of knowing, a way of seeing the world and our place in it, we are all computer people now.

[2004]

CHRISTOPHER CLAUSEN [b. 1942]

Against Work

Christopher Clausen received his Ph.D. from Queen's University in
Canada in 1972 and is now a retired professor of English at Pennsylvania State University. His research focuses on issues in philosophy, Vic-
torian literature, and contemporary American society. Clausen's books
include *The Place of Poetry: Two Centuries of an Art in Crisis* (1981), *The
Moral Imagination: Essays on Literature and Ethics* (1986), *My Life
with President Kennedy* (1994), and *Faded Mosaic: The Emergence of
Post-Cultural America* (2000). He has also published poems and essays
in the *Kenyon Review*, the *Virginia Quarterly Review*, and the *Sewanee
Review*.

In his essay "Against Work," originally published in the *American
Scholar* in September 2004, Clausen argues that Americans have an
unhealthy relationship with their work. Tracing the etymology of the
word "workaholism," he contends that, in comparison to those of
other cultures, Americans pursue work and employment status almost
religiously, often at the expense of happiness and other forms of
fulfillment.

A history of my suburban early ambitions would sound utterly conventional. At the age of six I wanted to be a cowboy. At twelve I decided
instead to become a professional football player, which, for someone
who would never weigh more than a hundred and thirty pounds, was
even more hopeless. In high school I made up my mind to be a writer. As
in most such cases, it wasn't the work of writing that appealed to me. It
was that, secretly, I never wanted to do any work at all. But teenagers are
rarely of one mind, and their inconsistent wishes seldom come true in a
recognizable way.

"What is the use of having money if you have to work for it?" Violet
Malone disdainfully asks her father-in-law, a self-made Irish-American
billionaire, in George Bernard Shaw's play *Man and Superman*. A century ago, when Shaw was writing, the different valuation that Americans

Christopher Clausen, "Against Work." From the *American Scholar,* Volume 73, No. 4,
Autumn 2004. Copyright © 2004 by Christopher Clausen. Reprinted by permission of
the author.

and Europeans set on work as an abstract ideal was already evident to anyone who had a chance to compare them. By that time the "gospel of work" preached by Thomas Carlyle, who repeated endlessly that "work is alone noble," was a mid-Victorian relic.

To her perfectly reasonable question, the Englishwoman Violet receives no answer. She would be just as baffled a hundred years later. If humans are the only animal that doesn't think the purpose of life is to enjoy it, Americans are an especially hard case. Today those of us with full-time employment typically put in several hundred more hours per year than western Europeans—the equivalent of seven additional weeks, according to some surveys. Even the proverbially hardworking Germans spend only about three-quarters as many hours on the job and retire younger. Our disposable income is correspondingly higher, though when asked whether we would prefer more leisure to greater wealth, most of us opt for leisure. Statistics on voluntary overtime, however, suggest that we may not be telling the truth. A long American tradition leads people to define themselves not just by their occupations but also by the amount of labor they put in.

Captain John Smith's declaration that those who do not work shall not eat is the real national motto, ratified by subsequent authorities from Benjamin Franklin to Donald Trump. Rockefellers and Kennedys, whose international counterparts would spend all their time collecting works of art, instead work conspicuously hard at finance or politics. The American way is to prove one's worth by long hours, almost regardless of what one actually accomplishes. The fact that many people appear to work hard while actually coasting through the week merely confirms the gap between what they think they should be doing and their actual preferences.

Consider the fate of the word *workaholism*, coined by W. E. Oates in 1968 to identify a disturbing psychological obsession—an "addiction," a "compulsion"—that Oates had noticed around him. Others took up the new term enthusiastically. "The workaholic, as an addict is called, neglects his family, withdraws from social life, and loses interest in sex," the *Sydney Bulletin* explained ominously in 1973. But within a decade the term lost all connotation of pathology and became a compliment. "Unlike their workaholic American cousins," *Time* reported in 1981, "Europeans tend to see lengthy vacations as somehow part of the natural order of things." Today the word is most often heard in the proud boast "I'm a workaholic," recited ad nauseam by type A personalities in corporations, politics, and the professions. Carlyle lives, if only in America.

Why on earth do we do it? Do most of us really prefer to work—to spend our lives in labor as an end rather than as an unavoidable means to our own or others' happiness? Of course not. Most jobs are boring at best, with few psychic rewards. Nobody works on an assembly line or at Wal-Mart, or recites the weather on Channel 9, simply for lack of a pleasanter way to spend two thousand hours every year. It's true that the most energetic and gregarious of us, the kind who have been claiming since high school that they "want to work with people," often find even jobs like these a relief from loneliness. One suspects, though, that if they suddenly didn't need the money or respect, they would quickly turn to playing games instead, or traveling the world, or finding innovative new ways to cope. The upper-middle-class professions are supposed to be a different story. Doctors, lawyers, and college professors usually think of themselves as "committed," with the implication that there is nothing they would rather be doing.

Speaking from experience, I can attest that being a senior academic is one of the more privileged assignments in life, although anyone who thinks universities are relaxed, humane centers for the free play of intellect hasn't spent much time in one lately. Plenty of hard work goes into getting a Ph.D., achieving tenure, and practicing a profession that despite its flattering self-image involves as much stress, conformity, and tedium as other occupations. In response to charges made a few years ago that professors are slackers, the Department of Education released a survey concluding that the average full-time university faculty member puts in between forty-five and fifty-five hours a week. Some of what I do for a living is fun—though I discovered early that writing anything meant to be read by others involves a good deal of labor—and the rest is pleasanter than what many people have to do. But still. Most of your waking hours for forty years?

There is something deeply conflicted about the devotion to work, vocation, career as an ideal in any society, but especially in one that has zealously cast off so many of its other repressions. Americans at the beginning of the twenty-first century pursue pleasure with the same avid desperation as upscale high school students pursue getting into the right college—that is, with a hell of a lot of work. We have all been so oversocialized that an unnatural devotion to toil leaves its mark on every area of life. It could even be argued that the most highly prized pleasures have themselves become a form of work, complete with their own uniforms, disciplines, and special lingo.

My own conflicted attitude probably owes something to the fact that during the summer between high school and college, I worked as an information clerk for the National Heart Institute in a suburb of the capital. As a temporary, I spent my days keeping track of offprints from medical journals, answering requests for the Heart Institute's own publications, and cleaning out the primitive photocopier. Much of the time there was not enough work to keep me busy, and like other low-level civil servants, I soon discovered that the Washington summer in a building with no air conditioning called for a relaxed approach to the public's business.

Most mornings I stayed in my office filling orders from schoolteachers 10 for our most popular publication, a garish poster titled "The Living Pump." Having answered the mail as best I could, I generally retreated in the heat of the afternoon to the comfortable underground vault where our own materials and hundreds of articles on heart disease were stored. This fastness lay beneath a building that had been constructed with nuclear attack in mind. In addition to a normal basement, it had four sub-basements reached by a freight elevator that no one else seemed to use. Once I got to the bottom, I made my way through nearly half a mile of corridors filled with abandoned office furniture. I never encountered another human being down there, just thousands of desks and chairs and filing cabinets that nobody wanted anymore. After several hours in this environment, it was easy to believe the world had ended, and all that was left of the United States government was one GS-2 surrounded by acres of junk five levels below ground zero. It seemed odd to me that reams of Living Pumps would survive Armageddon while the doctors who ran the National Institutes of Health turned into dust, but eighteen-year-olds have a high tolerance for irrationality. That's one reason they make good soldiers. I catalogued the contents of my bunker, restocked as necessary, composed juvenile light verse, and read a lot of novels in the cool silence. Some July afternoons I thought seriously about canceling my college plans and staying underground in the government forever.

The Department of Health, Education, and Welfare, as it was then called, had its headquarters on Independence Avenue in downtown Washington. Olive, a Southern widow who must have been in her fifties, presided over the Heart Institute's offices there. She had worked in similar offices since the New Deal and had seen bosses come and go. A slim woman of vast charm and presence, she liked young men who would spend Friday afternoons in her office drinking coffee and conversing. I retain only the general impression of an elegant lady from a different world where manners and human contact counted for nearly everything and bureaucratic procedures for nothing. Without ever saying so, she conveyed through her demeanor that the government was too absurd to worry about. My guess, although I really have no idea, is that Olive did her job very well, if in an unconventional fashion. Whoever was nominally her superior must have had a difficult time until he tacitly agreed that everything she did would be done her way.

As I look back, it's hard for me to believe what her way meant to my weekly routine. Every Thursday I would receive a slip entitling me to take a pickup truck out of the motor pool on Friday and drive it down-town to HEW. On alternate Friday mornings I would load the truck with publications from the bunker. Then I would have lunch, drive to Olive's office, unload the truck, and spend the afternoon listening, like a young man out of a Faulkner novel. The next Friday I would drive an empty truck to HEW, load it up with the same publications I had delivered the previous week, and return them to Bethesda. It sounds worse than it seemed at the time. Perhaps I'm forgetting some deliveries that served a real purpose beyond bringing me into Olive's presence. The possibility that my cheerful, unambitious colleagues would object to these excur-sions did not occur to me, and nobody ever did.

Everyone has met people who boast (sometimes repetitively) of loving their work so much that they rarely take vacations and can't bear the thought of retirement. Star athletes, successful artists, and research sci-entists are sometimes credible when they make these assertions. Occa-sionally an obstetrician goes on delivering babies into his nineties, and the local newspaper praises his enthusiasm for life. But who believes middle managers when they claim to spend the weekend looking for-ward to Monday? Who takes teachers seriously in June when they say they can't wait for September? If hypocrisy is the tribute vice pays to virtue, the oddity here is that so many people believe work as such, work divorced from any particular achievement, is especially virtuous. Work-ing to earn one's bread is something few people can escape. Working out of moral vanity is sheer self-deception.

Of course Americans didn't invent the idea. As with so many things, we merely perfected it. To get people to do their best over a long period of time, it has always been necessary to make what they do seem both a duty and a pleasure, something like rearing children. Seneca assured affluent Roman parents, "Nothing is so certain as that the evils of idle-ness can be shaken off by hard work." In a similar vein, Voltaire wrote, "Work keeps us from three great evils, boredom, vice, and need." These are the homilies of the fortunate. Those who have been forced to work hard are often more realistic about what is at stake. "I don't like work—no man does, "Joseph Conrad's alter ego Marlow announces in *Heart of Darkness*, and then adds, "—but I like what is in work—the chance to find yourself. Your own reality—for yourself, not for others—what no other man can ever know." The self-respect that comes from being financially self-supporting, as well as capable of some useful accomplishment for oneself or others, is a worthy goal for anyone. Fetishizing the labor itself is merely a form of bondage, workaholism in the true, perverse sense.

Because it serves so many different practical and psychic purposes, it's 15 no wonder that, in the celebrated words of C. Northcote Parkinson, "work expands so as to fill the time available for its completion." Still, much can be said not just for the strenuous, cultivated leisure that hardworking professionals sometimes allow themselves to imagine as an alternative to virtuous toil, but for bone-idleness. There is in fact no indication that those who work are happier than those who choose not to. After surveying a mass of research on what it takes to make people happy, the psychologist David Watson declares, "With the notable exception of involuntary unemployment, we see little evidence that occupational and employment status have a major impact on well-being. Generally speaking, people in seemingly uninteresting, low-status jobs report levels of happiness and life satisfaction that are quite comparable to those of individuals in high-status occupations. Moreover, the employed and voluntarily unemployed report extremely similar levels of affect and well-being." He concludes, "One particularly interesting implication of this literature is that people apparently devote much of their lives to striving after things—education, marriage, money, and so on—that ultimately have little effect on their happiness." Although having some goals in life seems to work better than having none, "happiness is primarily a subjective phenomenon . . . not highly constrained by objective circumstances."

If your work won't make you or anyone else happier, why do more of it than you have to? Believers in the gospel of work typically consider happiness irrelevant. Deep down, they think we have a duty to be miserable. As usual, the bullying Carlyle put it most brutally: "'Happy,' my brother? First of all, what difference is it whether thou art happy or not! . . . The only happiness a brave man ever troubled himself with asking much about was, happiness enough to get his work done. Not 'I can't eat!' but 'I can't work!' that was the burden of all wise complaining among men." Men must work, and women must weep, as Carlyle's friend Charles Kingsley decreed. Work itself, work as a sacred abstraction, had become a substitute for the God that Carlyle and many of his readers no longer believed in.

In America this grim pseudo-religion continues to draw worshippers on a scale no longer seen elsewhere in the Western world. The only major change is that women are now expected to work like men. We speak in reverent tones of the "work ethic"; politicians praise "working families" and, even in times of relatively low unemployment, make job creation an issue in every campaign. A few years ago, cutting the work week was a central promise in a French election, and the government actually passed laws on the subject. In the United States, by contrast, legislation has been introduced to make overtime easier for companies to afford. We abolished mandatory retirement in the 1980s. Despite the growth in productivity and affluence over the past decades, all the social

179

pressures are for working longer hours and later in life rather than cashing in on the promise of greater leisure—partly to take some of the pressure off Social Security and Medicare, but mostly because work is such an ingrained American value.

I don't know about the civil service, but not many Olives are left in major universities. Sometimes I dream of my vault full of Living Pumps. A colleague and I recently passed the time by talking speculatively of retirement. "You wouldn't actually retire at sixty-five, would you?" this proud workaholic asked with incredulity.

"Of course," I gulped, suddenly and unexpectedly defensive about my secret plan to quit at sixty-two. "Why not?"

He shrugged disdainfully and went back to writing his next book on 20 Chaucer. Truly, we are the last Puritans.

[2004]

JIB FOWLES   [b. 1940]

Advertising's Fifteen Basic Appeals

Born in Hartford, Connecticut, **Jib Fowles** was educated at Wesleyan University (B.A.), Columbia University (M.A.), and New York University (Ph.D.). After completing his doctorate, Fowles was a Fulbright scholar in India from 1963 to 1964. His distinguished academic career includes teaching positions at New York University and the University of Houston, where he presently chairs the program in Studies of the Future. As a researcher and writer, Fowles has studied aspects of American popular culture, focusing on the intersections of media, advertising, and celebrity. He has published several books related to his specialization, including *Mass Advertising as Social Forecast* (1976), *Television Viewers and Media Snobs: What TV Does for People* (1989), and *The Case for Television* (1999). Of his work, Fowles states: "My chief preoccupation is with an appreciative analysis of industrial culture—its past, present and future."

In his essay "Advertising's Fifteen Basic Appeals," Fowles examines the human psychology behind the attractive power of elemental advertising strategies.

EMOTIONAL APPEALS

The nature of effective advertisements was recognized full well by the late media philosopher Marshall McLuhan. In his *Understanding Media*, the first sentence of the section on advertising reads, "The continuous pressure is to create ads more and more in the image of audience motives and desires."

By giving form to people's deep-lying desires, and picturing states of being that individuals privately yearn for, advertisers have the best chance of arresting attention and affecting communication. And that is the immediate goal of advertising: to tug at our psychological shirt sleeves and slow us down long enough for a word or two about whatever

Jib Fowles, "Advertising's Fifteen Basic Appeals," from *Etc.* 39, No. 3. Reprinted with permission of the International Society for General Semantics, Concord, California.

is being sold. We glance at a picture of a solitary rancher at work, and "Marlboro" slips into our minds.

Advertisers (I'm using the term as a shorthand for both the products' manufacturers, who bring the ambition and money to the process, and the advertising agencies, who supply the know-how) are ever more compelled to invoke consumers' drives and longings; this is the "continuous pressure" McLuhan refers to. Over the past century, the American marketplace has grown increasingly congested as more and more products have entered into the frenzied competition after the public's dollars. The economies of other nations are quieter than ours since the volume of goods being hawked does not so greatly exceed demand. In some economies, consumer wares are scarce enough that no advertising at all is necessary. But in the United States, we go to the other extreme. In order to stay in business, an advertiser must strive to cut through the considerable commercial hub-bub by any means available—including the emotional appeals that some observers have held to be abhorrent and underhanded.

The use of subconscious appeals is a comment not only on conditions among sellers. As time has gone by, buyers have become stoutly resistant to advertisements. We live in a blizzard of these messages and have learned to turn up our collars and ward off most of them. A study done a few years ago at Harvard University's Graduate School of Business Administration ventured that the average American is exposed to some 500 ads daily from television, newspapers, magazines, radio, billboards, direct mail, and so on. If for no other reason than to preserve one's sanity, a filter must be developed in every mind to lower the number of ads a person is actually aware of—a number this particular study estimated at about seventy-five ads per day. (Of these, only twelve typically produced a reaction—nine positive and three negative, on the average.) To be among the few messages that do manage to gain access to minds, advertisers must be strategic, perhaps even a little underhanded at times.

There are assumptions about personality underlying advertisers' efforts 5 to communicate via emotional appeals, and while these assumptions have stood the test of time, they still deserve to be aired. Human beings, it is presumed, walk around with a variety of unfulfilled urges and motives swirling in the bottom half of their minds. Lusts, ambitions, tendernesses, vulnerabilities—they are constantly bubbling up, seeking resolution. These mental forces energize people, but they are too crude and irregular to be given excessive play in the real world. They must be capped with the competent, sensible behavior that permits individuals to get along well in society. However, this upper layer of mental activity, shot through with caution and rationality, is not receptive to advertising's pitches. Advertisers want to circumvent this shell of consciousness if they can, and latch on to one of the lurching, subconscious drives.

In effect, advertisers over the years have blindly felt their way around the underside of the American psyche, and by trial and error have discovered the softest points of entree, the places where their messages have the greatest likelihood of getting by consumers' defenses. As McLuhan says elsewhere, "Gouging away at the surface of public sales resistance, the ad men are constantly breaking through into the *Alice in Wonderland* territory behind the looking glass, which is the world of subrational impulses and appetites."

An advertisement communicates by making use of a specially selected image (of a supine female, say, or a curly-haired child, or a celebrity) which is designed to stimulate "subrational impulses and desires" even when they are at ebb, even if they are unacknowledged by their possessor. Some few ads have their emotional appeal in the text, but for the greater number by far the appeal is contained in the artwork. This makes sense, since visual communication better suits more primal levels of the brain. If the viewer of an advertisement actually has the importuned motive, and if the appeal is sufficiently well fashioned to call it up, then the person can be hooked. The product in the ad may then appear to take on the semblance of gratification for the summoned motive. Many ads seem to be saying, "If you have this need, then this product will help satisfy it." It is a primitive equation, but not an ineffective one for selling.

Thus, most advertisements appearing in national media can be understood as having two orders of content. The first is the appeal to deep-running drives in the minds of consumers. The second is information regarding the good[s] or service being sold: its name, its manufacturer, its picture, its packaging, its objective attributes, its functions. For example, the reader of a brassiere advertisement sees a partially undraped but blandly unperturbed woman standing in an otherwise commonplace public setting, and may experience certain sensations; the reader also sees the name "Maidenform," a particular brassiere style, and, in tiny print, words about the material, colors, price. Or, the viewer of a television commercial sees a demonstration with four small boxes labelled 650, 650, 650, and 800; something in the viewer's mind catches hold of this, as trivial as thoughtful consideration might reveal it to be. The viewer is also exposed to the name "Anacin," its bottle, and its purpose.

Sometimes there is an apparently logical link between an ad's emotional appeal and its product information. It does not violate common sense that Cadillac automobiles be photographed at country clubs, or that Japan Air Lines be associated with Orientalia. But there is no real need for the linkage to have a bit of reason behind it. Is there anything inherent to the connection between Salem cigarettes and mountains, Coke and a smile, Miller Beer and comradeship? The link being forged in minds between product and appeal is a pre-logical one.

People involved in the advertising industry do not necessarily talk in 10 the terms being used here. They are stationed at the sending end of this communications channel, and may think they are up to any number of things—Unique Selling Propositions, explosive copywriting, the optimal use of demographics or psychographics, ideal media buys, high recall ratings, or whatever. But when attention shifts to the receiving end of the channel, and focuses on the instant of reception, then commentary becomes much more elemental: an advertising message contains something primary and primitive, an emotional appeal, that in effect is the thin end of the wedge, trying to find its way into a mind. Should this occur, the product information comes along behind.

When enough advertisements are examined in this light, it becomes clear that the emotional appeals fall into several distinguishable categories, and that every ad is a variation on one of a limited number of basic appeals. While there may be several ways of classifying these appeals, one particular list of fifteen has proven to be especially valuable. Advertisements can appeal to:

1. The need for sex
2. The need for affiliation
3. The need to nurture
4. The need for guidance
5. The need to aggress
6. The need to achieve
7. The need to dominate
8. The need for prominence
9. The need for attention
10. The need for autonomy
11. The need to escape
12. The need to feel safe
13. The need for aesthetic sensations
14. The need to satisfy curiosity
15. Physiological needs: food, drink, sleep, etc.

MURRAY'S LIST

Where does this list of advertising's fifteen basic appeals come from? Several years ago, I was involved in a research project which was to have as one segment an objective analysis of the changing appeals made in post–World War II American advertising. A sample of magazine ads would have their appeals coded into the categories of psychological needs they seemed aimed at. For this content analysis to happen, a complete roster of human motives would have to be found.

The first thing that came to mind was Abraham Maslow's famous four-part hierarchy of needs. But the briefest look at the range of appeals made in advertising was enough to reveal that they are more varied, and more profane, than Maslow had cared to account for. The search led on to the work of psychologist Henry A. Murray, who together with his colleagues at the Harvard Psychological Clinic has constructed a full taxonomy of needs. As described in *Explorations in Personality*, Murray's team had conducted a lengthy series of in-depth interviews with a number of subjects in order to derive from scratch what they felt to be the essential variables of personality. Forty-four variables were distinguished by the Harvard group, of which twenty were motives. The need for achievement ("to overcome obstacles and obtain a high standard") was one, for instance; the need to defer was another; the need to aggress was a third; and so forth.

Murray's list had served as the groundwork for a number of subsequent projects. Perhaps the best-known of these was David C. McClelland's extensive study of the need for achievement, reported in his *The Achieving Society*. In the process of demonstrating that a people's high need for achievement is predictive of later economic growth, McClelland coded achievement imagery and references out of a nation's folklore, songs, legends, and children's tales.

Following McClelland, I too wanted to cull the motivational appeals 15 from a culture's imaginative product—in this case, advertising. To develop categories expressly for this purpose, I took Murray's twenty motives and added to them others he had mentioned in passing in *Explorations in Personality* but not included on the final list. The extended list was tried out on a sample of advertisements, and motives which never seemed to be invoked were dropped. I ended up with eighteen of Murrays' motives, into which 770 print ads were coded. The resulting distribution is included in the 1976 book *Mass Advertising as Social Forecast*.

Since that time, the list of appeals has undergone refinements as a result of using it to analyze television commercials. A few more adjustments stemmed from the efforts of students in my advertising classes to decode appeals; tens of term papers surveying thousands of advertisements have caused some inconsistencies in the list to be hammered out. Fundamentally, though, the list remains the creation of Henry Murray. In developing a comprehensive, parsimonious inventory of human motives, he pinpointed the subsurface mental forces that are the least quiescent and most susceptible to advertising's entreaties.

FIFTEEN APPEALS

1. *Need for sex.* Let's start with sex, because this is the appeal which seems to pop up first whenever the topic of advertising is raised. Whole books have been written about this one alone, to find a large audience of mildly titillated readers. Lately, due to campaigns to sell blue jeans, concern with sex in ads has redoubled.

The fascinating thing is not how much sex there is in advertising, but how little. Contrary to impressions, unambiguous sex is rare in these messages. Some of this surprising observation may be a matter of definition: the Jordache ads with the lithe, blouse-less female astride a similarly clad male is clearly an appeal to the audience's sexual drives, but the same cannot be said about Brooke Shields in the Calvin Klein commercials. Directed at young women and their credit-card carrying mothers, the image of Miss Shields instead invokes the need to be looked at. Buy Calvins and you'll be the center of much attention, just as Brooke is, the ads imply; they do not primarily inveigle their target audience's need for sexual intercourse.

In the content analysis reported in *Mass Advertising as Social Forecast* only two percent of ads were found to pander to this motive. Even *Playboy* ads shy away from sexual appeals: a recent issue contained eighty-three full-page ads, and just four of them (or less than five percent) could be said to have sex on their minds.

The reason this appeal is so little used is that it is too blaring and 20 tends to obliterate the product information. Nudity in advertising has the effect of reducing brand recall. The people who do remember the product may do so because they have been made indignant by the ad; this is not the response most advertisers seek.

To the extent that sexual imagery is used, it conventionally works better on men than women; typically a female figure is offered up to the male reader. A Black Velvet liquor advertisement displays an attractive woman wearing a tight black outfit, recumbent under the legend, "Feel the Velvet." The figure does not have to be horizontal, however, for the appeal to be present as National Airlines revealed in its "Fly me" campaign. Indeed, there does not even have to be a female in the ad; "Flick my Bic" was sufficient to convey the idea to many.

As a rule, though, advertisers have found sex to be a tricky appeal, to be used sparingly. Less controversial and equally fetching are the appeals to our need for affectionate human contact.

2. *Need for affiliation.* American mythology upholds autonomous individuals, and social statistics suggest that people are ever more going it alone in their lives, yet the high frequency of affiliative appeals in ads

belies this. Or maybe it does not: maybe all the images of companionship are compensation for what Americans privately lack. In any case, the need to associate with others is widely invoked in advertising and is probably the most prevalent appeal. All sorts of goods and services are sold by linking them to our unfulfilled desires to be in good company.

According to Henry Murray, the need for affiliation consists of desires "to draw near and enjoyably cooperate or reciprocate with another; to please and win affection of another; to adhere and remain loyal to a friend." The manifestations of this motive can be segmented into several different types of affiliation, beginning with romance.

Courtship may be swifter nowadays, but the desire for pair-bonding is 25 far from satiated. Ads reaching for this need commonly depict a youngish male and female engrossed in each other. The head of the male is usually higher than the female's, even at this late date; she may be sitting or leaning while he is standing. They are not touching in the Smirnoff vodka ads, but obviously there is an intimacy, sometimes frolicsome, between them. The couple does touch for Martell Cognac when "The moment was Martell." For Wind Song perfume they have touched, and "Your Wind Song stays on his mind."

Depending on the audience, the pair does not absolutely have to be young—just together. He gives her a DeBeers diamond, and there is a tear in her laugh lines. She takes Geritol and preserves herself for him. And numbers of consumers, wanting affection too, follow suit.

Warm family feelings are fanned in ads when another generation is added to the pair. Hallmark Cards brings grandparents into the picture, and Johnson and Johnson Baby Powder has Dad, Mom, and baby, all fresh from the bath, encircled in arms and emblazoned with "Share the Feeling." A talc has been fused to familial love.

Friendship is yet another form of affiliation pursued by advertisers. Two women confide and drink Maxwell House coffee together; two men walk through the woods smoking Salem cigarettes. Miller Beer promises that afternoon "Miller Time" will be staffed with three or four good buddies. Drink Dr. Pepper, as Mickey Rooney is coaxed to do, and join in with all the other Peppers. Coca-Cola does not even need to portray the friendliness; it has reduced this appeal to "a Coke and a smile."

The warmth can be toned down and disguised, but it is the same affiliative need that is being fished for. The blonde has a direct gaze and her friends are firm businessmen in appearance, but with a glass of Old Bushmill you can sit down and fit right in. Or, for something more upbeat, sing along with the Pontiac choirboys.

As well as presenting positive images, advertisers can play to the need 30 for affiliation in negative ways, by invoking the fear of rejection. If we don't use Scope, we'll have the "Ugh! Morning Breath" that causes the male and female models to avert their faces. Unless we apply Ultra Brite or Close-Up to our teeth, it's good-bye romance. Our family will be cursed with "House-a-tosis" if we don't take care. Without Dr. Scholl's antiperspirant foot spray, the bowling team will keel over. There go all the guests when the supply of Dorito's nacho cheese chips is exhausted. Still more rejection if our shirts have ring-around-the-collar, if our car needs to be Midasized. But make a few purchases, and we are back in the bosom of human contact.

As self-directed as Americans pretend to be, in the last analysis we remain social animals, hungering for the positive, endorsing feelings that only those around us can supply. Advertisers respond, urging us to "Reach out and touch someone," in the hopes our monthly bills will rise.

3. *Need to nurture.* Akin to affiliative needs is the need to take care of small, defenseless creatures—children and pets, largely. Reciprocity is of less consequence here, though; it is the giving that counts. Murray uses synonyms like "to feed, help, support, console, protect, comfort, nurse, heal." A strong need it is, woven deep into our genetic fabric, for if it did not exist we could not successfully raise up our replacements. When advertisers put forth the image of something diminutive and furry, something that elicits the word "cute" or "precious," then they are trying to trigger this motive. We listen to the childish voice singing the Oscar Mayer weiner song, and our next hot-dog purchase is prescribed. Aren't those darling kittens something, and how did this Meow Mix get into our shopping cart?

This pitch is often directed at women, as Mother Nature's chief nurturers. "Make me some Kraft macaroni and cheese, please," says the elfin preschooler just in from the snowstorm, and mothers' hearts go out, and Kraft's sales go up. "We're cold, wet, and hungry," whine the husband and kids, and the little woman gets the Manwiches ready. A facsimile of this need can be hit without children or pets: the husband is ill and sleepless in the television commercial, and the wife grudgingly fetches the NyQuil.

But it is not women alone who can be touched by this appeal. The father nurses his son Eddie through adolescence while the John Deere lawn tractor survives the years. Another father counts pennies with his young son as the subject of New York Life Insurance comes up. And all over America are businessmen who don't know why they dial Qantas Airlines when they have to take a trans-Pacific trip; the koala bear knows.

4. *Need for guidance.* The opposite of the need to nurture is the need 35 to be nurtured: to be protected, shielded, guided. We may be loath to admit it, but the child lingers on inside every adult—and a good thing it

does, or we would not be instructable in our advancing years. Who wants a nation of nothing but flinty personalities? Parent-like figures can successfully call up this need. Robert Young recommends Sanka coffee, and since we have experienced him for twenty-five years as television father and doctor, we take his word for it. Florence Henderson as the expert mom knows a lot about the advantages of Wesson oil.

The parent-ness of the spokesperson need not be so salient; sometimes pure authoritativeness is better. When Orson Welles scowls and intones, "Paul Masson will sell no wine before its time," we may not know exactly what he means, but we still take direction from him. There is little maternal about Brenda Vaccaro when she speaks up for Tampax, but there is a certainty to her that many accept.

A celebrity is not a necessity in making a pitch to the need for guidance, since a fantasy figure can serve just as well. People accede to the Green Giant, or Betty Crocker, or Mr. Goodwrench. Some advertisers can get by with no figure at all: "When E.F. Hutton talks, people listen."

Often it is tradition or custom that advertisers point to and consumers take guidance from. Bits and pieces of American history are used to sell whiskeys like Old Crow, Southern Comfort, Jack Daniel's. We conform to traditional male/female roles and age-old social norms when we purchase Barclay cigarettes, which informs us "The pleasure is back."

The product itself, if it has been around for a long time, can constitute 40 a tradition. All those old labels in the ad for Morton salt convince us that we should continue to buy it. Kool-Aid says "You loved it as a kid. You trust it as a mother," hoping to get yet more consumers to go along.

Even when the product has no history at all, our need to conform to tradition and to be guided are strong enough that they can be invoked through bogus nostalgia and older actors. Country-Time lemonade sells because consumers want to believe it has a past they can defer to.

So far the needs and the ways they can be invoked which have been looked at are largely warm and affiliative; they stand in contrast to the next set of needs, which are much more egoistic and assertive.

5. *Need to aggress.* The pressures of the real world create strong retaliatory feelings in every functioning human being. Since these impulses can come forth as bursts of anger and violence, their display is normally tabooed. Existing as harbored energy, aggressive drives present a large, tempting target for advertisers. It is not a target to be aimed at thoughtlessly, though, for few manufacturers want their products associated with destructive motives. There is always the danger that, as in the case of sex, if the appeal is too blatant, public opinion will turn against what is being sold.

189

Jack-in-the-Box sought to abruptly alter its marketing by going after older customers and forgetting the younger ones. Their television commercials had a seventy-ish lady command, "Waste him," and the Jack-in-the-Box clown exploded before our eyes. So did public reaction until the commercials were toned down. Print ads for Club cocktails carried the faces of octogenarians under the headline, "Hit me with a Club"; response was contrary enough to bring the campaign to a stop.

Better disguised aggressive appeals are less likely to backfire: Triumph 45 cigarettes has models making a lewd gesture with their uplifted cigarettes, but the individuals are often laughing and usually in close company of others. When Exxon said, "There's a Tiger in your tank," the implausibility of it concealed the invocation of aggressive feelings.

Depicted arguments are a common way for advertisers to tap the audience's needs to aggress. Don Rickles and Lynda Carter trade gibes, and consumers take sides as the name of Seven-Up is stitched on minds. The Parkay tub has a difference of opinion with the user; who can forget it, or who (or what) got the last word in?

6. *Need to achieve.* This is the drive that energizes people, causing them to strive in their lives and careers. According to Murray, the need for achievement is signalled by the desires "to accomplish something difficult. To overcome obstacles and attain a high standard. To excel one's self. To rival and surpass others." A prominent American trait, it is one that advertisers like to hook on to because it identifies their product with winning and success.

The Cutty Sark ad does not disclose that Ted Turner failed at his latest attempt at yachting's America Cup; here he is represented as a champion on the water as well as off in his television enterprises. If we drink this whiskey, we will be victorious alongside Turner. We can also succeed with O.J. Simpson by renting Hertz cars, or with Reggie Jackson by bringing home some Panasonic equipment. Cathy Rigby and Stayfree Maxipads will put people out front.

Sports heroes are the most convenient means to snare consumers' needs to achieve, but they are not the only one. Role models can be established, ones which invite emulation, as with the profiles put forth by Dewar's scotch. Successful, tweedy individuals relate they have "graduated to the flavor of Myer's rum." Or the advertiser can establish a prize: two neighbors play one-on-one basketball for a Michelob beer in a television commercial, while in a print ad a bottle of Johnnie Walker Black Label has been gilded like a trophy.

Any product that advertises itself in superlatives—the best, the first, 50 the finest—is trying to make contact with our needs to succeed. For many consumers, sales and bargains belong in this category of appeals, too; the person who manages to buy something at fifty percent off is seizing an opportunity and coming out ahead of others.

7. *Need to dominate.* This fundamental need is the craving to be powerful—perhaps omnipotent, as in the Xerox ad where Brother Dominic exhibits heavenly powers and creates miraculous copies. Most of us will settle for being just a regular potentate, though. We drink Budweiser because it is the King of Beers, and here comes the powerful Clydesdales to prove it. A taste of Wolfschmidt vodka and "The spirit of the Czar lives on."

The need to dominate and control one's environment is often thought of as being masculine, but as close students of human nature advertisers know, it is not so circumscribed. Women's aspirations for control are suggested in the campaign theme, "I like my men in English Leather, or nothing at all." The females in the Chanel No. 19 ads are "outspoken" and wrestle their men around.

Male and female, what we long for is clout; what we get in its place is Mastercard.

8. *Need for prominence.* Here comes the need to be admired and respected, to enjoy prestige and high social status. These times, it appears, are not so egalitarian after all. Many ads picture the trappings of high position; the Oldsmobile stands before a manorial doorway, the Volvo is parked beside a steeplechase. A book-lined study is the setting for Dewar's 12, and Lenox China is displayed in a dining room chock full of antiques.

Beefeater gin represents itself as "The Crown Jewel of England" and uses no illustrations of jewels or things British, for the words are sufficient indicators of distinction. Buy that gin and you will rise up the prestige hierarchy, or achieve the same effect on yourself with Seagram's 7 Crown, which ambiguously describes itself as "classy." [55]

Being respected does not have to entail the usual accoutrements of wealth: "Do you know who I am?" the commercials ask, and we learn that the prominent person is not so prominent without his American Express card.

9. *Need for attention.* The previous need involved being *looked up to,* while this is the need to be *looked at.* The desire to exhibit ourselves in such a way as to make others look at us is a primitive, insuppressible instinct. The clothing and cosmetic industries exist just to serve this need, and this is the way they pitch their wares. Some of this effort is aimed at males, as the ads for Hathaway shirts and Jockey underclothes. But the greater bulk of such appeals is targeted singlemindedly at women.

To come back to Brooke Shields: this is where she fits into American marketing. If I buy Calvin Klein jeans, consumers infer, I'll be the object of fascination. The desire for exhibition has been most strikingly played to in a print campaign of many years' duration, that of Maidenform lingerie. The woman exposes herself, and sales surge. "Gentlemen prefer Hanes" the ads dissemble, and women who want eyes upon them know what they should do. Peggy Fleming flutters her legs for L'eggs, encouraging females who want to be the star in their own lives to purchase this product.

The same appeal works for cosmetics and lotions. For years, the little girl with the exposed backside sold gobs of Coppertone, but now the company has picked up the pace a little: as a female, you are supposed to "Flash 'em a Coppertone tan." Food can be sold the same way, especially to the diet-conscious; Angie Dickinson poses for California avocados and says, "Would this body lie to you?" Our eyes are too fixed on her for us to think to ask if she got that way by eating mounds of guacomole.

10. *Need for autonomy.* There are several ways to sell credit card ser- 60 vices, as has been noted: Mastercard appeals to the need to dominate, and American Express to the need for prominence. When Visa claims, "You can have it the way you want it," yet another primary motive is being beckoned forward—the need to endorse the self. The focus here is upon the independence and integrity of the individual; this need is the antithesis of the need for guidance and is unlike any of the social needs. "If running with the herd isn't your style, try ours," says Rotan-Mosle, and many Americans feel they have finally found the right brokerage firm.

The photo is of a red-coated Mountie on his horse, posed on a snow-covered ledge; the copy reads, "Windsor—One Canadian stands alone." This epitome of the solitary and proud individual may work best with male customers, as may Winston's man in the red cap. But one-figure advertisements also strike the strong need for autonomy among American women. As Shelly Hack strides for Charlie perfume, females respond to her obvious pride and flair; she is her own person. The Virginia Slims tale is of people who have come a long way from subservience to independence. Cachet perfume feels it does not need a solo figure to work this appeal, and uses three different faces in its ads; it insists, though, "It's different on every woman who wears it."

Like many psychological needs, this one can also be appealed to in a negative fashion, by invoking the loss of independence or self-regard. Guilt and regrets can be stimulated: "Gee, I could have had a V-8." Next time, get one and be good to yourself.

11. *Need to escape.* An appeal to the need for autonomy often co-occurs with one for the need to escape, since the desire to duck out of our social obligations, to seek rest or adventure, frequently takes the form of one-person flight. The dashing image of a pilot, in fact, is a standard way of quickening this need to get away from it all.

Freedom is the pitch here, the freedom that every individual yearns for whenever life becomes too oppressive. Many advertisers like appealing to the need for escape because the sensation of pleasure often accompanies escape, and what nicer emotional nimbus could there be for a product? "You deserve a break today," says McDonald's, and Stouffer's frozen foods chime in, "Set yourself free."

For decades men have imaginatively bonded themselves to the 65 Marlboro cowboy who dwells untarnished and unencumbered in Marlboro Country some distance from modern life; smokers' aching needs for autonomy and escape are personified by that cowpoke. Many women can identify with the lady ambling through the woods behind the words, "Benson and Hedges and mornings and me."

But escape does not have to be solitary. Other Benson and Hedges ads, part of the same campaign, contain two strolling figures. In Salem cigarette advertisements, it can be several people who escape together into the mountaintops. A commercial for Levi's pictured a cloudbank above a city through which ran a whole chain of young people.

There are varieties of escape, some wistful like the Boeing "Some day" campaign of dream vacations, some kinetic like the play and parties in soft drink ads. But in every instance, the consumer exposed to the advertisement is invited to momentarily depart his everyday life for a more carefree experience, preferably with the product in hand.

12. *Need to feel safe.* Nobody in their right mind wants to be intimidated, menaced, battered, poisoned. We naturally want to do whatever it takes to stave off threats to our well-being, and to our families'. It is the instinct of self-preservation that makes us responsive to the ad of the St. Bernard with the keg of Chivas Regal. We pay attention to the stern talk of Karl Malden and the plight of the vacationing couples who have lost all their funds in the American Express travelers cheques commercials. We want the omnipresent stag from Hartford Insurance to watch over us too.

In the interest of keeping failure and calamity from our lives, we like to see the durability of products demonstrated. Can we ever forget that Timex takes a licking and keeps on ticking? When the American Tourister suitcase bounces all over the highway and the egg inside doesn't break, the need to feel safe has been adroitly plucked.

We take precautions to diminish future threats. We buy Volkswagen 70 Rabbits for the extraordinary mileage, and MONY insurance policies to avoid the tragedies depicted in their black-and-white ads of widows and orphans.

We are careful about our health. We consume Mazola margarine because it has "corn goodness" backed by the natural food traditions of the American Indians. In the medicine cabinet is Alka-Seltzer, the "home remedy"; having it, we are snug in our little cottage.

We want to be safe and secure; buy these products, advertisers are saying, and you'll be safer than you are without them.

13. *Need for aesthetic sensations.* There is an undeniable aesthetic component to virtually every ad run in the national media: the photography or filming or drawing is near-perfect, the type style is well chosen, the layout could scarcely be improved upon. Advertisers know there is little chance of good communication occurring if an ad is not visually pleasing. Consumers may not be aware of the extent of their own sensitivity to artwork, but it is undeniably large.

Sometimes the aesthetic element is expanded and made into an ad's primary appeal. Charles Jordan shoes may or may not appear in the accompanying avant-grade photographs; Kohler plumbing fixtures catch attention through the high style of their desert settings. Beneath the slightly out of focus photograph, languid and sensuous in tone, General Electric feels called upon to explain, "This is an ad for the hair dryer."

This appeal is not limited to female consumers: J&B scotch says "It 75 whispers" and shows a bucolic scene of lake and castle.

14. *Need to satisfy curiosity.* It may seem odd to list a need for information among basic motives, but this need can be as primal and compelling as any of the others. Human beings are curious by nature, interested in the world around them, and intrigued by tidbits of knowledge and new developments. Trivia, percentages, observations counter to conventional wisdom—these items all help sell products. Any advertisement in a question-and-answer format is strumming this need.

A dog groomer has a question about long distance rates, and Bell Telephone has a chart with all the figures. An ad for Porsche 911 is replete with diagrams and schematics, numbers and arrows. Lo and behold, Anacin pills have 150 more milligrams than its competitors; should we wonder if this is better or worse for us?

15. *Physiological needs.* To the extent that sex is solely a biological need, we are now coming around full circle, back toward the start of the list. In this final category are clustered appeals to sleeping, eating, drinking. The art of photographing food and drink is so advanced, sometimes these temptations are wondrously caught in the camera's lens: the crab meat in the Red Lobster restaurant ads can start us salivating, the Quarterpounder can almost be smelled, the liquor in the glass glows invitingly. Imbibe, these ads scream.

STYLES

Some common ingredients of advertisements were not singled out for separate mention in the list of fifteen because they are not appeals in and of themselves. They are stylistic features, influencing the way a basic appeal is presented. The use of humor is one, and the use of celebrities is another. A third is time imagery, past and future, which goes to several purposes.

For all of its employment in advertising, humor can be treacherous, 80 because it can get out of hand and smother the product information. Supposedly, this is what Alka-Seltzer discovered with its comic commercials of the late sixties; "I can't believe I ate the whole thing," the sad-faced husband lamented, and the audience cackled so much it forgot the antacid. Or, did not take it seriously.

But used carefully, humor can punctuate some of the softer appeals and soften some of the harsher ones. When Emma says to the Fruit-of-the-Loom fruits, "Hi, cuties. Whatcha doing in my laundry basket?" we smile as our curiosity is assuaged along with hers. Bill Cosby gets consumers tickled about the children in his Jell-O commercials, and strokes the need to nurture.

An insurance company wants to invoke the need to feel safe, but does not want to leave readers with an unpleasant aftertaste; cartoonist Rowland Wilson creates an avalanche about to crush a gentleman who is saying to another, "My insurance company? New England Life, of course. Why?" The same tactic of humor undercutting threat is used in the cartoon commercials for Safeco when the Pink Panther wanders from one disaster to another. Often humor masks aggression: comedian Bob Hope in the outfit of a boxer promises to knock out the knock-knocks with Texaco; Rodney Dangerfield, who "can't get no respect," invites aggression as the comic relief in Miller Lite commercials.

Roughly fifteen percent of all advertisements incorporate a celebrity, almost always from the fields of entertainment or sports. The approach can also prove troublesome for advertisers, for celebrities are human beings too, and fully capable of the most remarkable behavior. If anything distasteful about them emerges, it is likely to reflect on the product. The advertisers making use of Anita Bryant and Billy Jean King suffered several anxious moments. An untimely death can also react poorly on a product. But advertisers are willing to take risks because celebrities can be such a good link between producers and consumers, performing the social role of introducer.

There are several psychological needs these middlemen can play upon. Let's take the product class of cameras and see how different celebrities can hit different needs. The need for guidance can be invoked by Michael

Landon, who plays such a wonderful dad on "Little House on the Prairie"; when he says to buy Kodak equipment, many people listen. James Garner for Polaroid cameras is put in a similar authoritative role, so defined by a mocking spouse. The need to achieve is summoned up by Tracy Austin and other tennis stars for Canon AE-1; the advertiser first makes sure we see these athletes playing to win. When Cheryl Tiegs speaks up for Olympus cameras, it is the need for attention that is being targeted.

The past and future, being outside our grasp, are exploited by adver- 85 tisers as locales for the projection of needs. History can offer up heroes (and call up the need to achieve) or traditions (need for guidance) as well as art objects (need for aesthetic sensations). Nostalgia is a kindly version of personal history and is deployed by advertisers to rouse needs for affiliation and for guidance; the need to escape can come in here, too. The same need to escape is sometimes the point of futuristic appeals but picturing the avant-garde can also be a way to get at the need to achieve.

ANALYZING ADVERTISEMENTS

When analyzing ads yourself for their emotional appeals, it takes a bit of practice to learn to ignore the product information (as well as one's own experience and feelings about the product). But that skill comes soon enough, as does the ability to quickly sort out from all the non-product aspects of an ad the chief element which is the most striking, the most likely to snag attention first and penetrate brains farthest. The key to the appeal, this element usually presents itself centrally and forwardly to the reader or viewer.

Another clue: the viewing angle which the audience has on the ad's subjects is informative. If the subjects are photographed or filmed from below and thus are looking down at you much as the Green Giant does, then the need to be guided is a good candidate for the ad's emotional appeal. If, on the other hand, the subjects are shot from above and appear deferential, as is often the case with children or female models, then other needs are being appealed to.

To figure out an ad's emotional appeal, it is wise to know (or have a good hunch about) who the targeted consumers are; this can often be inferred from the magazine or television show it appears in. This piece of information is a great help in determining the appeal and in deciding between two different interpretations. For example, if an ad features a partially undressed female, this would typically signal one appeal for readers of *Penthouse* (need for sex) and another for readers of *Cosmopolitan* (need for attention).

196

It would be convenient if every ad made just one appeal, were aimed at just one need. Unfortunately, things are often not that simple. A cigarette ad with a couple at the edge of a polo field is trying to hit both the need for affiliation and the need for prominence; depending on the attitude of the male, dominance could also be an ingredient in this. An ad for Chimere perfume incorporates two photos: in the top one the lady is being commanding at a business luncheon (need to dominate), but in the lower one she is being bussed (need for affiliation). Better ads, however, seem to avoid being too diffused; in the study of post–World War II advertising described earlier, appeals grew more focused as the decades passed. As a rule of thumb, about sixty percent have two conspicuous appeals; the last twenty percent have three or more. Rather than looking for the greatest number of appeals, decoding ads is most productive when the loudest one or two appeals are discerned, since those are the appeals with the best chance of grabbing people's attention.

Finally, analyzing ads does not have to be a solo activity and probably 90 should not be. The greater number of people there are involved, the better chance there is of transcending individual biases and discerning the essential emotional lure built into an advertisement.

DO THEY OR DON'T THEY?

Do the emotional appeals made in advertisements add up to the sinister manipulation of consumers?

It is clear that these ads work. Attention is caught, communication occurs between producers and consumers, and sales result. It turns out to be difficult to detail the exact relationship between a specific ad and a specific purchase, or even between a campaign and subsequent sales figures, because advertising is only one of a host of influences upon consumption. Yet no one is fooled by this lack of perfect proof; everyone knows that advertising sells. If this were not the case, then tight-fisted American businesses would not spend a total of fifty billion dollars annually on these messages.

But before anyone despairs that advertisers have our number to the extent that they can marshal us at will and march us like automatons to the check-out counters, we should recall the resiliency and obduracy of the American consumer. Advertisers may have uncovered the softest spots in minds, but that does not mean they have found truly gaping apertures. There is no evidence that advertising can get people to do things contrary to their self-interests. Despite all the finesse of advertisements, and all the subtle emotional tugs, the public resists the vast majority of the petitions.

197

According to the marketing division of the A.C Nielsen Company, a whopping seventy-five percent of all new products die within a year in the marketplace, the victims of consumer disinterest which no amount of advertising could overcome. The appeals in advertising may be the most captivating there are to be had, but they are not enough to entrap the wiley consumer.

The key to understanding the discrepancy between, on the one hand, the fact that advertising truly works, and, on the other, the fact that it hardly works, is to take into account the enormous numbers of people exposed to an ad. Modern-day communications permit an ad to be displayed to millions upon millions of individuals; if the smallest fraction of that audience can be moved to buy the product, then the ad has been successful. When one percent of the people exposed to a television advertising campaign reach for their wallets, that could be one million sales, which may be enough to keep the product in production and the advertisements coming.

In arriving at an evenhanded judgment about advertisements and their emotional appeals, it is good to keep in mind that many of the purchases which might be credited to these ads are experienced as genuinely gratifying to the consumer. We sincerely like the goods or service we have bought, and we may even like some of the emotional drapery that an ad suggests comes with it. It has sometimes been noted that the most avid students of advertisements are the people who have just bought the product; they want to steep themselves in the associated imagery. This may be the reason that Americans, when polled, are not negative about advertising and do not disclose any sense of being misused. The volume of advertising may be an irritant, but the product information as well as the imaginative material in ads are partial compensation.

A productive understanding is that advertising messages involve costs and benefits at both ends of the communications channel. For those few ads which do make contact, the consumer surrenders a moment of time, has the lower brain curried, and receives notice of a product; the advertiser has given up money and has increased the chance of sales. In this sort of communications activity, neither party can be said to be the loser.

STEPHANIE COONTZ   [b. 1944]

A Nation of
Welfare Families

Stephanie Coontz teaches history and family studies at The Evergreen
State College in Olympia, Washington. Educated at the University of
California–Berkeley and the University of Washington, Coontz has
devoted her career to debunking myths about marriage and the American family. A former Woodrow Wilson Fellow, she has presented her
research findings to the House Select Committee on Children, Youth,
and Families, and is currently Director of Research and Public Education for the Council on Contemporary Families. Coontz has been a frequent guest on radio and TV and has contributed articles both to
general-interest publications such as the *New York Times* and *Harper's*
and academic journals such as *The Chronicle for Higher Education* and
Journal of Marriage and Family. Her books include *The Way We Never
Were: American Families and the Nostalgia Trap* (1992) and *The Way We
Really Are: Coming to Terms with America's Changing Families* (1997).

In her essay "A Nation of Welfare Families," Coontz argues that,
contrary to popular belief, government aid to families is not a new
thing, nor will it morally corrupt the institution. Since the early begin-
nings of our nation, families have depended on the federal government
for support.

The current political debate over family values, personal responsibility,
and welfare takes for granted the entrenched American belief that dependence on government assistance is a recent and destructive phenomenon.
Conservatives tend to blame this dependence on personal irresponsibility
aggravated by a swollen welfare apparatus that saps individual initiative.
Liberals are more likely to blame it on personal misfortune magnified by
the harsh lot that falls to losers in our competitive market economy. But
both sides believe that "winners" in America make it on their own, that
dependence reflects some kind of individual or family failure, and that the
ideal family is the self-reliant unit of traditional lore—a family that takes
care of its own, carves out a future for its children, and never asks for

handouts. Politicians at both ends of the ideological spectrum have wrapped themselves in the mantle of these "family values," arguing over *why* the poor have not been able to make do without assistance, or whether aid has exacerbated their situation, but never questioning the assumption that American families traditionally achieve success by establishing their independence from the government.

The myth of family self-reliance is so compelling that our actual national and personal histories often buckle under its emotional weight. "We always stood on our own two feet," my grandfather used to say about his pioneer heritage, whenever he walked me to the top of the hill to survey the property in Washington State that his family had bought for next to nothing after it had been logged off in the early 1900s. Perhaps he didn't know that the land came so cheap because much of it was part of a federal subsidy originally allotted to the railroad companies, which had received 183 million acres of the public domain in the nineteenth century. These federal giveaways were the original source of most major Western logging companies' land, and when some of these logging companies moved on to virgin stands of timber, federal lands trickled down to a few early settlers who were able to purchase them inexpensively.

Like my grandparents, few families in American history—whatever their "values"—have been able to rely solely on their own resources. Instead, they have depended on the legislative, judicial, and social support structures set up by governing authorities, whether those authorities were the clan elders of Native American societies, the church courts and city officials of colonial America, or the judicial and legislative bodies established by the Constitution.

At America's inception, this was considered not a dirty little secret but the norm, one that confirmed our social and personal interdependence. The idea that the family should have the sole or even primary responsibility for educating and socializing its members, finding them suitable work, or keeping them from poverty and crime was not only ludicrous to colonial and revolutionary thinkers but dangerously parochial.

Historically, one way that government has played a role in the well-being 5 of its citizens is by regulating the way that employers and civic bodies interact with families. In the early twentieth century, for example, as a response to rapid changes ushered in by a mass-production economy, the government promoted a "family wage system." This system was designed to strengthen the ability of the male breadwinner to support a family without having his wife or children work. This family wage system was not a natural outgrowth of the market. It was a *political* response to conditions that the market had produced: child labor, rampant employment insecurity, recurring economic downturns, an earnings structure in which

45 percent of industrial workers fell below the poverty level and another 40 percent hovered barely above it, and a system in which thousands of children had been placed in orphanages or other institutions simply because their parents could not afford their keep. The state policies involved in the establishment of the family wage system included abolition of child labor, government pressure on industrialists to negotiate with unions, federal arbitration, expansion of compulsory schooling—and legislation discriminating against women workers.

But even such extensive regulation of economic and social institutions has never been enough: government has always supported families with direct material aid as well. The two best examples of the government's history of material aid can be found in what many people consider the ideal models of self-reliant families: the Western pioneer family and the 1950s suburban family. In both cases, the ability of these families to establish and sustain themselves required massive underwriting by the government.

Pioneer families, such as my grandparents, could never have moved west without government-funded military mobilizations against the original Indian and Mexican inhabitants or state-sponsored economic investment in transportation systems. In addition, the Homestead Act of 1862 allowed settlers to buy 160 acres for $10—far below the government's cost of acquiring the land—if the homesteader lived on and improved the land for five years. In the twentieth century, a new form of public assistance became crucial to Western families: construction of dams and other federally subsidized irrigation projects. During the 1930s, for example, government electrification projects brought pumps, refrigeration, and household technology to millions of families.

The suburban family of the 1950s is another oft-cited example of familial self-reliance. According to legend, after World War II a new, family-oriented generation settled down, saved their pennies, worked hard, and found well-paying jobs that allowed them to purchase homes in the suburbs. In fact, however, the 1950s suburban family was far more dependent on government assistance than any so-called underclass family of today. Federal GI benefit payments, available to 40 percent of the male population between the ages of twenty and twenty-four, permitted a whole generation of men to expand their education and improve their job prospects without forgoing marriage and children. The National Defense Education Act retooled science education in America, subsidizing both American industry and the education of individual scientists. Government-funded research developed the aluminum clapboards, prefabricated walls and ceilings, and plywood paneling that comprised the technological basis of the postwar housing revolution. Government spending was also largely responsible for the new highways, sewer systems, utility services, and traffic-control programs that opened up suburbia.

In addition, suburban home ownership depended on an unprecedented expansion of federal regulation and financing. Before the war, banks often required a 50 percent down payment on homes and normally issued mortgages for five to ten years. In the postwar period, however, the Federal Housing Authority, supplemented by the GI bill, put the federal government in the business of insuring and regulating private loans for single-home construction. FHA policy required down payments of only 5 to 10 percent of the purchase price and guaranteed mortgages of up to thirty years at interest rates of just 2 to 3 percent. The Veterans Administration required a mere dollar down from veterans. Almost half the housing in suburbia in the 1950s depended on such federal programs.

The drawback of these aid programs was that although they worked 10 well for recipients, nonrecipients—disproportionately poor and urban— were left far behind. While the general public financed the roads that suburbanites used to commute, the streetcars and trolleys that served urban and poor families received almost no tax revenues, and our previously thriving rail system was allowed to decay. In addition, federal loan policies, which were a boon to upwardly mobile white families, tended to systematize the pervasive but informal racism that had previously characterized the housing market. FHA redlining practices, for example, took entire urban areas and declared them ineligible for loans, while the government's two new mortgage institutions, the Federal National Mortgage Association and the Government National Mortgage Association (Fannie Mae and Ginny Mae) made it possible for urban banks to transfer savings out of the cities and into new suburban developments in the South and West.

Despite the devastating effects on families and regions that did not receive such assistance, government aid to suburban residents during the 1950s and 1960s produced in its beneficiaries none of the demoralization usually presumed to afflict recipients of government handouts. Instead, federal subsidies to suburbia encouraged family formation, residential stability, upward occupational mobility, and rising educational aspirations among youth who could look forward to receiving such aid. Seen in this light, the idea that government subsidies intrinsically induce dependence, undermine self-esteem, or break down family ties is exposed as no more than a myth.

I am not suggesting that the way to solve the problems of poverty and urban decay in America is to quadruple our spending on welfare. Certainly there are major reforms needed in our current aid policies to the poor. But the debate over such reform should put welfare in the context of *all* federal assistance programs. As long as we pretend that only poor or single-parent families need outside assistance, while normal families "stand on their own two feet," we will shortchange poor families, overcompensate rich ones, and fail to come up with effective policies for helping out families in the middle. Current government housing policies are a case in point. The richest 20 percent of American households receives three times as much federal housing aid—mostly in tax subsidies—as the poorest 20 percent receives in expenditures for low-income housing.

Historically, the debate over government policies toward families has never been over *whether* to intervene but *how:* to rescue or to warehouse, to prevent or to punish, to moralize about values or mobilize resources for education and job creation. Today's debate, lacking such historical perspective, caricatures the real issues. Our attempt to sustain the myth of family self-reliance in the face of all the historical evidence to the contrary has led policymakers into theoretical contortions and practical miscalculations that are reminiscent of efforts by medieval philosophers to maintain that the earth and not the sun was the center of the planetary system. In the sixteenth century, leading European thinkers insisted that the planets and the sun all revolved around the earth—much as American politicians today insist that our society revolves around family self-reliance. When evidence to the contrary mounted, defenders of the Ptolemaic universe postulated all sorts of elaborate planetary orbits in order to reconcile observed reality with their cherished theory. Similarly, rather than admit that all families need some kind of public support, we have constructed ideological orbits that explain away each instance of middle-class dependence as "exception," an "abnormality," or even an illusion. We have distributed public aid to families through convoluted bureaucracies that have become impossible to track; in some cases the system has become so cumbersome that it threatens to collapse around our ears. It is time to break through the old paradigm of self-reliance and substitute a new one that recognizes that assisting families is, simply, what government does.

BRANDON AYERS

The Academic and Social Effects of Homeschooling

Stereotypes are things we assume about a certain culture, a certain race, or a certain gender. Stereotypes are everywhere and they only continue to become worse while new ones are created. According to *Oxford Dictionaries*, a stereotype is a "widely held but fixed and oversimplified idea or image of a particular type of person or thing." But there is nothing we can do about them because they are a person's assumption, and people will believe what they want to believe. "Stereotypes of homeschooled children often include labels such as 'backwards' or 'on the fringe' of society," according to Isaiah Cohen and Cynthia K. Drenovsky in "The Impact of Homeschooling on the Adjustment of College Students" (19). While stereotypes about homeschooled children seem to be true based on popular assumptions, the effects of homeschooling children are actually beneficial. Studies show that homeschooled children are not negatively affected by not going to public or private schools.

Homeschooling has been around since the colonial era, but in 1918, schooling laws were enacted that brought America's focus to institutionalizing education. The popularity of homeschooling began to rise in the 1960s because of several highly critical works on American public schools (Cohen and Drenovsky 20). Since then, homeschooling became much more prevalent, with about 1.5 million students being homeschooled just in the 1970s. "Homeschooling is considered the

204

fastest growing form of American education and is expected to continue to rise in the near future," write Cohen and Drenovsky (21). If homeschooling is the fastest growing form of education, why are homeschooled students considered outcasts in our society? Most "regular" students think that they have communication issues since they don't experience public schooling with other kids. But we're all wrong if we think that homeschooled children have communication problems. Just because they have to stay at home for school does not mean that they are in house prison and can't communicate with their peers in the outside world. Homeschooled children aren't held back from the public itself; they just don't go to public schools.

One example of homeschooled children communicating well with others is at the college level. When they reach college, according to Cohen and Drenovsky, surveys show that homeschooled children do not show any differences in self-esteem and actually have lower levels of depression than non-homeschooled children, which will cause them to perform better academically (28).

Cohen and Drenovsky also reported on the grades of homeschooled and non-homeschooled college students. Homeschooled students achieved better grades and as a whole viewed their college experience in a more positive light than students from public/private high schools. Out of 1,500 students that were asked to take a survey, only 185 answered; this is likely due to the target audience (college kids). But out of those 185, homeschooled children most likely had achieved As, whereas non-homeschooled kids had Bs. This survey showed that kids who took classes at home achieve better grades, even at higher levels (29).

Similarly, Michelle Wichers notes that "one-on-one education leads to another positive proponent of homeschooling: academic excellence"

(145). If you ask any student, public, private, or homeschooled, if they would rather have one-on-one learning or lectures here at WMU, they would say one-on-one because they would learn a lot easier. If a student doesn't comprehend the problem on the board, he is more likely to stop the teacher and ask questions if it's just the teacher and the student, as opposed to stopping the teacher in front of 30 people. Some people do not feel comfortable asking questions because of the people they're surrounded by.

Wichers also notes that individualized curricula help students progress quickly in learning information (145-146). As we've seen from both Cohen & Drenovsky and Wichers' reports, studies show that homeschooled children receive better grades and achieve greater academic success than public/private schooled kids. Hence, it seems highly possible that homeschooled children are receiving a better and more efficient education.

Works Cited

Cohen, Isaiah and Drenovsky, Cynthia K. "The Impact of Homeschooling on the Adjustment of College Students." *International Social Science Review* 87.1-2 (2012): 19-34. Electronic.

"Stereotype." *Oxforddictionaries.com.* Web. 30 Nov. 2012.

Wichers, Michelle. "Homeschooling: Adventitious or Detrimental For Proficiency in Higher Education." *Education* 122.1 (2001): 145-151. Electronic.

Research Writing: Summative Questions and Prompts

1. Perhaps your previous writing instructors have cautioned you against using the first-person in a research paper. Notice that many of the pieces in this section seamlessly blend data and secondary source material with the personal experiences and reactions of the writer. This combination can elevate an essay from a dry report to an engaging, humanized argument or conversation. Practice this style by answering the question, "What is one of the most interesting things you have learned in your college coursework?" Respond by citing an interesting fact, theory, or idea that you have learned this semester, then elaborate on why you find it interesting or relevant. Two hints: 1) Check your fact/theory/idea for accuracy. 2) Give credit to the appropriate scholar(s).

2. Write a paragraph-length summary of any one of the pieces in this section of the text. Use this writing exercise to practice different ways of integrating secondary sources into your essays. Make sure your paragraph contains all of the following:

   - Reference to the source by title and author.

   - At least one sentence that is *only* summary or paraphrase.

   - At least one long quotation that is a complete thought, introduced with a signal phrase.

   - At least one short quotation of a key phrase that is integrated into your own words.

3. Re-read Amitai Etzioni's "Working at McDonalds" and create a reverse outline in which you trace the progression of his argument. Begin by stating Etzioni's thesis, then summarize his main points in order of occurrence. Write all parts of the outline in your own words and make each main point a complete thought. Do not expect to find all of the main points in the first sentences of paragraphs, and recognize that most of his points span several paragraphs.